A TASTE OF AUSTRALIA

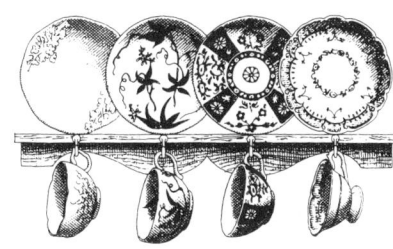

*Savouring Australia's past
in traditional recipes
and nostalgic photographs*

PETER TAYLOR

ANGUS
& ROBERTSON
PUBLISHERS

For Bob Williams
and all those who remember
Headfort Place

ANGUS & ROBERTSON PUBLISHERS

Unit 4, Eden Park, 31 Waterloo Road,
North Ryde, NSW, Australia 2113;
94 Newton Road, Auckland 1,
New Zealand; and
16 Golden Square, London W1R 4BN,
United Kingdom

First published in 1980
This revised edition first published
by Angus & Robertson Publishers in 1989

Copyright © Peter Taylor 1980, 1989

ISBN 0 207 16206 9

Produced by Taylor-Type Publications
(Australia) Pty Ltd

Typeset in 10 pt Clearface Medium by
Caxtons Pty Ltd, Adelaide
Printed in Singapore

Acknowledgements

The photographs in this book are reproduced by kind permission of the Mitchell Library, Sydney; the State Library of Victoria; the National Library of Australia; the South Australian State Archives; and Telecom Australia. The Mitchell Library in Sydney also gave permission to reproduce recipes from manuscripts in their collection: from Elizabeth Coghill's Diary, the recipes for bottled gooseberries and tomato sauce; from the notebook of Helenus Scott the younger, the recipes for beer and ginger beer; and from Mrs Mitchell's manuscript 'Receipes', those for mutton hams and Mother Eve's pudding.

My wife Rosemary bore up well under the strain of yet another cookery book, and my son Jonathan gave up much of his holiday to help me in the darkroom — I thank them both.

Finally I must thank all the people who suggested recipes and ideas and who listened patiently whilst I tried to put them all together.

Introduction

Is there a taste of Australia? The question was asked by many people when I was researching this book and it needs to be answered.

Australians are aware that many dishes familiar in this country had their origins in Britain, that they were imported by the early convicts and their guards and reinforced by those who came later. The belief is that Australian cooking is no different to that in England, and that it has developed alongside it since the late eighteenth century. It seems so logical that it is not surprising that it is so widely held, although an Australian travelling in Britain today often begins to doubt its truth.

When the first convicts and their guards arrived in Australia in 1788 they had every reason to feel that their prospects were even worse than had been intended. Botany Bay had been selected as the site for the penal colony on the basis of reports by Captain Cook and Sir Joseph Banks after their brief visit in 1770 and which indicated that the soil was fertile and capable of supporting a settlement. But the members of the First Fleet found instead that they had been sent to a country that could provide them with nothing—inhabited by Aborigines that were hunters and food gatherers, not growers. The country had no cultivated grain or vegetables, no fruit to speak of, and no milk-producing animals. If the Aborigine could live off the country, the European could not. Nor could the European readily adopt the itinerant life-style of the Aborigine as it was hardly compatible with the requirements of a penal settlement. In fact, with the exception of the macadamia nut, none of the food now cultivated in Australia was present when the First Fleet arrived. It has all been introduced since.

It is not surprising that the early settlers were close to starvation many times during the first few years. Nor is it surprising that the first seeds and animals came from England and that the food they eventually produced was recognizably English. They would naturally have had a preference for such food, and the fact that there was no alternative meant there was no incentive to adapt to a new diet.

But the story does not end there. As the settlers came to terms with the country they realized that they had many advantages that had not been so obvious to those who arrived with the First Fleet. Although early crops failed (because they were bred for a different climate) later they started to flourish. Livestock did well, fruit could grow in a profusion unknown in England, and the sea was abundant with fish.

Slowly, Australians selected from traditional English food those dishes that used the things that were plentiful, and it is that process of selection that has resulted in a taste of Australia. It is not so much that dishes were invented here (although some were), but that the availability of meat and seafood, for example, often made many dishes more popular here than in their country of origin. This combined to make a diet that is recognizably different. It is this fact that makes the Australian in London realize that he *does* eat differently to the English. His casual acceptance of Beef Wellington in Melbourne contrasts strongly with the respect (and cost) it justifies in London. Australia, then, has adapted those dishes that 'work' in Australia and, by and large, discarded those that don't. And by doing so we have created a taste of Australia without even realizing it.

In this book I have deliberately limited the contents to those dishes that reflect this adaptation of English cooking and that between them establish the taste of Australia. I have excluded Aboriginal cooking for two reasons: one is that it has had little influence on that of white Australia, and the other is that I feared that by including it I would be doing so for 'amazement', parading it, as it were, as an anthropological curiosity, and I would wish to have no part of that.

I have also had to exclude the very significant influence on Australian cooking made by migrants from other European countries and South-East Asia. Again there are two reasons for this: it came, on the whole, after the Second World War and therefore does not fit easily into this format; and it has been of such great importance that it is really the subject of a book on its own.

PETER TAYLOR

Billy Tea

The traditional drink of the Australian traveller and those living in the bush. Dry tea was easy to carry and only needed water, a container and a fire to make. The water could usually be found by an experienced bushman even in the arid Centre, although he often had to dig into the bed of the dry river to get enough. At first the container was a tin measuring jug with a side handle, but about 1850 this gave way to the familiar 'billy'. This had the advantage of having a lid, and a wire handle that made carrying easier and allowed the billy to be suspended over the fire. The origin of the word is unclear: one suggestion is that it comes from a French tinned soup called *bouilli* and that the empty tins were the forerunners of the billy; another is that it comes from an Aboriginal word *billa*, meaning a creek or river and from which we get 'billabong'. It might have come from the Scottish dialect word 'billypot', for a cooking vessel, or it might simply have been a man's name.

To make billy tea, the billy was filled with water and hung over the fire and when the water came to the boil a handful of tea was thrown in. Many stirred it with a stick, which often added its own flavour, whilst others just let it stand. The trick, though, was to get the leaves to settle to the bottom of the billy. One method was to hold the billy by the handle and to whirl the arm round in a wide circle as quickly as possible. Centrifugal force would drive the leaves to the bottom, but if the action was done timidly the result would be quite different. A safer, but less effective, method was to simply tap the side of the billy with a stick.

The tea was then poured into the pannikin (a tin mug) and sugar added to taste if it was available.

Swaggie, 1894. (Mitchell Library, Sydney)

Damper

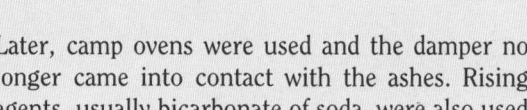

Damper, like billy tea, was the traditional and unmistakably Australian 'tucker' of the bush. It had the advantage, again like billy tea, of being made from dry ingredients that were easily carried and which only needed water to complete. It was made by mixing plain flour with water to make a dough, to which salt was added if it was available. The dough was made into a ball and then flattened with the hand to form a rough circle about 70 mm thick. The hot ashes of the fire were scooped out to make a depression, the damper placed in it, and more ashes raked over the top so that it was completely covered. The top ashes were removed after about half an hour and if the damper sounded hollow when tapped, it was considered to be cooked and taken from the fire. The adhering ash was removed as completely as possible and the damper eaten hot. It smelled delicious, but most 'new chums' were appalled at the uncleanliness of the cooking and probably only got used to it because there was no alternative.

Later, camp ovens were used and the damper no longer came into contact with the ashes. Rising agents, usually bicarbonate of soda, were also used to give a more pleasant texture.

The same basic mixture could be used to make a number of variations. Johnny cakes were made from one handful of the mixture cooked in the ashes or, carefully, in a frying pan. They were also fried in mutton fat and then they were known as leather-jackets. Devils-on-coals were even smaller, about the size of a biscuit, and were cooked on the fire and turned quickly.

'*The term* [leather-jacket] *is a very appropriate one, for tougher things cannot well be eaten; however with our keen appetites, we found them very good, and persons who cannot make a hearty meal on such tough fare should not venture any great distance from home.*'

Samuel Mossman,
Australia Visited and Revisited, 1853.

Transporting the wool clip; near Nelligen, New South Wales. (National Library of Australia)

Bacon and Egg Pie

Australian pubs were the dream of the traveller, sometimes the despair of women, and the nightmare of the wowsers. And perhaps they still are. From the city street to the arid outback, they are everywhere, or at least it seems so until you find yourself in need of one. They nearly all serve meals in the form of the counter lunch and counter tea and in the country can blend subtly into a general store as well. Although city pubs reflect the sophistication, or lack of it, of their locality, and change as that changes, country pubs often seem quite timeless. To take a counter tea in a bush pub, often isolated along its own unsealed and dusty road, is to come close to the prospectors, settlers, shearers and others who knew the same pub years ago and who would probably still recognize it.

Ingredients

250 g short crust pastry
8 bacon rashers
6 eggs
1 onion, sliced
1 tablespoon parsley, chopped
1 teaspoon chives, chopped
¼ teaspoon cayenne pepper
salt and pepper

Method

Make the pastry, roll it out on a floured board and divide it in half. Use one piece to line a 20-cm pie plate. Cut the rind from the bacon and cut the rashers into strips. Lay a third of the bacon in the bottom of the dish, break in two of the eggs and add some of the onion. Sprinkle with some of the parsley, chives and cayenne pepper and season. Fill the dish with two more layers in the same way. Put the remaining pastry over the top of the dish and seal it. Bake at 180°C for 30–35 minutes.

The Tilba Tilba Hotel, New South Wales. (National Library of Australia)

Bread

> 'At last some ears of wheat were displayed in Hindley-street, and the fact made patent that this cereal could be produced from the virgin soil of the young colony . . . Little did those who gazed on this specimen imagine that South Australia would wrest the prize from all the nations of the world for her superior wheat.'
>
> *Experiences of a Colonist* by 'An Old Hand', 1880.

Ingredients

4 cups plain flour
1 teaspoon salt
15 g butter
3 teaspoons compressed yeast
½ teaspoon sugar
tepid water

Method

Sift the flour and salt together and rub in the butter. Make a hollow in the centre and crumble in the yeast, then sprinkle the sugar over the yeast and mix both to a batter using about half a cup of tepid water. Some of the flour mixture can be mixed in at this stage, but leave most of it round the basin. Cover with a cloth and leave to stand in a warm place until the dough rises, which will take about 20 minutes. Then take the cover off and mix in the rest of the flour mixture, adding a little more water if necessary. Put the dough on to a floured board and knead well until it is springy and does not cling to the hands. Grease the basin and put the dough in it. Cut across the top several times, re-cover and stand in a warm place until it is well risen. Put the dough back on the floured board and knead again. Press into the shape required and leave to stand again for 10–15 minutes. Put in the oven and bake for 5–10 minutes at 250°C, then gradually reduce the heat to 180°C until the bread is cooked. It will take about 30 minutes.

Webster's Tea Room in Queen Street, Brisbane, in 1900. (John Oxley Library, Brisbane)

Roast Goose

'The top of Bourke-street appears to be the chief haunt of the Bohemian diners . . . See the placards: "Roast goose today!" "Goose and apple sauce!" "Try our prime rabbits", and so on. The shops are numerous, the odour issuing therefrom savoury. Bohemia, if it has sixpence, can eat and be filled.'

Marcus Clarke, *Australasian*, 3 July 1869.

'Roast goose is a common but favourite dish. It must be well stuffed with onion, sage, bread-crumbs, pepper, salt, and a little cayenne; with the liver, and the yolk of an egg. It must be well done, and served up with apple sauce; and garnish the dish with cut lemons.

'Roast goose is served up on Michaelmas Day in England because it is the day the Queen Elizabeth heard of the defeat of the Spanish Armada, and her chivalrous Highness ordered the dish to be invariably on the table afterwards; but other writers contend that this dish was eaten on Michaelmas Day in the time of Edward IV, before the Armada was thought of. In France they eat goose on St Martin's Day, Shrove Tuesday, and Twelfth Day; and in Denmark on St Martin's. We recommend the reader to eat it whenever he can get it, for it is a very good dish . . .'

E. Abbott, *The English and Australian Cookery Book*, 1864.

Rowes Café, Brisbane, about 1911. (John Oxley Library, Brisbane)

Billy Fruit Loaf

Although the billy can is usually associated with billy tea, it was often the only cooking utensil available and was put to many uses.

 Ingredients

3 cups plain flour
½ teaspoon salt
1½ teaspoons bicarbonate of soda
3 teaspoons cream of tartar
1 teaspoon mixed spice
1 tablespoon ground cinnamon
2 tablespoons sugar
1 cup bran
1 tablespoon butter
milk
1 tablespoon golden syrup
1 cup mixed fruit

 **Method**

Mix together the flour, salt, bicarbonate of soda, cream of tartar, spice, cinnamon, sugar and bran. Rub in the butter. Mix a little milk with the golden syrup and add this to the mixture. Then add more milk to the mixture, stirring all the time, to make a soft dough. Then add the mixed fruit. Grease and flour a billy and add the mixture. Put the lid on and bake in the ashes until done, which will be about 1½ hours, depending on the heat of the ashes.

Camped for the night in the bush, 1850. (National Library of Australia)

Pumpkin Soup

 ## Ingredients

500 g pumpkin, peeled and
  chopped
3 tomatoes, skinned
2 onions, chopped
4 cups chicken stock
salt and pepper
½ teaspoon ground nutmeg
1 cup milk or cream
1 tablespoon parsley, chopped

Method

Put the pumpkin, tomatoes and onions in a large saucepan
with the stock, salt, pepper and nutmeg. Bring to the boil,
cover and boil gently until the pumpkin is tender. Then
purée it or rub it through a sieve. Add more salt and pepper
and nutmeg if desired. Stir in the milk or cream to give the
required consistency and reheat gently. Do not boil. Serve
garnished with chopped parsley.

Outside the hotel, near Gundagai. (National Library of Australia)

Bottled Gooseberries

This recipe comes from the diary of Elizabeth Coghill and is dated 14 December 1859.

'The bottles to be dry. The fruit to be put in layers about two inches thick. Sprinkle each layer with sugar. When full, cork and then tie bladder over the cork. Allow about one inch bladder below your tie. Then place in a boiler with cold water up to the neck of the bottles. Put on a slow fire until the water boils, then allow the fire to die away slowly. When the water is cold remove the bottles to your store or any convenient place you have, but do not place them under your bed lest you break them.'

A house at Gulgong, New South Wales, 1872. (Mitchell Library, Sydney)

Avocado and Oysters

This simple and delicious dish is an example of how two ingredients, both freely available in Australia, are used in a way that would seem positively reckless in many other countries.

Ingredients

2 ripe avocados
12 fresh oysters
2 hard-boiled egg yolks
4 tablespoons olive oil
2 tablespoons lemon juice
salt and pepper
lemon wedges for garnish

Method

Cut the avocados in half lengthways and remove the stone. Brush the cut surface with a little lemon juice and put three oysters into each half. Mash the egg yolks until they are smooth and gradually add the olive oil. Blend until smooth and thick, then stir in the lemon juice and season with salt and pepper. Top each avocado half with this sauce. Place on individual dishes, garnish with the lemon wedges and serve with thinly sliced brown bread and butter.

Tuggeranong Homestead, New South Wales, 1911. (National Library of Australia)

Grilled Scallops

It is difficult to imagine Australia without its beaches, and so dependent upon them are most Australians in the summer that they would be pushed to know what to do if they suddenly weren't there. The kilometres of hot sand, the blue sea and sky, the tumbling white surf, the flags that indicate the area patrolled by life-savers, and the incredibly athletic surf-boarders riding the waves with deceptive ease, all make up a scene so familiar to most Australians as to be almost taken for granted. The familiar pictures of the life-savers marching behind their huge banners up Bondi Beach are known throughout the world and have made Bondi perhaps the best known of all Australian beaches.

Ingredients

12 scallops
melted butter
salt and pepper
hot buttered toast
1 tablespoon parsley, chopped
lemon wedges for garnish

Method

Rinse and dry the scallops carefully and put them on a buttered baking sheet. Brush them generously with the melted butter and season with salt and pepper. Place under a pre-heated grill for 5-6 minutes or until just brown. Serve on the hot buttered toast with a sprinkle of parsley and a wedge of lemon.

Bondi Beach, Sydney, on Boxing Day, 1906. (Mitchell Library, Sydney)

Corned Beef

The Overland Telegraph Line, which was completed in 1872, made possible rapid communication between Australia and Europe for the first time. The line ran for 3,000 kilometres between Adelaide and Darwin through some of the most inhospitable country in the world and was built in less than two years. Amongst the items used to supply the men were tins of beef made by J. V. Hughes at Booyoolee Station in South Australia. Known at first as Booyoolee Beef, it later became famous to soldiers everywhere as bully beef.

Ingredients

2 kg silverside
1 medium-sized onion
6 cloves
6 peppercorns
1 bay leaf
2 tablespoons vinegar
1 tablespoon brown sugar
water

Method

Put all the ingredients into a large saucepan, cover with water and bring to the boil. Then reduce the heat and simmer for about 2 hours or until the meat is tender. If serving hot, add parsnips and carrots for the last 30 minutes. If serving cold, let the meat cool in the liquid for added flavour.

Men of the Overland Telegraph Line at the Roper River Depot, Northern Territory, in 1872. (Telecom Australia)

Potted Prawns

Cricket has been played in Australia since the days of the First Fleet and remains the national summer game. By 1826 there were a number of organized clubs. The first interstate game, between Victoria and New South Wales, was played in 1856. The first English team came out in 1861, and what is now regarded as the first Test match was played in Melbourne in 1877. Australia won by 45 runs, although England won the second Test, played a few days later, by four wickets. Picnic food has always been a part of cricket, from meat pies on the outer to the more elegant dishes in the members' stands.

Ingredients

500 g prawns, cooked and
shelled
250 g butter
1 teaspoon powdered mace
½ teaspoon powdered ginger
¼ teaspoon cayenne pepper
salt to taste

Method

Chop the prawns into small pieces. Gently melt three-quarters of the butter, stir in the prawns and spices and season with salt to taste. Continue stirring over a low heat until the prawns have absorbed most of the butter, then scrape into small pots and press the mixture down. Melt the remainder of the butter and pour it over the top of the mixture to seal it. Refrigerate until set and firm. To serve, turn out and cut into wedges.

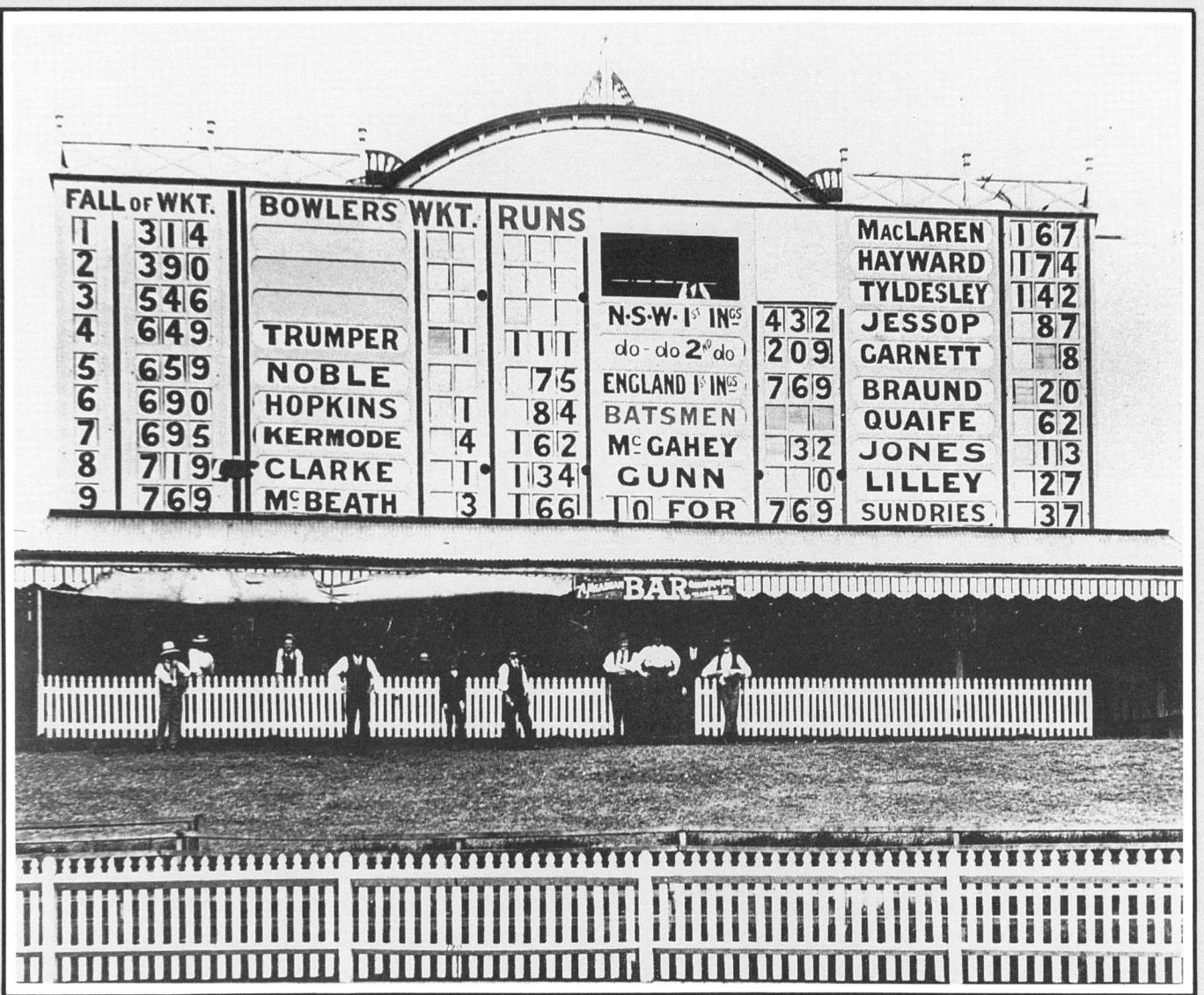

England piling it on against New South Wales at the Sydney Cricket Ground during their 1901/02 Tour. (Mitchell Library, Sydney)

Short Ribs of Beef

When the First Fleet disembarked at Sydney Cove in January 1788, a 'portable canvas house' was erected for Governor Phillip on the eastern side of the cove. On 15 May the foundation stone for a more substantial Government House was laid at the south-west corner of Phillip and Bridge Streets and, under the supervision of James Bloodworth (a builder who had been sentenced to seven years in 1785), the building was finished by early June. The original foundation stone, together with its commemorative copper plate, was discovered by workmen in 1899 and both are now preserved in the Mitchell Library. The site of the building is marked by a plaque erected by the Royal Australian Historical Society.

Ingredients

1.5 kg short ribs of beef, cut into portions
1 tablespoon fat
1 medium-sized onion, sliced
1 beef stock cube
1½ cups water

SEASONED FLOUR
1 cup flour
1 teaspoon salt
¼ teaspoon pepper

Method

To make the seasoned flour, sift the flour into a bowl, add the salt and pepper and blend thoroughly. Take a quarter of a cup (the rest can be bottled for future use) and rub well into the meat. Heat the fat in a pan over a moderate heat, add the meat and brown it. Then drain off any surplus fat, add the onion, stock cube and water and cover the pan tightly. Bring to the boil, then reduce the heat and simmer for 1½–2 hours until the meat is tender. Serve the meat hot.

An old house in Pitt Street, Sydney. Although it has been claimed, wrongly, to be the first Government House built by Governor Phillip in May 1788, it was probably built about the same time. (Mitchell Library, Sydney)

Lamb Breasts with Fruit

Ingredients

3 or 4 breasts of lamb with the bones in
1 large onion, chopped
1 tablespoon butter
2 tablespoons curry powder
1 cooking apple, peeled and chopped
¼ cup dried apricots
2 tablespoons brown sugar
1½ cups water
1 teaspoon salt
¼ cup raisins

Method

Cut the lamb between the bones into strips 3 cm wide, leaving two bones in each strip. Put the strips in a baking dish and cook at 220°C for 30 minutes to brown, turning them a few times. Meanwhile, sauté the onion in butter until soft. Add the curry powder, then the apple, apricots, brown sugar and water. Stir, cover and simmer gently for 30 minutes. Drain the fat from the lamb strips and pour the fruit mix over them through a sieve. Season with salt and sprinkle on the raisins. Cover the dish with foil and cook at 180°C for 30–45 minutes or until tender. Skim off the excess fat and serve with hot rice and salad.

Shepherds hut on Moira Station, Victoria, 1869. (National Library of Australia)

Baked Bananas

Ingredients

4 bananas
melted butter
1 tablespoon cornflour
¼ cup water
3 tablespoons raisins
15 g butter
3 tablespoons clear honey
3 tablespoons lemon juice
¼ teaspoon ground cinnamon

Method

Peel and slice the bananas lengthways and brush them with a little melted butter. Arrange them in the bottom of an ovenproof dish. Then mix together the cornflour and water and cook gently for 10 minutes. Add the raisins, butter, honey, lemon juice and cinnamon and stir well until well blended. Pour the sauce over the bananas and bake at 180°C for 30 minutes. Serve hot with ice cream or cream.

A shop at Gulgong, New South Wales. (Mitchell Library, Sydney)

Ginger Beer

Travel in Australia even in the late nineteenth century was often far from comfortable. The railway system was still limited and a journey from one country town to another was usually made either by a Cobb & Company coach or by a local wagon. In either case, summer heat or flash floods would do little to make it a pleasant experience. Cobb & Co. started their first coach service in 1853 between Melbourne and Castlemaine and dominated country transport until their last run in 1924 from Yeulba to Surat in Queensland. In 1870, Cobb & Co. covered 45,000 km each week and harnessed 6,000 horses every day.

Method

From the notebook of Helenus Scott the younger, 1822.
'Take 1 oz of ginger root sliced, 2 dr of Cream of Tartar, the juice and peel of one lemon, 1 lb of loaf sugar and one gallon of water—

'Boil the water and ginger together for about ½ hour over a slow fire, then add them to the other ingredients. When milk warm add one tablespoon of yeast. After the yeast is added let it stand 24 hours covered with a cloth. Lastly strain it through a fine cloth and bottle it in stone bottles taking care to tie the corks and put the beer in a cool place. It is fit for drinking in 18 hours or if wanted before put a few bottles in the sun and it will be fit for use in 2 hours.'

Cobb & Co. coach on the route between Corowa and Urana, 1890. (National Library of Australia)

Camp Pie

The discovery of gold transformed Australia. It made it wealthy, brought in people, opened up the bush and, perhaps more incidentally, did much to foster the Australian concept of 'mateship'. After the easy alluvial gold had been worked out of the river valleys it became necessary to sink deep shafts in the surrounding hills to work the underground seams. The prospector slowly gave way to companies that had to be formed to raise the capital necessary to buy and establish the heavy machinery that was now required.

Ingredients

700 g shin beef
250 g bacon
1 teaspoon salt
mace
cayenne pepper
½ teaspoon mustard
1 tablespoon gelatine
1 egg, beaten

Method

Mince the beef and bacon, then add the salt, a little mace and cayenne, the mustard and gelatine. Bind the mixture with the beaten egg and pack it tightly into a billy. Cover with buttered paper and put the lid on. Steam for 2½ hours. Then take it from the fire, remove the lid and put a weight on the pie until it is firm.

Family group on the goldfields, New South Wales, 1872. (Mitchell Library, Sydney)

Plum Duff

> 'Well, we are now at work, sinking a round hole about five feet in diameter, and have sunk three feet since morning; and when the time comes, home we go to dinner. Tea, fried mutton, and a damper is the general dish with diggers for breakfast, dinner and supper; but on Sunday, plum dough for dinner is "all the go".'
>
> John Sherer, *The Gold-Finder of Australia*, 1853.

Ingredients

¼ cup plain flour
¼ cup self-raising flour
pinch salt
½ teaspoon bicarbonate of soda
60 g suet
1 egg
2 tablespoons sugar
1 cup cooked prunes
1 teaspoon mixed spice

Method

Sift together the flour, salt and bicarbonate of soda. Shred the suet and rub it into the flour. Beat the egg, add the sugar, then add the prunes after cutting them into small pieces. Gently fold in the flour and stir in the spice. Tip the mixture into a floured pudding cloth, gather it up and tie securely. Put it into a large saucepan of boiling water and boil for 3 hours.

Currants and sultanas can be used instead of prunes, and the pudding can be steamed by putting the mixture in a basin, covering with greased brown paper and standing in boiling water for about 45 minutes.

Gold miners, New South Wales, 1872. (Mitchell Library, Sydney)

Boned Shoulder of Lamb

Although Governor Phillip brought the first sheep to Australia in 1788 it was the introduction of the merino that paved the way for Australia's wool industry. Since then wool has been a vital part of the Australian economy. With a sheep population of about 165 million, the country now produces 900 million kilograms of wool each year, about a third of the world's total.

Ingredients

1 shoulder of lamb, boned

STUFFING:
1 tablespoon butter
1 cup fresh breadcrumbs
¼ teaspoon salt
pepper
1 tablespoon parsley, chopped
pinch dried herbs
a little grated nutmeg
1 egg

Method

Mix all the stuffing ingredients together, using the egg to moisten the mixture. Wipe the meat with a damp cloth, fill it with the stuffing and tie securely. Put the meat in a baking dish with the fat side up and cook in a moderate oven, allowing about an hour for each kilo. Turn the meat about halfway through the cooking time, and put potatoes and pumpkin in the dish about an hour before the meat is cooked. When cooked, remove the meat and untie. Serve with the vegetables.

Loading the wool clip. (Mitchell Library, Sydney)

Beef Wellington

> '*Is anyone aware that there is in Melbourne a cafe where one may get a French dinner and a bottle of wine for the modest sum of one shilling and sixpence? It is so . . . "I am told," said Sporboy, "that there is a house at which one can EAT, not feed, not gorge, not cram, Sir, but EAT!"'*
>
> Marcus Clarke, *Leader Supplement*, 2 April 1881.

Ingredients

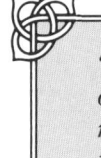

1 kg fillet steak
60 g butter
125 g mushrooms, sliced
salt and pepper
¼ cup brandy
340 g puff pastry
60 g liverwurst
1 egg yolk

RED WINE GRAVY:
1 tablespoon flour
1 stock cube
½ cup claret
½ cup water

Method

Sauté the mushrooms in half the butter until soft, season with salt and pepper, then drain and remove them from the pan. Add the other half of the butter to the pan and, when hot and foaming, add the fillet and brown it well all over. Pour the brandy over it and set it alight. Remove and allow to cool. Keep the pan juices on one side for making the sauce.

Roll the pastry out thinly. Then put the fillet at one end and spread the liverwurst and cooked mushrooms over the top. Moisten the edges of the pastry and enclose the fillet, sealing the edges well by pressing them firmly together. Decorate with pastry trimmings and brush all over with the egg yolk. Place on a baking sheet and cook at 220°C for 35 minutes or until cooked to taste.

To make the gravy, re-warm the pan juices and blend in the flour. Add the stock cube, the claret and water and stir until smooth and thickened. Simmer for one minute and season with salt and pepper. Serve separately.

Annual Dinner of Woman Journalist's Association, 1912. (Mitchell Library, Sydney)

Lambs Fry and Bacon

Popular throughout the whole of Australia, this dish is a familiar item on the menu of the traditional 'counter tea'.

Ingredients

1 lamb's liver
175 g fat bacon
1½ tablespoons flour
½ teaspoon salt
pepper
parsley
pinch of herbs
1 teaspoon dripping
Worcestershire sauce
300 ml water

Method

Wash the liver in warm water and dry it well. Remove the rind from the bacon, cut into strips and thread about half of them on to a skewer as a garnish. Cut the liver down from the thin end into strips and dip each strip into a mixture of the flour, salt, pepper, parsley and herbs. Cook the bacon in a frying pan, remove and keep hot. Heat the bacon fat in the pan, add the dripping and then add the pieces of liver. Fry for 5 minutes then turn them and cook for another 4 minutes, keeping the pieces moving so that they do not burn. Remove the liver and keep hot. Drain off the surplus fat from the pan to leave about a tablespoonful, then add the flour mixture that was used to coat the liver. Stir until brown, then add the water and Worcestershire sauce to taste. Bring to the boil and thicken, stirring all the time. Put the liver pieces back in the pan and simmer for 8 minutes. Serve hot with the skewered bacon.

A commercial traveller's wagonette outside the Palace Hotel, Central Tilba, New South Wales. (National Library of Australia)

Grilled Barramundi

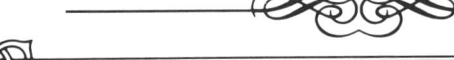

There are more than 2,000 species of fish in Australian coastal waters and although many are edible, the members of the First Fleet found them difficult to catch. There are also about 150 species of freshwater fish, although some, like trout, are not natives. The Murray cod can reach 60 kg whilst the barramundi, one of our best eating fish, can grow to 14 kg in the warm waters of northern Australia.

Ingredients

4 barramundi cutlets
lemon juice
4 tablespoons clarified butter
2 tablespoons shallots, chopped
black pepper
parsley

Method

Squeeze some lemon juice over the cutlets and put them on one side for 15 minutes. Then brush them with the clarified butter and grill for about 8 minutes each side. Sauté the shallots in the rest of the butter and pour over the cutlets. Season with black pepper and garnish with parsley.

Ted Sheather and his son with a large Murray cod. Gundagai, about 1900. (National Library of Australia)

Meat Loaf

Although fresh meat was not available during the first few years after the colony was established, by the middle of the nineteenth century it was cheap and plentiful and had become an essential part of Australian cooking. By the end of the century the annual consumption of meat in Australia was 125 kg per head, compared with 50 kg per head in Great Britain.

Ingredients

500 g steak, finely minced
500 g sausage meat
100 g bacon, chopped
½ cup white breadcrumbs
1 medium-sized onion, finely chopped
1½ tablespoons chopped parsley
1 clove garlic, crushed
1 egg
2 tablespoons tomato sauce
1 teaspoon Worcestershire sauce
salt and pepper

Method

Using a large bowl, combine the minced steak, sausage meat, bacon, breadcrumbs, onion, parsley and garlic. Beat the egg and mix it with the tomato sauce and the Worcestershire sauce, then stir in to the meat mixture. Season with salt and pepper. Pack the mixture into a well-greased loaf tin and cover with greased foil. Bake at 175°C for 1¼–1½ hours, then remove the foil and bake for a further 15 minutes. Drain off the excess fat and turn the loaf out on to a plate. Serve hot or cold.

The butcher at Tilba Tilba in 1895. (National Library of Australia)

Stewed Oxtail

Bullocks provided the heavy transport of nineteenth-century Australia, taking supplies to remote settlers and bringing back the wool clip. Although they only covered about 8 km a day, they could take their heavy loads almost anywhere and their tracks are the origins of many twentieth-century roads. Unlike other travellers, the bullockies could carry ample supplies for their own use and their hospitality in the bush was legendary. So, too, was their language.

Ingredients

1 oxtail
1 cup seasoned flour
1 onion, sliced
1 tablespoon flour
1.7 litres stock
1 bouquet garni
1 teaspoon lemon juice
1 carrot, sliced

Method

Take the fat off the oxtail and cut it into joints. Coat each joint with the seasoned flour. Put a little fat in a large saucepan, add the onion and cook until it is brown. Then add the meat, flour, stock, bouquet garni and lemon juice and simmer gently for 4 hours. Then add the carrot and simmer for another hour. Remove the bouquet garni and if necessary thicken the gravy with flour. Serve hot with vegetables.

Teamsters making camp, 1871. (National Library of Australia)

Rabbit Casserole

Once very popular, the rabbit is to many Australians an unpleasant reminder of the Depression, when there was little else to put on the table. Nor did the introduction of myxomatosis do much to enhance its culinary appeal. All of which is unfortunate as they still make very good eating.

Ingredients

1 whole rabbit, about 1 kg
seasoned flour
3 bacon rashers
1 medium-sized onion, chopped
1 cup sliced carrot
1 cup sliced parsnip
2 tablespoons flour
1 chicken stock cube mixed with water
salt and pepper
parsley for garnish

Method

Soak the rabbit for 30 minutes in warm water, then dry it and cut into joints. Coat each piece with seasoned flour and put on one side. Cut the bacon into 5 cm pieces, fry until the fat is clear and then take them from the pan. Put the pieces of rabbit in the same pan, fry them until they are brown all over and then put them in a casserole. Put the onion, carrot and parsnip in the frying pan and cook until lightly browned. Stir in the flour and cook until it goes a pale brown. Add the stock and stir until it boils and thickens. Season with salt and pepper and pour over the rabbit. Put the pieces of bacon on the top, cover the casserole and bake at 175°C for 1½–2 hours or until the meat is tender. Garnish with parsley.

The rabbito, about 1900. (National Library of Australia)

Lamingtons

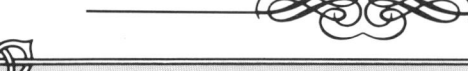

'*Nearly every colonial girl learns something of household work, and can cook some sort of a dinner . . .*'
Richard Twopenny, *Town Life in Australia*, 1883.

Ingredients

2 cups self-raising flour
pinch of salt
¾ cup sugar
125 g butter
3 eggs
vanilla essence
½ cup milk

CHOCOLATE ICING:
2 cups icing sugar
4 tablespoons cocoa
125 g butter
1 teaspoon lemon essence
warm water
2 cups desiccated coconut

Method

Sift the flour and salt. Cream the sugar and butter and add the eggs and vanilla essence. Beat well, then fold in the flour and salt mixture and add the milk. Grease a lamington tin and add the mixture. Bake at 180°C for 30–35 minutes and allow to cool on a wire rack. Meanwhile, make the chocolate icing by sifting the icing sugar and cocoa together. Melt the butter, add the lemon essence and beat into the sugar and cocoa mixture. Beat well and add enough water to give the required consistency. Dip each lamington in the icing and then roll in the desiccated coconut while the icing is still moist.

Miss Fowler's cooking class, Adelaide, 1913. (South Australian Archives)

Aberdeen Sausage

Ingredients

500 g beef steak
6 rashers bacon
2 cups breadcrumbs, browned
1 egg
¼ teaspoon pepper
½ teaspoon salt
1 tablespoon Worcestershire
  sauce

Method

Mince the steak and bacon and pound all the ingredients except the breadcrumbs together until well blended. Add the beaten egg to bind the mixture. Make into a roll and tie a cloth round it, putting a stitch in the middle if neccessary. Put into boiling water and boil for 2 hours, making sure that the roll is always well covered with the water. Lift out the roll and let it stand for a few minutes, then turn it out of the cloth and cover with the breadcrumbs. Serve cold.

Teamsters at a meal break. (National Library of Australia)

Chicken and Almond Casserole

Gundagai is a typical Australian country town. Built on the banks of the Murrumbidgee River and halfway between Sydney and Melbourne, it now has a population of more than two thousand. Although much has changed since it was first laid out in 1840 it is still an important stopping place for overland travellers.

Ingredients

1 chicken, about 1.25 kg
thyme
salt and pepper
seasoned flour
1 large onion, chopped
½ cup blanched almonds, sliced
2 cups chopped celery
2 tablespoons flour
1½ tablespoons butter
½ cup cream

Method

Joint the chicken and put the pieces into a saucepan with the thyme. Cover with boiling water to which a little salt and pepper have been added and simmer gently for an hour. Remove the chicken pieces (reserve the stock), take the meat from the bones and cut into small cubes, then toss in seasoned flour. Fry the onion, almonds and celery until lightly browned, stirring all the time. Then add the chicken cubes and keep turning them until they are lightly browned. Remove, drain and put them in a casserole. Cover with the onion, almond and celery mixture. Blend the flour into the fat remaining in the pan, add the cream and reserved chicken stock and stir until the mixture thickens. Lightly season and pour into the casserole. Cover and cook at 175°C for about 40 minutes or until the chicken is tender.

Country lady, Gundagai, about 1900. (National Library of Australia)

How to cure mutton hams

From Mrs Mitchell's manuscript book of 'Receipes' written in 1827 and now in the Mitchell Library, Sydney.

'It is necessary that the mutton should be very fat. Two ounces of raw sugar must be mixed with an ounce of common salt and half a spoon full of saltpeter. The meat is to be rubbed well with this and then placed in a turee. It must be beaten and turned twice a day during three consecutive days. And the scum which comes from the meat having been taken off, it is to be wiped and again rubbed with the mixture.

'The next day it should be again beaten and the two operations should be repeated alternately during ten days, care being taken to turn the meat each time. It must then be exposed to the smoak for ten days.

'These hams are generally eaten cold.'

House on the goldfields, Gulgong, New South Wales, 1872. (Mitchell Library, Sydney)

Pavlova

One of the few dishes to originate in Australia, the pavlova was invented in Perth by Herbert Sachse when Pavlova was touring Western Australia. Needing a sure touch to make well, one housewife in any rural community will be recognized as the best pavlova-maker, although she will be expected to defend that reputation at each Annual Show. They are also made commercially, usually by small bakeries, and they too are very jealous of their reputation.

Ingredients

4 egg whites
pinch of salt
1 cup castor sugar
1 teaspoon cornflour
1 teaspoon vinegar
1 teaspoon vanilla essence
whipped cream
passionfruit (traditionally) or
    strawberries

Method

Beat the egg whites with the salt until very stiff, then gradually blend in the sugar until it is all dissolved. Continue beating and add the cornflour, vinegar and vanilla essence. Pile the mixture thickly on to a 35-cm pavlova tray and bake near the bottom of the oven at 140°C for about 1½ hours or until quite firm to touch. Turn the heat off and leave the pavlova in the oven until cool. Fill with whipped cream and garnish with the fruit.

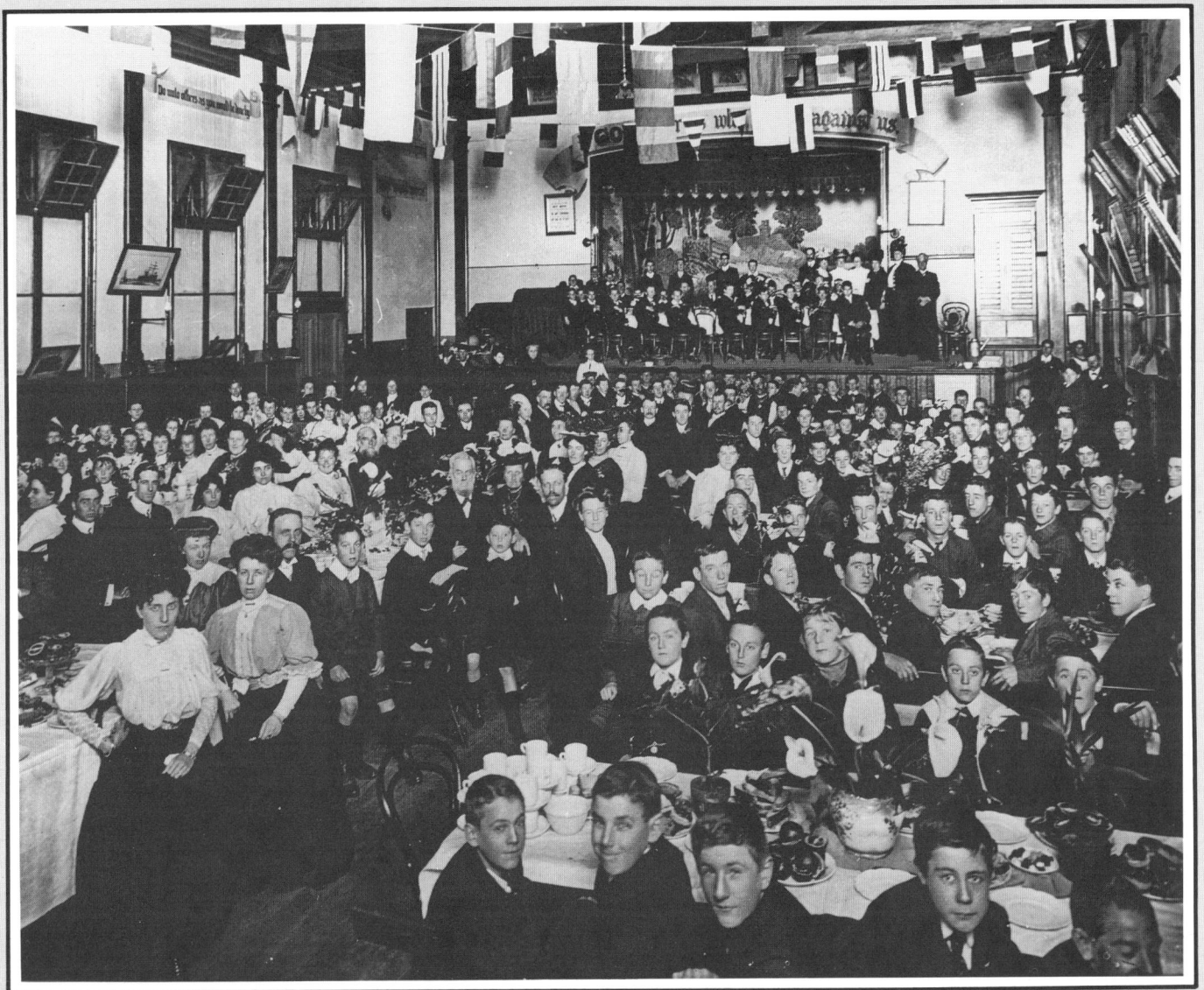

Try Boys Pound Night, Melbourne, 1907. (La Trobe Collection, State Library of Victoria)

Rock Melon Fruit Salad

The first photograph in Australia was taken in Sydney in May 1841, little more than a year after the techniques of photography had been explained in Europe by Daguerre. The name of the photographer is not known, but it is thought that he was probably a Frenchman who was in Sydney on business. The first Australian photographer was G. B. Goodman who in 1842 opened his business at the Royal Hotel in George Street, where Dymocks bookshop now stands. The dry plate was introduced in the 1880s, and as the process became more manageable it was quickly taken up by a growing number of wealthy amateurs.

Ingredients

SYRUP:
½ cup castor sugar
6 tablespoons water
2 tablespoons maraschino

1 large rock melon
1 punnet of small strawberries
1 cup pineapple pieces
3 bananas, sliced
lemon juice

Method

Slice the top third off the melon and put it on one side for later use. Take the larger part of the melon, remove and discard the seeds, then, using a melon scoop or a large spoon, scoop out the flesh and put it in a bowl. Hull and wash the strawberries, sprinkle the slices of banana with lemon juice to prevent them discolouring, and add the strawberries and bananas to the bowl together with the pineapple pieces. Allow to chill.

To make the syrup, put the sugar and water into a small pan. Stir over a low heat until the sugar dissolves, then bring to the boil. Remove from the heat, add the maraschino, allow to cool and then pour over the fruit in the bowl. Just before serving, heap the fruit and syrup into the melon shell and replace the top.

Photographic society outing near Melbourne, probably about 1890. (La Trobe Collection, State Library of Victoria)

Avocado with Crab Meat

A simple dish that draws on ingredients readily available in Australia, if not elsewhere.

Ingredients

2 ripe avocados
lemon juice
125 g crab meat
1 tablespoon mayonnaise
2 tablespoons thickened cream
1 teaspoon French dressing
salt and pepper

Method

Halve the avocados, remove the stones and sprinkle the flesh with lemon juice. Mix all the other ingredients together gently and season with salt and pepper. Spoon this mixture into the centre of each avocado half. Serve with lemon wedges and slices of brown bread and butter.

Bush wedding near Bundaberg, Queensland, about 1904. (National Library of Australia)

Anzac Biscuits

The word Anzac was made from the initials of the Australia and New Zealand Army Corps, but was applied to all soldiers from the two countries during the First World War. Anzac Day, 25 April, is held as a public holiday each year to mark the landing of the troops at Gallipoli in 1915, when, pinned down under withering fire, they tried to establish a beachhead. Anzac Day is marked by solemn ceremonies and marches, followed by reunions that are a good deal less solemn. The biscuits called Anzacs seem far removed from all that.

Ingredients

1 cup plain flour
1 cup rolled oats
¾ cup desiccated coconut
¾ cup sugar
½ teaspoon baking powder
125 g butter
2 tablespoons golden syrup

Method

Sift the flour and combine it with the oats, coconut, sugar and baking powder in a bowl. Melt the butter and add the golden syrup, stirring over a low heat until the syrup is melted. Stir the melted butter mixture into the dry ingredients and mix to a smooth batter. Roll the mixture into small balls, put them on a greased oven tray and flatten each ball slightly with the heel of the hand. Bake in a slow oven, 150°C, for about 15 minutes.

Australian Field Artillery in the First World War. (Mitchell Library, Sydney)

Mother Eve's Pudding

From Mrs Mitchell's *'Receipes'*, 1872, now in the Mitchell Library, Sydney:

'If you'd have a good pudding pray mind what you're taught
Take two pennyworth of eggs when they're twelve for a groat
Take of the same fruit, with which Eve did once cozen
Well pared and well chopped at least half a dozen
Three ounces of bread, let your maid eat the crust
The crumbs must be grated as small as the dust
Three ounces of currants from the stones you must sort
Lest they break out your teeth and spoil all your sport
Three ounces of sugar'll not make it too sweet
Some salt and some nutmeg to make it compleat
Three hours let it boil without any flutter
Nor is it so good without sugar and butter.'

Unloading apples from a river steamer for overseas shipment. Hobart, Tasmania. (Mitchell Library, Sydney)

Barbecued Steak

Although eating outdoors has always been popular in Australia, barbecuing is a relatively recent social development. For a long time, cooking outside was a necessary chore when travelling the long distances between settlements and was not regarded with any great enthusiasm, although the results were often pleasant enough. More recently, of course, barbecuing has become part of the Australian way of life. Varying in sophistication from the bush barbecue that has much in common with those early travellers, to three course meals produced in wealthy suburbs, they all hope to combine good food, good company and good weather.

The steak should preferably be thick and of a quality cut. Trim off the surplus fat, but be careful not to pierce the meat as that will allow juices to escape as it is cooked and make it dry. Do not add salt as that will also draw out the juices. Make the fire good and hot, but if using wood, the heat should come from the bed of ashes, not from leaping flames. Then put the steak on an open grill above the fire and leave it alone—there is no need to push it or prod it, and it certainly should not be turned unnecessarily. Wait until the juices form on the top of the steak and *then* turn it over—not before. Cook the other side until the juices appear once again, take it off the grill and serve it immediately. This method produces a steak that is slightly rare—for a medium steak, allow the juices to gather a little longer.

The barbecue flavour comes from the juices which drop from the steak on to the fire below and which are then vaporized back up to the meat by the heat of the fire. It follows from this that provided the meat is on an open grill the choice of fuel is unimportant, although a wood fire will add a smoky flavour of its own. Dry gum leaves thrown on the fire will also add flavour, but this should be done towards the end of the cooking as the flavour can become intrusive if done too soon.

Bush picnic. (National Library of Australia)

Kangaroo Tail Soup

Although a few smaller species are found in New Guinea, most marsupials are unique to Australia. Kangaroos were first reported by François Pelsaert in 1629 when his ship was wrecked on the coast of Western Australia, and again by Captain Cook in 1770, although it is now thought that they both saw wallabies, not kangaroos. In Colonial Australia, the kangaroo was widely used as food and Kangaroo Tail Soup is perhaps the most famous Australian dish. Although at the time opinion differed as to its merits, John Sherer made no attempt to restrain his enthusiasm for it in *The Gold-Finder of Australia* in 1853: *'The pannikin was washed out and found perfectly water tight, when I was despatched to fill it at the pond I had discovered. The distance was fully a mile from our encampment; but who would grudge three times that distance for half-a-pint of kangaroo tail soup in our circumstances? a dish fit for an alderman; rivalling the most superb ox-tail ever cooked in the most esteemed refectory of London.'*

Ingredients

2 kangaroo tails
butter
3 carrots, sliced
4 onions, sliced
bunch of herbs
500 g gravy beef, sliced
salt and pepper
3.5 litres water

Method

Cut the tails into joints and fry them in butter until they go brown. Then add the carrots and onions and fry until they just turn brown. Put the tail joints and vegetables into a large saucepan together with the herbs and gravy beef and season with salt and pepper. Add 3.5 litres of water, bring to the boil, then allow to simmer for about four hours. Then take out the tail joints, strain the stock and thicken with flour, return the joints and boil for a further ten minutes before serving.

Prince Alfred starting for a kangaroo hunt at Campbell House Station, South Australia, about 1868. (Mitchell Library, Sydney)

Kangaroo Steamer

'Take the most tender part of the kangaroo, being careful to remove all the sinews. Chop it very fine, about the same quantity of smoked bacon (fat); season with finely-powdered marjoram, pepper and a very little salt. Let it "steam", or "stew", for two hours; then pack or press tight in open-mouthed glass bottles; the bung must be sealed down, and the outside of the bottles washed well with white of egg, beaten; preserved in this way it will keep "good" for twelve months or more. When needed for use, the vessel containing the preserve should be put into a saucepan of cold water, and allowed to boil for fifteen minutes (if a large bottle); when dished, pour a little rich brown gravy over it, flavoured with mace, salt, and pepper; garnish with forcemeat balls. If required for immediate use, half an hour will cook it sufficiently; no gravy will be necessary. Forcemeat balls without bacon will be found a great improvement.

'Mrs Sarah Crouch, the lady of the respected Under-Sheriff of Tasmania, obtained a Prize Medal for the above at the Exhibition of 1862, and has allowed us to make public the recipe. The dish was partaken of by the guests of the Acclimatisation Society, at the London dinner of that year, Lord Stanley in the chair. Several speakers commented on the goodness of the "steamer". Sir John Maxwell, a first rate judge, pronounced it excellent as a stew, and said that he should like to see it introduced into the Navy. It is understood that Prince Napoleon, one of the first gastronomers of the day, was desirous to acclimatise the kangaroo to France, for the sake of the "cuisine" the animal affords.'

E. Abbott, *The English and Australian Cookery Book*, 1864.

Dinner time on a station, 1882. (National Library of Australia)

Cheese

The popularity of cheese in Australia increased considerably with the setting up of cheese-making co-operatives, which took over the time consuming process from the dairy farmer.

'The process which the milk goes through after reaching the vats may be briefly described as follows:— By means of steam it is heated to about 85°F, when the rennet is introduced. The milk becomes completely curdled in half an hour, and is then cut up into little cubed shaped pieces by passing through it the curd cutter, an instrument composed of a number of sharp blades about an inch apart. The curd is again heated to about 100°, when the whey is drawn off by a syphon. This having been done the curd is cooled and salted, and then put into the press. Here it loses what whey may have been left in it after about a quarter of an hour to twenty minutes pressing. The cloth is then put on, and after the cheese has again been pressed it is taken out and trimmed, so as to present a neat and taking appearance. It is then put into the press again, and remains there for about eighteen hours being subject to pressure all the time, by weight as well as the lever screw presses . . . The cheeses, having been thoroughly pressed, are removed to the cheese room, where they are placed on shelves to mature prior to being sold.'

From the Melbourne *Age*, 26 July 1884.

Staff displaying cheese at the A.B.C. Co-operative Cheese Society Ltd, New South Wales, 1903. (National Library of Australia)

Pigs Trotters

Ingredients

8 pig's trotters (salted or plain)
1 onion, chopped
1 carrot, chopped
1 celery stalk, chopped
6 peppercorns
2 sprigs parsley
1 bay leaf

Method

Rinse the trotters well and scrub them to remove hairs. Bring a pot of water to the boil, drop in the trotters and boil them for five minutes. Drain off the water, then put the trotters, vegetables, peppercorns, parsley and bay leaf in the pot and cover with cold water. Bring it slowly to the boil, skim the liquid and reduce the heat. Cover the pot and simmer for 1½–2 hours or until tender. Allow the liquid to cool before removing the trotters. Serve cold with salad.

Wash day. (National Library of Australia)

Potted Meat

Not surprisingly, timber was the traditional building material of the bush: it was easily worked and freely available. Unlike the Americans, however, the Australian settler rarely used whole logs. Instead, he split them with wedges into slabs which were erected vertically with the curved side on the outside. This technique used less timber and gave a more weatherproof finish. The roof was made of bark that had been carefully stripped off the logs in sheets and then laid over the roof framework. Poles were hung from the ridge cap over the bark to keep it flat. Chimneys were always on the outside of one wall and were lined with mud or stones to make them fireproof.

Ingredients

500 g shin of beef
2 pig's trotters or 1 knuckle
  of veal
2 lamb shanks
1 carrot, diced
1 turnip, diced
1 onion, chopped
stick of celery, sliced
4 peppercorns
2 allspice
water
parsley

Method

Trim off the excess fat from the meat. Place all ingredients in a large saucepan with enough water to cover them. Bring to the boil, then cover and simmer for 3–4 hours, when the meat should be falling from the bones. Lift out the meat and chop it finely before putting it in a large basin. Skim the fat from the cooking liquid and pour enough of the liquid into the basin to cover the meat. Mix well, put into a mould and refrigerate overnight. Turn out on to the serving plate and garnish with the parsley.

A shepherd's hut, 1870. (National Library of Australia)

Christmas Cake

'The "Christmas dinner" truly seemed to me a most odd and anomalous affair. Instead of having won a seasonable appetite by a brisk walk over the crisped snow, well muffled in warm winter garments, I had passed the miserable morning, half-dead with heat, on the sofa, attired in the coolest muslin dress I possessed, sipping lemonade . . .'

Mrs Meredith, *Notes and Sketches of New South Wales*, 1844.

Ingredients

30 g ground almonds
3 large eggs
210 g plain flour
mixed spice

340 g currants
225 g sultanas
60 g cut mixed peel
110 g glace cherries
30 g glycerine
170 g soft brown sugar
170 g butter

Method

Mix all the fruit together, rub in the glycerine and leave it exposed in a large bowl for twenty-four hours. Cream the butter and sugar together with the ground almonds. Then add the eggs, having slightly warmed them first by standing them in a container in hot water for ten minutes. Sift the flour and the mixed spice together and lightly blend into the mixture. Add the fruit and mix gently until it is evenly distributed, but do not overmix. Put the mixture into a 20-cm tin which has been lined with double thickness of greaseproof paper. Bake for one hour at 137°C, then reduce the heat to 120°C and bake until the cake is firm to touch. If the top of the cake browns too quickly, cover it lightly with foil.

Afternoon tea at the homestead. (Mitchell Library, Sydney)

Peanut Butter

As much a part of Australian childhood as Blinky Bill, peanut butter sandwiches were the between-meal filler or the meal itself—the Australian equivalent of the jam butty of the north of England. Expatriate Australians often become nostalgic at the thought of it—I was once with one at the Ritz in London when he thought he might embarrass that hotel by ordering them for tea. In due course, and with probably little effort, they served them, although it was, as he said, the first time he had been given peanut butter sandwiches without the crusts.

Ingredients

2 cups peanuts, shelled and
with skins removed
½ teaspoon salt

Method

Put the peanuts through the mincer twice. Then add the salt and mince again. The oil in the peanuts should be sufficient to make a paste that will be ready to put into pots, but, if not, a little melted butter can be added and thoroughly mixed in.

Country children with their governess (centre). About 1898. (National Library of Australia)

Apple Cobbler

Bush boarding houses and hotels were often rough and ready affairs, although many were able to offer a fair degree of comfort and a reasonably good table. However good or bad, though, the traveller usually did not have much choice as they were often hundreds of kilometres apart, and the only alternative was to spend another night in the open.

Ingredients

2 cups stewed apples, drained but moist
1½ cups self-raising flour
30 g butter
1 tablespoon sugar
2 tablespoons grated lemon rind
1 egg
2/3 cup milk
2 tablespoons brown sugar
½ teaspoon cinnamon

Method

Put the apples in a greased cake tin. Sift the flour and rub in the butter; then add the sugar and lemon rind and mix to a soft dough with the beaten egg and milk. Shape the dough to fit the cake tin and put it on top of the apples. Slit it with a knife. Bake it in a hot oven, 200°C for about 25 minutes. Brush the top of the hot pie with milk and sprinkle it with the brown sugar and cinnamon. Serve hot with cream.

William Sam's boarding house at Gulgong, New South Wales. 1872. (Mitchell Library, Sydney)

Oysters in Bacon

Sydney rock oysters are justifiably famous throughout the whole of Australia. Because they are abundant (there is no closed season) and relatively cheap, they are widely distributed and much enjoyed. Sydney rock oysters grow naturally along the coast from the Victorian border to Brisbane, but because they are small, most oysters served on the table have come from one of the many oyster farms near Sydney. Most start their life in the waters off Port Stephens, where the small spats are collected on tarred sticks which are then sold to farmers. The sticks are kept in racks on the farm until the spats have become mature oysters. This takes about three years. In Tasmania, Pacific oysters are bred in hatcheries and grown individually to maturity in beds of grit, producing oysters that are larger and more uniform in shape.

Ingredients

1 dozen oysters
500 g thin streaky bacon
cayenne pepper
lemon juice
Worcestershire sauce

Method

Remove the rind from the bacon and cut the rashers into strips about 100 mm long. Wash the oysters in their own liquor and place one on each strip of bacon. Squeeze a little lemon juice over them and then add a dash of cayenne pepper. Roll each up in its strip of bacon and fasten with a skewer. Put them in a hot oven (about 250°C) and cook for 8–10 minutes. To serve, replace in the warmed shells and add a dash of Worcestershire sauce.

Fernandez oyster shop in William Street, Sydney, in the early 1900s. (Telecom Australia)

Chicken with Wine and Peaches

The first officially organized race meeting in Australia was held at Sydney's Hyde Park in 1810. The Governor gave the convicts the afternoon off, trusting that they would conduct themselves in 'a sober, discrete and orderly manner'. They didn't.

Ingredients

1 chicken about 1.5 kg
1 orange, peeled, with pith removed, and cut into quarters
1 medium-sized onion, peeled and cut in half
1 bay leaf
60 g butter
1 cup white wine
500 g can peach slices, drained
½ cup juice from the peaches
salt and pepper

Method

Season the chicken inside and out with salt and pepper. Stuff the cavity with the orange, onion and bay leaf and put the chicken in a roasting dish. Rub the butter into the breast and pour on the white wine and the peach juice. Cover with foil and bake at 190°C for 30 minutes, then remove the foil and bake for another hour and a quarter or until done. Put the chicken on a serving dish. Simmer the pan juices gently until thickened, then add the peach slices and heat through. Pour over the chicken and serve.

Randwick racecourse, Sydney. (Mitchell Library, Sydney)

Tomato Sauce

Some people might suggest that if there is a taste of Australia, then it is the taste of tomato sauce. No pub meal would be complete without it and, like flies, it is inevitably present at a barbecue. But if it is sometimes used more generously than might be necessary, it cannot be denied that it is an ideal sauce for many of the meat dishes that are such an important part of Australian cooking. This recipe, from about 1866, comes from Elizabeth Coghill's manuscript diary, which is now in the Mitchell Library, Sydney.

Ingredients

20 lb tomatoes
2 lb onions, chopped
1 lb sugar
½ lb salt
½ lb horse radish, grated
¾ oz cayenne pepper
½ oz cloves
½ oz allspice
½ oz mace
1 quart vinegar

Method

Simmer gently eight hours. Beat through a cullender. When cold, bottle and cork tightly. Boil in enamelled saucepans to preserve the colour.

Prince of Wales Hotel, Gulgong, New South Wales, 1872. (Mitchell Library, Sydney)

Curried Prawns

Ingredients

1 kg prawns
1 onion, diced
butter
1 tablespoon flour
1 tablespoon curry powder
salt
1½ cups stock
lemon juice
boiled rice
1 marrow, thickly sliced in
    rings, steamed and with
    seeds removed
lemon wedges

Method

Fry the onion in the butter, then add the flour and curry powder and a pinch of salt. Slowly add the stock, stirring all the time to keep the mixture smooth. Simmer for thirty minutes, then add the prawns and a little lemon juice. Put the marrow rings on the boiled rice on the serving dish and fill the rings with the prawn mixture. Serve with lemon wedges.

Bush picnic. (National Library of Australia)

Lemon Fish

Captain Phillip explored Sydney Harbour on 23 January 1788 and immediately decided it was a better place for a settlement than Botany Bay. Moving the small fleet into the Harbour on 26 January he hoisted the British flag near the site of the present Customs House and named the spot Sydney Cove. Colonel George Barney turned it into an orderly waterfront between 1837 and 1844 and called it Semi-circular Quay, which was soon shortened to its present but less accurate name, Circular Quay. The fastest clipper ships in the world tied up alongside during their golden age, but as that age came to an end, the Quay took on its present role as the terminal of the Harbour Ferries.

Ingredients

1 kg fish fillets
1 egg yolk
1 tablespoon chopped onion
1 cup cooked rice
¼ cup melted butter
juice from ½ lemon
salt
pepper

Method

Lightly beat the egg yolk. Sauté the onion in a little butter and mix with the egg yolk, the rice and three teaspoons of melted butter. Season with salt and pepper and add half the lemon juice. Lay half the fish fillets in a greased ovenproof dish and spoon some of the mixture over each one. Lay the rest of the fillets on top, season with salt and pepper and pour on the rest of the melted butter and lemon juice. Cook at 200°C for 25–30 minutes, basting frequently with juices in the dish.

Circular Quay about 1892 looking towards the present site of the Opera House. (Mitchell Library, Sydney)

Cumquat Marmalade

The Chinese have a long history in Australia. They first came as shepherds after the end of transportation, but the gold rushes brought many more. By 1888 there were about 50,000 Chinese in Australia and, although many returned home, a large number stayed as market gardeners, craftsmen and businessmen.

Method

Slice the cumquats and add 4 cups of water to every kilogram of fruit. Allow to stand overnight and the next day boil until the fruit is tender. Then add 3 cups of sugar to every kilogram of cooked fruit and boil again until the mixture jells, which will take about 45 minutes.

Chinese market gardener, Katoomba, about 1890. (Mitchell Library, Sydney)

Sticker-up-Cooking

E. Abbott, in *The English and Australian Cookery Book*, 1864, quotes the following passage from *Home in Tasmania* by Mrs Meredith.

'Here I was first initiated into the bush art of "Sticker-up cookery", and for the benefit of all who go "a-gypsying", I will expound the mystery. The orthodox material here is of course the kangaroo, a piece of which is divided nicely into cutlets, two or three inches broad and a third of an inch thick. The next requisite is a straight, clean stick, about four feet long, sharpened at both ends. On the narrow part of this, for the space of a foot or more, the cutlets are spitted at intervals, and on the end is placed a piece of delicately rosy fat bacon. The strong end of the stick-spit is now stuck fast and erect in the ground, close to the fire, to leeward, care being taken that it does not burn. Then the bacon on the summit of the spit, speedily softening in the genial blaze, drops a lubricating shower of rich and savoury tears upon the leaner kangaroo cutlets below, which forthwith frizzle and steam and splutter with as much ado as if they were illustrious Christmas beef grilling in some London chop-house under the gratified nose of the expectant consumer. "And, gentlemen," as dear old Hardcastle would have said, if he had dined with us in the bush, "to men that are hungry, stuck-up kangaroo and bacon are very good eating." Kangaroo is, in fact, very much like hare.'

Miner's hut, Mount Dromedary. (National Library of Australia)

Carpetbag Steak

Although probably not an original Australian dish, carpetbag steak is a good example of how Australian cooking combines ingredients that are plentiful here, but scarce or expensive elsewhere. In this case, steak and oysters are used to produce a popular dish which would be prohibitively expensive in many other countries.

Ingredients

Fillet or rump steak, about
    5 cm thick
3 or 4 oysters
salad oil
lemon juice
chopped parsley

Method

Trim excess fat from the steak and with a sharp knife make a slit in the steak to form a pocket. Fill the pocket with oysters and fasten with cocktail sticks or by sewing with nylon thread. Mix the oil and lemon juice and marinade the steak for an hour or longer. Then grill the steak, turning carefully to avoid piercing the meat. Alternatively, cook the steak in a pan and after removing it, add the chopped parsley to the pan juices and perhaps a little sherry and pour over the steak.

Butchers shop, Gulgong, New South Wales. (Mitchell Library, Sydney)

Australian Meat Pie

> The most popular Australian snack, meat pies are sold by the thousand every day, in milk bars, in hotel bars, at sporting events, in fact wherever Australians gather. Usually made commercially by large manufacturers, this recipe captures all the flavour of this national dish.

Ingredients

750 g topside
2 lambs kidneys
1 tablespoon cooking oil
onion powder
¼ teaspoon M.S.G.
2 beef stock cubes
1 teaspoon Vegemite
2 tablespoons cornflour
salt and pepper
500 g puff pastry
1 egg, beaten

Method

Dice the topside and kidneys into small pieces (do not mince). Heat the oil in a saucepan, then add the meat and stir until it is browned. Add a good shake of onion powder, then the M.S.G., stock cubes and Vegemite. Add enough hot water to cover the meat, cover and simmer gently for about 1½ hours or until tender. Then mix the cornflour with enough cold water to make a thin cream and slowly add this to the meat. Bring to the boil until the mixture has a soft jelly consistency—adding more cornflour water mixture if necessary. Season with salt and pepper and allow the mixture to cool.

Roll out the puff pastry and line the inside of six individual pie tins which have been previously buttered. Fill with the meat mixture. From the remaining pastry cut circles slightly larger than the tins. Dampen the edges and fit them over the tins, pressing the edges down firmly. Make a small slit in the top and brush them with beaten egg. Preheat the oven to 230°C and cook for about 30 minutes until the pies are a deep golden brown.

Pie and coffee shop on the New South Wales goldfields, 1872. (Mitchell Library, Sydney)

Seafood Special

Ingredients

1.5 kg crayfish, cooked
2 blue swimmer crabs, cooked
1 kg prawns, cooked
500 g Balmain bugs, cooked
18 oysters, in their half-shells

DIP:
1 cup mayonnaise
¼ cup tomato ketchup
2 cloves garlic, crushed

DRESSING:
1 tablespoon oil
½ cup lemon juice
salt and pepper

Method

Take the tails off the crayfish and cut the rest into thick pieces, separating the claws. Cut the crabs into portions and rinse in cold water. Peel and remove the veins from the prawns. Remove the soft shell from underneath the bugs and rinse them in water. Arrange them all on a serving dish with the oysters, lettuce and lemon wedges and chill. When ready, pour the dressing over the seafood and serve the dip separately.

The ocean beach at Manly, Sydney. (Mitchell Library, Sydney)

Potato Salad

A squatter, photographed at his homestead near Wagga Wagga in 1900. The son of a Scottish Minister, he arrived in Victoria when he was sixteen with £7 in his pocket. At twenty-six he selected land in the Riverina district and at thirty he married. In 1900, at the age of sixty, he owned all his land and 75,000 sheep and showed an annual profit of £12,000.

Ingredients

6 large potatoes
3 eggs, hard boiled
3 tablespoons olive oil
2 tablespoons white wine
   vinegar
1 teaspoon salt
pepper
1 medium-sized onion,
   chopped
1 tablespoon chopped parsley
pepper
mayonnaise
capers

Method

Boil the potatoes in their skins until they are just tender, then peel and slice them whilst they are still warm. Peel and slice the eggs. Make the dressing with the oil, vinegar, salt and pepper. Put alternate layers of sliced potatoes and sliced eggs in a serving dish and sprinkle each layer with onion and parsley and pour on a little dressing. Finish with a layer of potato and allow to cool. Cover with mayonnaise and garnish with capers before serving.

Jugged Hare

 **Ingredients**

1 hare
1 cup flour
110 g bacon, diced
2 onions, sliced
herbs to taste
6 cloves
3 allspice
½ teaspoon black pepper
lemon peel
2 tablespoons butter
pepper and salt
1 teaspoon red currant jelly
small glass port

Method

Wash the hare and cut it into joints. Flour each one and fry them until they are lightly brown. Then add the bacon and fry lightly. Cover the bacon and joints with boiling water and add the rest of the ingredients, except jelly and port. Simmer for 3–4 hours or until tender. Then take the meat out. Strain the gravy, thicken it with butter and flour, and boil for 3 minutes. Then return the meat and add a teaspoon of red currant jelly and a small glass of port. Serve with fried forcemeat balls.

Shooting party at 'Sherringham', Central Tilba, about 1903. (National Library of Australia)

Australian Goose

An optimistic name for a dish familiar to all early Australians.

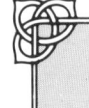

Ingredients

Shoulder of mutton with the
    bone removed
3 or 4 carrots, chopped
2 large onions, chopped
1 tablespoon dripping
1 cup claret

STUFFING:
1 onion, chopped
1 clove garlic, crushed
½ teaspoon marjoram
½ teaspoon thyme
¼ teaspoon sage
2 tablespoons parsley,
    chopped
1½ cups soft breadcrumbs
2 eggs, beaten

Method

Make the stuffing by mixing all the ingredients together. Open out the shoulder as much as possible and spread the stuffing inside. Roll it up tightly and sew with strong thread. Heat the dripping in a large saucepan, add the carrots and onions and lightly brown. Then put the shoulder on top of the vegetables, cover with a well-fitting lid and cook slowly over a gentle flame, allowing 30 minutes for each 500 g of meat. Turn the meat frequently whilst cooking and add the claret halfway through the cooking time. The pan juices can be used to make a very good sauce. Serve hot.

Backwoodsman, New South Wales about 1890. 'I came here seventeen years ago. First I put up a tent, then I made a shed and then it "growed" into what you see. I brought up seven children here.' (Mitchell Library, Sydney)

Rolled Mutton Flaps

'The working-man's food here is also immeasurably better and cheaper. Mutton he gets almost for the asking, and up-country almost without it.'

Richard Twopenny, *Town Life in Australia*, 1883.

Ingredients

1 boned flap of mutton
sausage meat
salt and pepper

Method

Spread the sausage meat over the inner side of the flap, thickly or thinly as preferred, and season with salt and pepper. Then roll the flap like a roly-poly, wrap it with netting and tie securely. Put it into boiling water and boil hard for a few minutes, then reduce the heat and simmer for three hours. Remove the netting and serve the meat cold with salad.

Sheep shearers at Currawallinghi, New South Wales. The cook is on the left. (National Library of Australia)

Australian Salad

Popular outdoors, though often seen at its worst as the ubiquitous accompaniment at barbecues, the true Australian salad is an attractive blend of salad greens and fruit.

Ingredients

6 tomatoes
salt
pepper
sugar
3 tablespoons grated cheese
1 tablespoon chopped
  pineapple and nuts
4 tablespoons finely chopped
  lettuce
1 teaspoon finely chopped
  parsley
1 teaspoon spring onion

Method

Cut off the tops of the tomatoes and scoop out the centres. Sprinkle the insides with salt, pepper and sugar. Mash the pulp and mix in the other ingredients. Fill the tomato cases with the mixture, sprinkle with a little cayenne pepper and cover with thick mayonnaise. Put each tomato on a lettuce leaf and serve chilled.

A family picnic. (Mitchell Library, Sydney)

Banana Cake

The local store was an important centre in any rural community, indeed often the only centre. It had to cater for a wide variety of local needs, often drawing its supplies from a town many kilometres away. A mixture of hardware, groceries, medicines and clothes, it often had a cave-like atmosphere in contrast to the harsh light outside, and a blend of smells that was unique.

Ingredients

½ cup butter
½ cup sugar
2 eggs
2 small bananas
vanilla
½ teaspoon bicarbonate of
   soda dissolved in
   1 tablespoon milk
2 cups self-raising flour

Method

Cream the butter and sugar together and add the eggs one at a time, beating them in well. Mash the bananas and add a few drops of vanilla. Add them to the mixture together with the milk and soda. Fold in the flour and bake at 180°C for 45–50 minutes. Cover with lemon icing.

Otto May's store, Tilba Tilba, about 1899. (National Library of Australia)

Beer

With a country where temperatures of 40°C are common, it is not surprising that the beer consumption per head in Australia is one of the highest in the world. The first Australian beer was brewed by James Squire only seven years after the arrival of the First Fleet, and in 1812 he harvested his first crop of hops at Ryde, near Sydney. Philip King, who became Governor in 1800, encouraged brewing as an alternative to the heavy consumption of rum. It was difficult at first as slow transport and high temperatures did little to improve the product, and it was not until much later in the nineteenth century that it was discovered that the beer could be made more stable by increasing the amount of cane sugar and thereby starving the yeast. Since then, brewing, and Australians, have never looked back.

This home brew comes from the notebook of Helenus Scott the younger, 1822.

Ingredients

10 lb sugar
10 oz hops
2 lb siftings
12 gall water (which boils
   down to 10 gallons)

Method

Boil the sugar in the water until all the scum is taken off—then add the hops and boil for 25 minutes—put it when cooled a little into a 10 or 11 gallon keg, hops included. (When the above liquor is boiling, pour about one gallon of boiling water over the siftings and strain—you will get about 2 quarts of liquor, which is added to the liquor in the keg.) When the liquor is sufficiently cooled add a teacupful of yeast and place the keg on its end leaving a hole for the beer to work and cover from dust. It will work a week more or less. When clear, probably in a fortnight or three weeks, it may be bottled for use, or drunk.

Mr McCutcheon, licensee of Walker's Family Hotel Gundagai in the early 1900s. (National Library of Australia)

Index

QUEST FOR LOVE

Memoir of a Child Sex Slave

ANNEKE LUCAS

*"The accumulated darkness of ages is dispelled at once by
bringing the light in, not by trying to chase the darkness out."*

~ Paramahansa Yogananda

Cover photos: Front: private archive of the author, photo of the author taken in 1974. Back: private archive of the author.

Interior photos: private archive of the author.

Quote on Title Page by Paramahansa Yogananda from "*Scientific Healing Affirmations*," published by Self Realization Fellowship, Los Angeles, CA and reprinted with permission.

This book is published under ISBN number 979-8-9862558-0-4.

Printed in the United States of America.

Cover design by Ranjini Chatterjee.
For more information, visit www.designjini.in or contact ranjini.chatterjee@gmail.com

CONTENTS

Dedicated to All the Victims and Survivors of the World-wide Network

In Honor of the Memory of these Victims of the Belgian Network:

My little friend Wouter
The young woman
The 12-year old Moroccan boy
The thin girl with long ash blonde hair (sickly fairy)
The blonde boy
Peter Bosmans
The 9-year old girl with wavy brown hair and bangs

and

Julie Lejeune
Melissa Russo
An Marchal
Eefje Lambrecks

*Thank you for all the kind and generous messages of support
you have sent over the years. These messages have encouraged
and uplifted me more than I can adequately express.*

*Special thanks for the invaluable support in the
creation and publication of this book:*

Dixie Waldrip, my fellow survivor and editor extraordinaire;

Douglas De Coninck, for fact-checking the information
regarding the Dutroux case in this book;

Kurt Ossenfort, whose support has been steadfast from the start;

and

Sam Hiyate at the Rights Factory, my trusted literary agent.

IMPORTANT NOTICE:

This is a general trigger warning for intense material such as extreme child neglect, sadism, sex trafficking, and graphic descriptions of sexual and physical abuse, violence and murder.

The attachment of the child narrator to her perpetrators, and the confusion this creates in the child's mind, may be a trigger for anyone who has ever experienced incest, sexual, physical or emotional abuse by a parental figure, teacher, or any authority figure during childhood or adulthood.

If the reading of this memoir evokes experiences in any way similar to those described, it may be important to be able to reach out to a therapist or a safe person.

It is easy to sensationalize extreme conditions of a childhood such as mine. Creating sensation is a form of exploitation, and shows lack of understanding. It requires courage to read my story, which sheds light on a truth that has been successfully hidden for too long. Absorbing this truth is the most important and the most helpful thing one can do, and I am awed by all those can receive these facts in the spirit in which they were shared.

NOTICE ABOUT NAMES:

I grew up with the first name Ann, of which there are several diminutives in Flemish and French, such as Annie and Anneke, used by different people in the book. I started going exclusively by Anneke in 1985 upon my arrival in the U.S. and currently do not respond to the name Ann.

My surname at birth was Michielsen and my stepfather's name was Geens. I obtained an official name change in 2001 when I was naturalized as a U.S. citizen.

The name d'Auriac is the fictional name for a family whose children were exposed to the network. To protect the child victims' identities, the surname and all first names of the members of this family, as well as other potentially identifying details, have been changed throughout this book.

I have chosen to omit various names for personal reasons. It has taken much soul searching to make the most ethical as well as practical choices in communicating my story. The process has taught me, above all, to be patient, and trust there is a right time for everything.

INTRODUCTION

Most of this book was written in 2004. It was read back then by two literary agents, whose basic commentary was that, although the manuscript was a page-turner, the content was too heavy. The content has not changed, but the world has, and I believe that the time has now come for this story to be told.

People's ability to absorb the dark facts of my childhood, which give a glimpse into how the elite secretly functions, has steadily increased. The world's greatest curse is power abuse, which sabotages the best initiatives. Part of this curse is the temptation for anyone making headway in any area—although often starting out with great ideals and authentic creative gifts—to succumb to the ways of power somewhere along the way, perverting original integrity and intentions and give in to selfishness, greed, theft and lies, as modeled at the top levels of power. My story shows where that road ultimately leads. As we work to remove our own blind spots, our lies and our greed, and heal from our own trauma, we also reach greater clarity about the deceit in the world. We are now in a time in which there is dire need to connect with deeper truths, so that massive lies and hypocrisy can be exposed and collective healing can begin.

Weeks after starting psychotherapy in the 1980's, I was confronted with the truth of my father's sexual abuse and broke out in tears. I cried for weeks, but from the moment grief hit, it also felt that I was finally dealing with something real; I was starting to find myself, like a tiny crack letting a single beam of light into a dark cave. Each time feelings or bodily reactions that had been repressed in trauma were consciously linked to their source, I learned something significant. Through healing, I also started to become conscious of how, through my unresolved trauma, I myself was blind to the mass deception imposed by some of the very people who had abused me in childhood. In observing my transformation, I could look back and understand former behaviors, habits, and beliefs I had adopted to cope with the trauma. Personal transformation is sacred, and the journey is spiritual, as the integration translates to an increase in empathy, understanding, and the ability to love.

Even though I merely describe what happened to me personally, my memoir is controversial, because extreme events involving known political figures can easily stir up one's own unhealed trauma and feelings towards authority figures, and can threaten one's core beliefs and worldview. Confronting personal trauma is synonymous with deprogramming from mass brainwashing. It demands courage; no one wants their past to include humiliation. Before healing, we are left only with a vague impression of horrendous shame, which, like a virus, is transmitted during the abuse, and causes dissociation, denial, and other defense mechanisms to avoid feeling it. Shame unattached to corrigible actions is unbearable, because it covers the soul with the lie that the "badness" is incorrigible, and thus innate. While my perpetrators did their best to turn this troubled emotional state into a complex belief system, for all their smarts and heady theories that justified their evil actions, they were blindly perpetuating their own abuse, too scared to face their own truth, and the truth about their own childhood authority figures. In the thirty-plus years of my healing journey, I have waded through that muck of shame, confronting the greatest of fears: that the messages about me which accompanied the abuse would be true. Only the experience of facing those fears yields the answer: that these messages are lies and that we are all, at our essence, pure souls.

Twenty-five years ago, it seemed unimaginable that I would ever publicly share my past. However, around that same time in my home country of Belgium, unbeknownst to me, other network survivors, labeled X-Witnesses to safeguard their anonymity, were revealing all they knew to police in the Dutroux case. The case had sparked outrage and grief in the wake of the rescue of two girls from Marc Dutroux' dungeon, and the subsequent discovery of four girls' bodies in nearby locations on the grounds of properties owned by Dutroux.

In 1996, Marc Dutroux told the press he was a small cog in a giant wheel and alluded to his protection by highly placed government officials. The New York Times reported about the "deadly pornography ring."[1] It appeared as though the entire world was about to learn all about the network into which I had been sold as a child. I learned about the Dutroux case in a New York Times article when the Chief Investigator who had promised the distraught public to "get to the bottom of this," was fired for partiality because he had eaten a plate of spaghetti at a fundraiser for victims. This sincere judge's dismissal sent more than 300,000 people into the streets of Belgium in what were termed the White Marches, protesting government corruption in the wake of the child murders.[2]

Under the codename X1, Regina Louf testified to a team of dedicated investigators about her experiences of child sex slavery in the Belgian network. X1/Regina Louf recalled minutiae of interiors and inflicted wounds, as well as biographical and circumstantial data about victims and abusers. Her information enabled investigators to link her testimony to several unsolved child murder cases. However, an inquiry was ordered into the X1 investigation. Her trusted initial investigators were put on leave and replaced with a new team. The "investigation of the investigation" was found to be unsubstantiated on the first day, yet the inquiry remained open for over two years without yielding a single result. Moreover, a "rereading" of all the X1 files was ordered. The new team of investigators was suspicious of the X-witness testimonies from the get-go, and their rereading destroyed the

1. New York Times, Sept. 12, 1996: "King Forced to Step In/Pedophile Scandal Just One Of Many: Belgium's Confidence Crisis is Deepening"

2. New York Times Oct. 21, 1996: "275,000 In Belgium Protest Handling of Child Sex Scandal"

original investigation. During a press conference in 1998, eleven magistrates solemnly addressed the Belgian press, declaring, "Everything has been thoroughly examined, and X1's testimony is completely worthless."

In a book about the X-Witness testimonies,[3] the authors examined the entire transcript of the X1 deposition and the four reports of the rereading. The authors were able to establish that the new team of investigators changed quotes from the transcripts, or used isolated bits of text to prove certain points which lost their validity once the excerpts were seen in proper context. Almost none of the conclusions in the rereading reports survived the double-take. Meanwhile, the statute of limitations of the child murder cases which X1 had spotlighted had expired.

In 2004, eight years after Marc Dutroux was apprehended, when the case finally went to trial, it looked like the Belgian network had been forgotten by the international media. Previous reports about a larger network were ignored and the single-perpetrator theory was widely embraced.[4] All testimony and evidence regarding the existence of a ring involving VIPs had been cut off from the case, and relegated to a new case file, "Dutroux-bis" which was quietly closed months after Marc Dutroux was sentenced to life in prison. Belgium had gone from national outrage to wide-scale indifference and denial. In an ironic twist, those who banded together as "disbelievers" believed the official story—that survivors of the network were mythomaniacs. Those who suspected that corrupt, highly placed officials sabotaged the case to cover up their own and their friends' crimes, were labeled "believers."

Thanks to X1/Regina Louf, I was armed with awareness of the treatment which survivors of the Belgian network could expect once they gathered the courage to speak out. It would take several more years before I would

---

3.   *French Title: Les Dossiers X: Ce que la Belgique ne devait pas savoir sur l'Affaire Dutroux*
      Flemish Title: De X-dossiers: Wat België niet mocht weten over de zaak-Dutroux (The
      X-Files: What Belgium was not supposed to know about the Dutroux Case) by Annemie
      Bulté, Douglas De Coninck and Marie-Jeanne Van Heeswyck. Publisher: Epo/Houtekiet,
      copyright 1999

4.   *New York Times, March 2, 2004: "Belgian Faces Trial At Last In Sex Killings"*

feel ready to withstand the inevitable disbelief, disrespect, mockery, threats, and personal attacks that were sure to come my way if I would start sharing my own history. In 2013, I was interviewed about my work in prisons, which marked the first time I publicly revealed my past in the Belgian network.[5]

It may be worth noting that I never came across Marc Dutroux, who is only seven years older than me, and was not active in the network in the years I was there. My memoir begins in 1973, after I had already been abused in the network for four years, and centers around the tumultuous relationship with one of my abusers, who was not a VIP.

Maybe my story can be a tiny beam of light in a large, dark cave. Many other stories can never be told because the victims are dead. Other stories are being told, as more survivors of organized abuse and mind control are speaking out. However, as survivors of extreme abuse, we cannot possibly be expected to ever go public, considering the extensive trauma and the obvious potential for re-traumatization, not only from the retelling of horrific events, but from the massive, uncensored victim blaming that is sure to follow, not to mention the threats and intimidation tactics by the network. The message that was most deeply embedded in the network, and the apparent reason for much of the horror and violence, was and still is all about secrecy.

Elite pedophilia is the world's best protected secret. And it makes sense, because the perpetrators need to ensure that you, the reader, will never focus on them. They prefer that we all keep busy with the many distractions they throw at us to keep us divided: dysfunctional siblings of the global family, with psychopaths and narcissists for parents. We should do anything but look to the source of Western society's ills, which is the utter selfishness of the leadership, so extreme that it is an emotional disease, of which symptoms such as heartlessness and superiority turn its hosts into monsters. Those who do what it takes to belong to the power establishment are the most lost, the most emotionally infantile, the most broken, and

---

5.   DNA Info March 13, 2013: "New York City Child Sex Trafficking Victim Finds Peace Teaching Rikers Inmates Yoga"

the most evil among us. They do not deserve our trust, our confidence, our acceptance of their political savvy and expertise, or our admiration for their power or wealth—it is all smoke and mirrors. If we can absorb the reality that many of the most rich and famous rape and kill children with impunity, how can we possibly continue arguing and vilifying each other over differences of opinion?

Here is my story; my hard truth. Thank you for having the courage to look.

CHAPTER ONE

Belgium, 1973

I am normal. My family, house, village, school, even my country, are as normal as it gets. We are known for chocolates and waffles, for Bruges and the rain, for our relative wealth, for an easygoing lifestyle, and for our beer. We are a Catholic country; I have been at an all-girls school with the Sisters of the Annunciate Order since pre-K. My grades are average, no honors. We are a church-going, middle-class family of four, and we live in an average-sized house with a yard. Our language is Germanic, our reserve Nordic, our religion Southern, and our culture confused. The Second World War is still doing damage in my mother's secret heart; my stepfather, who fought in it, is kind of dead. And all of this is normal in these parts, in these times.

It is Saturday afternoon and I am watching TV, still extremely normal. My mother, whom I call Mama, warns my little brother that this is his bedtime.

Though the sky is gray, it is still light outside; the Flemish antique brass wind-up clock says that it is twenty minutes after four. My little brother's bedtime changes daily. The time does not matter, what matters is that this is my cue. He protests, "Why doesn't Ann have to go to bed?"

"Because she is older than you," answers Mama.

This is true. I am four years older than my brother. He is six and I am ten. But when my stepfather is home, we sometimes do go to bed at the same time, and usually much later. When my stepfather is home, I have a different cue.

Mama accompanies my brother to his bedroom. I stay behind in the quiet, half-dark living space, and stare at the corner of the roughly-hewn slate shelf of the fireplace. It disappears, and so does everything else. Space and time. Even me. Everything is gone.

Mama enters the room and looks at me. I get up and tell her I have to get ready. I go to the bathroom, lock the door, and begin my ritual. I look in the mirror.

There I am: normal, bland, ugly, ashamed, bad; Mama's girl.

I observe my image, and tear off the invisible swathes that cover my face to create what Mama needs to see, also covering my eyes to the truth of who she is. Looking in the mirror now reveals structure and sensuality in my features. My lips swell into an involuntary pout, my nose takes on a definitive shape, my skin tone evens out, cheekbones appear, and my eyes are larger. As I transmute, everything becomes clear.

I brush my hair. It has grown over my shoulders. I brush it for a long time, continuing to look at my face. I hear Mama's hushed voice outside the door.

"Ann, are you ready?"

"Almost."

Though her voice is a whisper that keeps my brother asleep, I hear that she is impatient, anxious. I brush my hair, peaceful in a moment of stolen time, free from Mama. Only after the cue has been given, though. In our normal life I would not do or think anything that could upset Mama. The door shakes in its hinges.

"We're going to be late if you don't hurry."

When I unlock and open the door, Mama gives me an irritated look. I pull an anorak from the coat rack and loosely throw it on before following Mama to the front door and to her car parked in the driveway. Night has fallen. Shivering, I get in the passenger's seat.

Mama checks the rear-view mirror, pointed towards her face instead of the back window. She releases the hand break and lets the car roll down the driveway. I stiffen, sensing her breathless tension. This is our time out of time, when the shadow appears, when darkness reflects nothing, when the black hole sucks up the here and now—the same hole that has my mother's soul and left her a poor beast in a shell of human flesh. I know the beast cannot be spoken to. In a society of humans, Mama wants to be human— she keeps checking that mirror—so the beast that drives the car has to hide, especially from itself.

What is happening is not actually happening. That is the silent message I receive. Mama loves secrets.

She turns the key, maneuvers the car, clumsily turns it around, and we are off into the dark. Once we pass the windmill and get on the paved road, she will turn left onto the square, though I never know which way we will go once we reach the church in the town center.

Left. This means the ride will probably be short. When we pass the church of the next village, I expect that we will turn left again, and after a few minutes will end up on a lane leading to a large vacant mansion. But instead we go straight, towards the Brussels highway.

I hear the noiseless sound of my blood flowing, flushing, faster, expanding, tightening my veins, tightening my heart. At the orgies around Brussels, whether in bars, villas or castles, you never know what may happen. The Brussels atmosphere is bloodthirsty. The network, though it is my reality and I have to know it, is part of that shadow that cannot be known.

I count the triangular patches of light we pass through, falling from the enormous light poles on the expressway, the ones that make Belgium visible on night satellite photos, like a great orange spider web.

Eighty-seven...

Eighty-eight...

Eighty-nine...

We drive through ancient woods, up a boulevard alongside the forest, then turn onto a road running through a Brussels suburb, onto the driveway of a small castle, ivy climbing up its walls, tucked away between peaceful pastures and forest. Mama stops the car off to the side, away from the main entrance.

"This is a nice place," comments Mama.

My state of extreme fear causes my concentration to hone in on the smallest details and every little movement or nuance, as I listen for something in Mama's voice.

"The Countess d'Auriac told me it's going to be special tonight."

Mama sounds like she is trying to prove that she is an insider, and not just my chauffeur. She must have been impressed hearing names. Big names mean big danger.

Castle, Belgium,
one overcast afternoon sometime in 1973

I walk through a hallway, looking up at stately portraits, perhaps of the ancestors of the family who inhabits this castle. Through open double doors I enter a salon; endless oak parquet floors reflect the gray sky. A group of old men are talking by a wide-open liquor cabinet. The boss is there; I don't know his name but call him Polo. He is the biggest boss, the biggest sadist, and has some high post in Belgian politics. He is with the polished-looking Gaspard (I believe that is his last name) and a few of his other shady friends.

There is another small group of four foreign visitors, one of whom translates from French into Italian for the shortest among them, a man with a receding hairline, badly hunched shoulders, and a hawkish face. The three other Italians lean towards the little fellow while he only moves his eyeballs. *This is my guy.* Someone calls him by his name. I will call him "A."

"Come here!" Polo calls out in Flemish, since he believes that is my native tongue. The truth is that my first language was French, and I learned Flemish only after Mama got married and we moved from Brussels to Flanders when I was three. After four years in the network, I am fluent. I won't tell Polo, because the more I understand, the more I am considered a danger to his secrets.

With all eyes focused on me, I carefully approach the group. Though I am only ten years old, I am the girl always used for The Game. I was properly trained abroad, under the auspices of a foreign, world-renowned VIP and global network Big Shot, who is revered in the Belgian network. While none of that reverence rubbed off onto me, Polo is getting plenty of use out of the training that prepared me for the world's elite. The perpetrators never need say a word—I anticipate their every whim, and fluidly, automatically, fulfill their deepest emotional needs and sexual desires.

Gaspard gathers up papers spread out on the salon table and neatly puts them in folders. I am a part of this arms contract, one weapon that is not on paper. Gaspard mumbles something under his breath to Polo, who quickly turns his head away, only 20 degrees or so. However, the effect is enormous: Gaspard slumps, suddenly looking rumpled and wrinkled. He nervously excuses himself and hurries out the room, clutching the papers.

"So, which one?" Polo asks me.

That question is the starting shot of the game. I smile at Polo without moving my lips, as if I would choose him if I could. I sit in a large armchair and fold my hands, looking ahead to get into the zone, while I hear the blood pumping out of my heart. I won't be killed over making the wrong choice, but you never know what the man might do to make sure no one will ever find out.

"Sirs!" Polo booms as he gestures towards me. "Have you forgotten how to court a lady? Where are your manners?"

The Italians laugh, including A. Still, someone hurries to translate. Next, they are all talking at once, until the translator comes to sit in the chair next to mine.

"What is your name?" he asks in French that sounds Italian, smiling bravely.

I look silently at him and wait for the right moment to answer. As I wait, his smile changes as he raises his brows. He is sort of funny and charming, but looks at me as if I am just a child, and that is his mistake.

The Belgians down their tumblers and get ready to leave, but Polo's attention is with the Italians. The translator breaks eye contact and turns to the others, asking something in Italian.

"She understood you very well," Polo calls out, his tone implying that the Italian might be the one with trouble understanding. "But I doubt she's going to waste any more time on you!"

Everyone laughs. I overhear the words *"molto bella,"* and Polo winks at me as he leaves the salon with the other Belgians. I almost see a comical look on the translator's face next to me. I like him best; he is the least scary of the bunch, but he is out of the game and I have to ignore him.

I focus on a black-haired thug with dead eyes that glare suspiciously: *why are you looking at me?* In the sidelines of my vision, I see A. watching me, grabbing his chin like someone absorbed in a story. I make my eyes dead like the thug's and stare him down. In this zone, I read his energy. My survival instinct is activated, which I was trained to use to gather information from perpetrators in a flash. From this thug, I get that he is used to killing men, but that he would never touch a child. He clearly does not suspect that a young girl like me might be more dead inside than he is. In response to my stare, he looks a little surprised, and then sad. The trauma inflicted during my training was designed to systematically kill off all my hopes and feelings, so that I would be dead inside and appear super grown up. In the zone, I automatically bypass the rational brain, and comply with the perpetrators without any feelings or thoughts interfering. The point of the training was that I would never again experience natural reactions such as fear, horror, surprise, or sadness, unless a perpetrator desired I experience them. My deadened feelings make me appear mature in the same way that the perpetrators also only appear mature: they don't have control over their feelings like truly mature people; their feelings are deadened. My own deadness ensures that they will never be faced with the reality that they are hurting a child. The most insecure and immature men need power the most, because they are the most deadened.

I avert my head away from the thug, just like Polo did to Gaspard, and notice, without looking, that the big shot of this little group, A. is almost smiling.

The second to last contender looks ruthless, intelligent, and ugly. His lazy eyes flatten me into a little object, and he smiles flirtatiously. A. energetically draws me in and as we lock eyes, his are twinkling softly.

"*Sièditi qui!*" says the ugly one, tapping his leg.

Staying attuned to A., I move towards the ugly one and lean on his lap so as not to put any weight on his leg. He smiles so all his white teeth show, though his eyes are still lazy.

"So, what do you like, eh?" he says quietly.

The ugly one speaks to me in Italian, which is not a language I have mastered. Nevertheless, his confidence that I will understand him is supreme, and I gather what he means from the energy behind the words. This is one of the things that can happen in that zone beyond thought. A. is still watching, not ready yet. I look the ugly one in the eyes, thinking, *I'm here to do what you like.*

"I can show you," the ugly one whispers.

I smile as if to mean I am sure he can make me feel really good, and put my full weight on his legs. His breath stinks of whiskey. I take his tumbler and smile at him as I have a sip, remedy against the smell, the nausea. The ugly one thinks that I am choosing him.

This is the moment A. has been waiting for. I jump off the man's lap and quickly join A. as we walk resolutely out the door together.

Bedroom in castle, Belgium, 1973

"Yuk."

With a small horsewhip, I examine A.'s testicles.

"Two rotten pears...."

I maneuver the loop of the whip up and down A.'s limp penis.

"...From a sad old tree."

A. lies naked on the floor while I stand over him. I catch him sneaking a peek.

"Don't look at me, creepy old bastard."

With all my might, I whip his thigh. A. becomes aroused.

"On hands and knees," I command.

I kick A. into position and lash his buttocks, several times, hard.

"Open your legs."

Standing behind him, I administer quick taps so the leather stings his testicles, which greatly excites him.

"You like this too much. Turn around. On your back!"

I kick him again. He falls into the fetus posture and crosses his arms protectively over his face. I push him on his back and straddle him.

"You can't do anything without help, can you?"

I push his chin up with my hand, so his head arches back.

"You just want to look. I told you no."

"*Not allowed*" are the words A. needs to hear. He puts pressure on my hands, tries to lower his gaze, a desperate grimace on his face, his shoulders pathetically hunched. When he is about to come, I stand up and cover his eyes with my foot.

"I'm gonna piss on you."

"*Si!*" exclaims A.

As urine flows over his face and neck, semen flows over his stomach. He shivers, huddles, cold, wet, and miserable.

It is all a game. We are playing roles: me, the powerless slave/ruler; he, the powerful ruler/slave. A bigger-than-life self is fun, but not real. Neither is the groveling, smelly bad boy. We are like infants, shaped by the psychic energy of those around us, condemned to turn everyone into a mother. Feeling all, we take everything personally; only complete subservience bears no insult. We live in a void, our sense of self lost, killed long ago by a slew of humiliations. Without self-esteem, lies fill the emptiness: egos raw and rampant, never checked or civilized by a caring adult. Whether we re-experience the humiliation or repel it by humiliating others, it always haunts us, and it has turned A. into a slave to power.

He shoots me a fearful glance. I kneel beside his head. Now the hardest part of the job begins: I have to hide my disgust and get myself into a space from which I can love. A. pulls me close. I cradle his head on my lap and touch his face. My hand slides over his skin, along his neck to his arm. I smooth the oxidized sweat back into his pores, caressing the shoulder, wishing I could ease it down and release the burden resting there. I give and give and give the tender love A. never received, which he has always needed, still needs, and always will. A. meekly, sweetly looks me in the eye, like a docile little boy.

It makes me hopeful that my one wish can be fulfilled. I only need a small sign; I will recognize it in the tiniest gesture. The mind control training was not 100% successful, because I am not completely dead inside; I want to know if true love exists. That is all. In this moment, in this situation, is this man able to give what he is taking? Energy flows through my hands, and with each stroke, A. looks more fulfilled. When he glows like a well-fed baby, he brusquely rises, and without another look, hurries to an adjoining bathroom.

I feel like I am dying. Once again, it seems that power is obtained through theft of love, and love is the energy which the powerless give to the powerful to obtain love, and that neither the power nor the love is real.

Castle Van Revelingen,
Rhode-Saint-Genese, Belgium, fall 1973

The orgy is in full swing. I am let in at the late stages, after those who are not considered "ripe" for children have left. Lights low, I pretend to notice nothing and no one, like the Count d'Auriac having sex with a skinny, naked blonde woman, crouched on all fours on a stuffed chair. The count's face is deformed by contempt, pulling his brows up and mouth corners down. His shirt and tie are on properly, he even wears his jacket, but his trousers are down just enough. He is always in the same role; there is no play in him.

There is Polo, huddled together with his ever-present friends and acolytes. I try to slip away, but Gaspard, the polished-looking one, throws me a significant glance. When I come to stand near him, he runs his hand across my jeans, my buttocks and the inside of my thighs, while carrying on a conversation with a tall, thin man with a long, wrinkly face whom I have never seen before.

Ignoring me as he fondles me, Gaspard is showing that I am available for sex. The guest watches, entirely impassive—strange for a newcomer, who usually betrays agitation at this point. This man is either not new or he does not like girls. Gaspard pushes his fist up between my legs, obliging me to widen my stance, helping the guest understand he can do anything at all to me. I feel myself blush. The wrinkly newcomer smiles. Gaspard nudges him, but the newcomer subtly shakes his head. Gaspard dismisses me with a disdainful glance, as if I were too dirty to please anyone. My role is to take on all that which he so painstakingly tries to wash off himself. And I do feel dirty.

Men have gathered in small groups, by appearances casually talking and drinking while their eyes hungrily dart about the salon as couples form, strip, and engage. Someone makes eye contact with me. As I slowly approach him, I transform under his gaze: I am now awfully small, thin and delicate, and look at him very shyly. As he offers for us to sit, I sense his arousal, as if my attunement turned me into his energetic suffix. I catch the glance of another man from another cluster. Sitting next to man number one, I keep shooting looks at the second, who is younger and looks slightly better. My eyes say, *"Come and save me!"*

For the brief instances in which my eyes meet those of man number two, I metamorphose into a playful, mischievous girl, bored out of her mind. The purpose of this game is to win as much time as possible before having to go upstairs with anyone.

Man number two heads over, shakes hands with man number one and company, and sits in an armchair across from me. Man number one notices why man number two is there, and agitatedly begins to tell a story, placing his hand on my thigh, as if I were his girlfriend.

I notice someone else who is new and wonder if he is one of the kids. He looks really young, maybe just too old to be one of us. Very tall, with white-blonde shoulder-length hair, he is wearing jeans instead of a suit and tie. He limps a little, and as if to make up for it, his vigorous energy explodes through the room. My heart races. He strikes me as a fierce survivor with impossible hurdles: too sensitive, too intelligent, and too hurt.

He turns his head, looks at me, and abruptly changes his course in my direction. As he makes his way over, his gaze briefly slides down to my thigh with the man's hand on it. I jump out of my seat and advance into the room to meet him. The adrenaline pumps through my body as I take him in, plying my senses in attunement. I seem to take on the glow and proportions of a glorious goddess, but my face, strangely, is just my own, as if I can finally be me. When he stands before me, I smile.

"So, you like your job, do you, you little whore?" he says softly, quickly.

Incredibly indignant, I ask, "You think I like it here?"

He stares at me in shock. The ferocity of my reaction surprises me too, but surely it is just part of the game, sensing what he likes.

As the young blonde man continues to stare, the surroundings, the room and all the people in it cease to exist. His eyes transmit an entire universe of emotion. I see all the feelings that have ever been experienced by humans throughout the ages, all together and at once. The myriad of feelings coagulates into one, all others exist only in relation to the presence or the absence of the one; his eyes become a mellow, bright blue ocean of love.

"Thanks for getting my drink for me!"

Florence's words alone are more than enough to break up the moment, but with a nasal snigger, she also deftly positions herself between us, her back to me, facing the young blonde one, nodding at the glass of champagne in his hand.

Florence is the ten-year old daughter of the Count and Countess d'Auriac, with long hair, high cheekbones, and worldly confidence.

"Here you go," says the young blonde man, upon which he hands Florence the glass and turns on his heel, leaving us both.

Florence shrugs, saunters over to the bosses, sits next to the new guest with the wrinkly face, and chats. He answers, but frowns, displaying not the slightest interest.

Maybe he likes boys, I think. It is just a hunch, but he strikes me that way, sitting there as if he were a little boy himself, knees closed, hands neatly on his lap, well-behaved and pleased as pie to be part of the Big Boys' club.

Polo taps his thigh, and Florence crawls on his lap. I rejoin my suitors. Man number one possessively puts his hand on my thigh and sends a smile that says, "I'm not going to let you escape again." I lower my eyes and lift them to meet the amused gaze of man number two. Behind him, I can't help but notice the young blonde man again, advancing purposefully towards Polo's group, this time with Michel Nihoul in tow.

Michel Nihoul's businessman exterior makes him look like his god Polo, only younger and shorter. Even though he has not been around for long, Nihoul has quickly made himself indispensable as the middleman between the child victims, pimps, pedophiles, and Polo. He arranges everything at the orgies, running around tirelessly to please the big shots.

The young blonde one has an animated discussion with the bosses. Now and then he turns his head towards Nihoul, who dutifully seconds him. From the way the blonde one confidently addresses the group, it is clear he is not one of the lowly pimps. Polo shakes his head with a wry smile.

The wrinkly new guest nervously wriggles his fingers, eyes wide and worried. Though he is very ugly and the young blonde one very beautiful, both have the same build and the same narrow, long face-shape; they look related.

Polo holds out an open hand, as if to say, "go ahead, have it your way." The tall blonde one, once again heads straight towards me, this time with Nihoul following close behind.

If he went and asked Polo for me, this young new guest is amazingly defiant of the network game rules.

"Would you like to accompany me?" he asks quietly, politely, though he brazenly ignores the bedazzled looks of the men around me.

He makes it sound as if I had a choice. As I begin to follow him, he lets his open hand trail behind, offering for me to take it. I respond, of course, but his way suggests that it would have been perfectly okay if I had not.

Our sour-faced bellboy Michel Nihoul leads us up a staircase and through a quiet, wide hallway to a corner room, fingering a set of keys, unlocking the door and entering to switch on some lights. The young man releases my hand to indicate the sprawling room.

"Do you like it?" he asks.

Assuming he is making fun of me, I glare. He smiles and mumbles, "Okay," then dismisses a petulant Nihoul with a swift nod. Nihoul usually gets off on being the gopher, but the blonde one is not only very young, he is also full to the brim with derisive authority. Whatever his game, he is good at it. There is something about him that reminds me of something about me that I don't want to know.

Alone with the young blonde man, I am suddenly overtaken by fear. My entire body trembles: hands, arms, legs—even my lips are shaking.

"I'm not going to hurt you," says the man in his gentle voice, which has an immediate soothing effect.

I feel very bright and beautiful. An unearthly light threatens to dissolve the structure of every known foundation, and seems to unravel the room.

The room. Why are we here?

"Don't worry," he says. "I'm not going to touch you."

He leans against the wall and casually crosses his arms and feet.

What does he mean?

He laughs as if in reply.

So, then what? I think.

He widens his eyes slightly and smiles. *It's up to you*, he nods. I look at the large bed in the comfortable surroundings. I climb up thinking it would be nice just to sleep, though I don't dare say it.

Standing on the bed, I look at him. In this moment, he looks very young, like a boy, but his face has not looked exactly the same twice since we met. He looks like he has what I have, as if he never solidified out of infancy into a set personality. I have many parts, with different characteristics or skills, fluidly transforming according to the need of the moment. The young man looks like he grew up too fast, awkwardly. I picture him among teens and sense that he is an outcast, like myself. As I think this, his awkwardness is suddenly reflected in his expression, and he limps towards the bed with a sheepish smile.

"Isn't this better than downstairs?" he asks.

With me standing on the bed, our heads are level. The look on his face is so sweet my arms shoot out and I place my hands on his shoulders.

"Yes, it is."

He responds with a brilliant smile. I am struck by his exquisiteness. His pale skin tone evens out and lights up with a deep, purifying glow. He lifts me off the bed and holds me with his hands, moving me up and down to demonstrate how light I am. I don't even have to kiss him. His game is very different.

The first thing I notice when I awake the following morning is that I am lying in clean, soft sheets under a comfortable cover. The second is that my underwear are still on.

Patrick is sleeping, the corners of his mouth turned up in a slight smile that looks as if it is trying to decide between peace and sarcasm. I slide off the bed and move to a tall window to absorb the magnificently colorful autumn landscape and the events of last night. It seems impossible, but there was no sex of any kind. A rustle calls me back to the bed. Patrick puts his hands behind his head and smiles. He looks so at ease and attractive, I am drawn to kiss him, but don't. He pats the pillow next to his head. As I stretch out next to him, he leans on one elbow and places his hand lightly on my cheek. I tremble in fear. He brings his lips close to mine. As I look into his eyes, I notice his pupils are dangerous pins bobbing on a tumultuous ocean of blue. I back my head into the pillow, maybe an inch. Patrick jumps up and pulls on his jeans and shirt.

"I'm hungry. Are you?" he asks. I nod.

"I'll be right back."

Ten minutes later, he returns with a large breakfast tray. With a wide grin, he places it down by one of the windows and, taking a jug of steaming milk in his right hand, he lifts it, while with his left he pours the hot chocolate, aiming the milk so it dramatically cascades into the bowl and froths. Deeply suspicious, I observe the activities.

"I made them melt the chocolate," he divulges, and unceremoniously pours the rest of the milk in his coffee, adding, "That is why I took so long."

When he smiles, I stare coldly. Undeterred, he busily drops four sugar cubes in his cup. I can't figure out his game.

"You might need some, too," he says, extending the bowl of sugar. "I don't believe the chocolate is sweet."

The chocolate indeed tastes bitter and I follow his example, dropping four sugar cubes into the bowl. Then I follow his example again and dip the tip of a croissant into the liquid. The taste explodes into vibrant good feeling. The doughy, buttery sweetness in my mouth, the beautiful autumn view out the windows, and the familiar-looking young man; this must be the most nurturing experience of my life.

I notice that Patrick is aware of my change, and is pleased. I am furious. I just got beaten at my own game.

CHAPTER TWO

Belgium, fall 1973

The d'Auriac family lives in a manor in a nearby town and I occasionally visit them. Florence and I ride horses at the same stable, which justifies our regular-life friendship. Her mother calls us down for dinner as her father, the Count d'Auriac, pulls up on the long driveway and parks his car. He enters, hands his coat to his wife, and immediately joins us at the kitchen table in suit and tie. After leading everyone in a mumbled prayer, he converses with Florence and her older brother in French, language of the aristocracy, and I, with my Mama's girl, day-to-day personality, can only understand Flemish.

The countess, with thin orange lips like a last sliver of sun setting on her harsh face, asks Florence to help her. I get up as well, but am categorically sent back to my seat, as if anything I'd touch would break. When Florence pulls salad dishes instead of appetizer plates out of the cupboard, her mother quietly shows her the difference.

During the meal, I am self-conscious about my table manners, especially when some green peas roll off my fork. A half smile appears on the count's contemptuous face. He throws Florence a look, and she smiles back. My brain shorts. After the glitch, I am a different girl. Full of glee, I realize we can play. I put my knife down and take the fork in my right hand, to stab at the peas. The count throws me severe looks out of the corner of his eye. I make a show of it, chasing the peas round and round on my plate. Florence and her brother jokingly comment in French, and I understand every word. The countess stares; the count glares. I pick up a pea, place it on my fork which I raise up high, and, amidst gales of laughter from the children, aim the pea straight into my wide-open mouth.

When I arrive home after a bike ride through pastures and fields, Mama is standing on the front doorstep, holding a wire basket of eggs, chatting with a lady with a round, open face whom I vaguely recognize. The lady laughs heartily, "Oh, and this is Ann? It's been a long time since I've seen you. You're growing up fast, coming home late and all."

"She had dinner at her friend Florence's home," Mama volunteers. "Whose family lives in a castle...."

"It's not a castle!" I point out.

"Ugh you!" Mama exclaims with mock irritation. Addressing the lady, she says, "You know what I mean, don't you?"

"Sure, sure," the woman says vaguely. "Well, I don't mean to keep you standing out here, pretty girl. I really should be going."

Overcome with shyness at the lady calling me "pretty girl," I try to suppress a budding smile. As soon as she leaves, Mama's ice-cold gaze freezes my heart. Sucked into a polar vortex of guilt, I follow Mama to the kitchen.

"Do you know her?" Mama asks in an extra light, sing-song tone—so incongruous with the cold glare of a few seconds prior, that I instantly doubt myself. The conviction that I must have been wrong blows away the mist of confusion. It makes much more sense that I am mistaken, because Mama is so nice.

"She brought some eggs. They're real peasants, simple people...she has no taste. And that hair; no style!" Mama comments, while she melts butter in a frying pan on the electric range and cracks two of the eggs. "She just keeps it short and lets it hang. And it's thin hair, like yours, and then it looks like she doesn't have any."

In my state of guilt, I hear Mama's criticisms with the same lightness with which she utters them: she doesn't mean anything by it.

"I just went to the hairdresser today but I feel she cut it too short. What do you think?" Mama asks.

"It looks fine to me."

"She pinned it up and she put a new extension in for the bun, but still, I didn't like it when I left. See? There's loose strands."

Mama smiles as she feels her head and finds and shows me one such strand. As Mama's girl, I think everything about her looks beautiful, and any imperfections only add to her charm.

When I join my little brother in the dark living room where he is watching TV, Mama serves him an omelet.

"It's not salty enough," he complains.

Mama heads to the cupboard to get the salt shaker, calling, "You want orange soda? Ann, you too?"

My brother and I grunt affirmations. Mama places two glasses of fizzing soda on the side table. *She is so nice, such a good mother.* I feel guilty for being lazy.

Glued to the TV screen when Mama re-enters the room after putting my brother to sleep, I ask, "Can I have chips?"

Mama returns to the kitchen. The crackle of the bag and the clatter of potato chips dropping in a bowl are the concentrated shapes of tension in the air. Handing me the bowl, Mama says, "Here, mistress. Whatever you do, don't get up yourself."

In a flash, I remember Countess d'Auriac asking for Florence's help (*Mama never asks!*) and my brother complaining about the salt (*she didn't criticize him!*). Lightning hits; my brain thunders to life; the game is on. I hold out the empty glass.

"More, please," I order.

Mama swipes the glass out of my hand and rushes to the kitchen. I play my role of the tyrant and she plays the abused slave. She hands me the glass. I accept it without taking my eyes off the TV and place it on the side table. Mama stands in front of me. I frown as though I didn't understand what she is still doing there. Mama's face is flustered. Her voice breaks.

"If you think I'm just going to run around for you and you're not even going to...." she sniffs. "You can't do this to me. I'm your mother. Say thank you!"

The sniffs turn into sobs.

"SAY THANK YOU!"

"You want to wake my brother up?"

Though I was not even trying to be clever, my question sounds Machiavellian. It seems as if I implied that if my brother were awake, she might act differently, and layers of meaning I never intended suddenly introduce themselves into my mind. Mama looks bewildered. She arches back as if I were about to kill her, and streams of tears spring from her glazed, wide-open eyes, which have a look of sheer terror in them.

"If you don't say thank you...I'm going to take you there again!"

As she waits, I wait, and when she speaks, in a voice ringing with lustful notes of vengeance, I mentally mouth along.

"Okay, I'm taking you back there!"

"Thank you."

Castle, Belgium, afternoon, fall 1973

"He screamed."

I am remembering Wouter, my little friend with short-cropped blonde hair and a high-pitched voice, who came from East-Flanders. The four or five times I had spent nights with him in the network, I had felt very protective, as if he were my little brother. I loved him. He was just seven, a bit slow, and I was nine.

I am lying on my stomach, face buried in a pillow to shut out the light of a side table lamp, hiding my tears. Heavy rain clobbers the window panes of the round castle tower. Patrick steadily caresses my back and asks me to confide in him. I don't understand why he wants to know. I do not really want to remember, but as I do, and as I cry, I feel warm and kind of good, because it feels safe to have feelings.

"He screamed. And that made things worse."

"How so?" Patrick wants to know.

"The adults around him, the ones that were going at him, they couldn't stand to hear his screams. He was so little. He had a piercing voice. The sound made the men crazy. And then they would go at him more. More brutally."

Patrick briefly touches my wet cheek, to let me know that he's aware of my tears.

"Why were you there?"

I see Wouter again, lying helplessly on the stone altar in the vaulted basement. I was being held down myself. *Why was that?* Then I remember.

"What?" Patrick puts his face level to mine to gaze intently into my eyes.

I turn my head away, too ashamed, unable to continue talking about what happened. It was as though I had switched sides. When Wouter screamed again, and then again, sensing the unbearable excitement and irritation of the adults, I too had felt that I wanted the screams to stop so that it would be over, so that his suffering would finally end. I had so wanted to protect him, and I failed; I feel responsible for his death. I turn to Patrick, dry-eyed, silent. With a look and a nod, he indicates that he understands.

"I swore then that I would never scream."

"You've never screamed?"

"Oh no, I did. Once. It was with Polo."

I sense a sharp, almost tense interest from Patrick. It makes me curious; I would like to know who Patrick is, why he elicits almost as much respect as Polo from the networkers. In the hope that Patrick will reveal some things to me, I begin to share.

"He took me to a little room, the first time I was alone with him in this sense. I undressed, and when I thought he was going to do the same, he cuffed me in the face, really, really hard. I'd not seen it coming, and my skin stung wildly, but I didn't show a reaction. When I looked at him, his eyes were twinkling, like we were about to play a game, or a match. The thought came to me: I'm stronger than him. He hit me again, this time in my stomach, with his fist, but I didn't even feel it; I was prepared. Then he went for my head, but for some reason that's the body part I'm least worried about."

"Which part are you most worried about?"

"I don't know."

"People say it's the Achilles' heel, but that's not really it. You know the most vulnerable spot on your body?"

"No, what?"

"The backs of your knees. That's what you really want to watch out for."

Patrick pulls up the right leg of his jeans and shows a bulging scar on the back of his knee. I want to ask him how he got it, how he got his limp, but he pulls his pant leg down, smiles, and shakes his head. I continue, "He kept on going, hitting harder and harder, all over. Then he picked me up and threw me through the room. My side hit the wall. Throughout most of this, we were looking at each other, me thinking I'm stronger than him, and he figuring I'm going to break down and scream, but I didn't. The bruises started showing, my whole left side hurt and my body was starting to get tired, but my spirit was wide awake. It gave me such pleasure to hold out against him...."

I want to say, "one of the most powerful men in the country," but I realize if I say that out loud I'll give away the secret of my game. Patrick caresses my head. His sad eyes seem to say that he understands me so deeply, it hurts him that I don't trust him more.

"Then Polo said: 'Just get your clothes and get out of here. You're so dead there's nothing to be done with you.' When he said that, he got to me. I felt terrible when I gathered my clothes, afraid that I'm dead."

"He's weak," Patrick says pensively.

Patrick's remark sounds like a note to himself, but he has broken network rule number one: Never Challenge the Absolute Power of The Bosses (Not Even in Thought). Patrick understands what I mean by "I'm stronger than Polo," which is about my inner world and how I survive. He seems to understand me on a level no one else could. I instantly feel more whole, more alive, and when I speak, I am less inhibited and even sound more like my age.

"The next time, my mother dropped me off at this villa in the middle of the day. Nihoul opened the door, took me by the arm, and, with this annoying smile, brought me over to Polo, who smiled the same way, though of course it's Nihoul mimicking Polo...."

I expect Patrick might smile or in some way agree with me, but his face is a mask, which directs me to act more grown-up.

"There was no one else in the house. They led me to the basement. It was light in there because there were arched windows below the ceiling and it was a sunny day. Nihoul carried a carton. They looked for a spot and found a half-full coal cellar, a deep narrow space with three walls, so they can look in, but I'm trapped. Then Nihoul cuts the box open, but he makes sure it stays shut. Now I've been scared the whole day; first my mother keeps me home from school—that's never good—then realizing it's just Nihoul and Polo. I was already shaking when we went down the stairs to the cellar, but now I'm shut in there with Nihoul and this box blocking the doorway, and

I think whatever's in there is going to kill me. I'm being killed because I didn't scream for Polo."

Maybe I don't have to go on. Maybe I'll just stop talking and focus on something else now, I think. I have never shared any of this with anyone; there is no point in starting now. This is very much against the rules. It is easier to pretend it never happened; it helps everyone, especially me.

I sit cross-legged on the bed, and Patrick, who is lying on his back, lays his hand on my knee. Whereas I am very used to being touched sexually, gentle, comforting touch is not part of my experience. Patrick's small gesture seems enormous: a sign that someone cares. I instantly feel a comforting warmth in my chest, and as I feel this, I am more aware of my vulnerability, and realize that my game is nothing but a buffer against the truth, and I wonder if I could even live if let myself know the truth.

"What was it?" Patrick asks.

"Bugs," I whisper.

I see once again how Nihoul nervously held the box out, opened the flaps quickly with one hand and then threw it at me, so a swarm of shiny black beetles landed on me, and all around, biting, pinching everywhere.

"I screamed."

"Were they biting insects?" Patrick asks with dry, scientific curiosity, which pulls me out of the gruesome past in the dirty coal cellar.

I nod, and breathe. As Patrick sits up to continue his businesslike inquiry, I proceed to describe the bugs, and he mumbles something under his breath that sounds like the French pronunciation of "helicopter."

"Was he satisfied?" Patrick asks, averting his gaze.

"I don't think so, not completely. He did laugh, but after the initial shock, I crouched down and went into another state. I felt the bugs crawl on my body and in my hair and I felt them bite, but it dawned on me that they were just natural creatures taken out of their environment, and that they were scared, like me, and not monsters...."

There is something I need to add that is intrinsic to the awareness that got me through my ordeal, and I would like to tell Patrick, but I don't feel that free.

"He was the monster!" Patrick says in a ringing voice and a knowing smile.

I remember how the beetles dissipated, disappeared into the stack of coals, onto the cement walls, and out the doorway. I got up, still in this state of extreme lucidity that made me calm and at peace with my conditions. It even seemed to affect the bugs; they seemed less aggressive, though maybe it was I who didn't experience their bites in the same way. Polo and Nihoul were gone. I pulled the last beetles out of my hair and brushed them off my body. Covered in soot and small bloody marks in the shape of arrow points, I climbed back up the stairwell to go find my clothes and wait for Mama.

As the memory of the insects begins to fade, the clarity of mind I had during the experience is transported to the present. Looking into Patrick's blue eyes, I see something shifty in them.

What is he hiding? I think.

I know nothing about his life. I still don't know why he wants to hear about my experiences in the network. He seems to read my mind...I feel men's thoughts so that I can respond to what they want, but Patrick doesn't need me for his survival.

Why is he attuned to me? What does he need from me?

Patrick's stare intensifies, and the crystal of his irises darkens to a midnight blue. A ferocious feline is revealed, sitting intently still as it watches, relishing its prey before the kill. Death has hung over my head often enough, and I never cared. Today, Patrick has kindled hope that love exists, that life seems worth something. The shudder that runs along my spine seems acutely linked to life energy—never have I been so afraid.

Patrick leans over and whispers in my ear, *"Je t'aime."* (I love you.)

CHAPTER THREE

Café, Belgium, afternoon, December 1973

It is cold and rainy as Mama and I shop for Christmas gifts in a nearby town, so we stay in a covered shopping gallery, and enter a smoky cafe with heavy, velvet chairs and uniformed waiters. Mama studies the menu when the waiter approaches.

"Ladies, have you decided?" he mumbles, ready to write.

In a high-pitched voice, on a drawn-out note, Mama says, "Yes?" as if she were really, really young. She giggles delightfully for the man, who ignores her. Mama picks up a loose strand of her pinned up hair and coquettishly twirls it around her pointing finger.

"I'm going to have a coffee and Steak Tartare please," Mama says, still in the little girl voice.

"Sandwich or salad plate?" drones the waiter, an amused twinkle playing in his eye.

Mama breaks out in a big, flirtatious smile, which is met by a benevolent grin.

"The salad plate, please," she answers, beaming, flirting blatantly, raising her eyebrows several times.

The waiter looks taken aback. Mama turns pale. I stare down into the table. The waiter turns to me with a friendly smile.

"And what will the young lady have?"

"Just a coke, thank you."

I feel Mama's ice-cold glare boring into me.

"And that's all? You're not hungry?" the waiter persists.

I shake my head, see friendly concern in his slightly sad smile, and quickly stare back into the table. I wonder if I unconsciously did something to attract him, if I unconsciously tried to steal his attention away from Mama. I know I didn't mean to do anything of the kind, but I can't shake the guilty feeling.

When we arrive home, Mama locks herself into the home office to make a phone call, and afterwards defrosts a box of creamed spinach on the electric range. She serves it at the dining table set for one and sits down across from me.

"You're not eating?"

"No," Mama mumbles. "I'm going to wait 'til later."

Mama absently stares down and nervously curls a strand of hair around her finger. I inhale the meal and soon scrape the last streaks of green out of the pot.

"Okay, we're going now," Mama says, jumping up from the chair.

Mama's expression is blank at first, but when she picks up her car keys, deep satisfaction settles on her features.

"Mama," I beg. "No, please. Not tonight."

Mama's mouth trembles as she fights the impulse to laugh.

"I didn't mean it," I continue, trying to apologize for the waiter smiling at me, or whatever I might have done to upset her.

Mama's cold, leveling gaze says that I am a killer, and that I know it.

"I'm really, really sorry."

"Oh, don't play innocent!" Mama retorts flatly. "And anyway, I can't do anything about it."

As she heads towards the lobby, she jingles the keys: my wake-up call. *She can't do anything about it?* I cross my arms in defiance.

"Come on, or we're going to be late," she says, turning back.

"I'm not going."

"Don't be ridiculous," she sneers.

"I'm not going," I repeat, as the adrenaline violently whooshes through my body, affecting every one of trillions of nerves.

After a slight hesitation, a little backwards jerk of the head and trembling of the shoulders, Mama suddenly lunges at me, grabs me by the hair, pulls, and drags me towards the front door.

"Let me go!"

I try to kick her, but have to tread along as I'm being pulled. I grab my head and try to remove her hands, but she seems stronger than ever, and before long, with never-before-seen authority, Mama has pushed me into the passenger seat, slammed the door, jumped in the driver's seat and started the car. As she backs up, I open the door, but the car is going too fast. Mama hits the brake, leans over me, pulls the door shut and brusquely elbows me, pinning me into my seat as I vainly attempt to break loose. I huddle up. My heart pounds like a sledgehammer about to tear through ribs and skin. We speed through the quiet country roads, whooshing past small-town centers, and before long, Mama stops in front of the gate of the manor where the d'Auriac family lives.

Dusk under the large beech trees is as dark as the darkest night. A shadow approaches from the manor. Mama tries to whip the car around, backs up too fast, and with a terrific thud hits a short cement marker on the edge of the driveway, denting the back fender of her car. The unearthed marker leans over like a wilted flower. I expect Mama will get out of the car and check the damage, but instead she speeds off, out of the lane. Florence's older brother materializes, and though it is quite dark, his enormous grin is very visible.

"Did your mother just hit something?"

I point a shy finger at the felled marker. Florence's brother opens the gate, fastens the doors with ground level latches and inspects the little heap of cement, grinning all the while.

"I came to meet you, because we're leaving right away," he informs me, smiling flirtatiously.

The car rolls out of the garage, crunching the sandy gravel. Florence's brother recounts the situation and the rest of the family pile out of the car to observe the damage. As the foursome huddle over the flattened little pole, they laugh and joke about the accident, and about the fact that my mother drove off without even talking to them. I wish that I could just laugh at Mama, like them, but instead I feel sorry for her.

Villa, Belgium,

Saturday evening, December 1973

After about an hour's drive, we arrive at an opulent villa near Ghent. Smiling obsequiously, Michel Nihoul opens the front door. Loud disco music and chatter from inside the house nearly drown out Nihoul's sincere Christmas wishes to the d'Auriac family. As I file in, Nihoul frowns.

"We have no need for you here!"

The countess stops dead in her tracks and gives Nihoul one of her ice-cold stares. Nihoul huffs apologetically.

"She's off-limits for now."

"What do you mean? What does that mean?" demands the countess.

Nihoul gesticulates defensively.

"There's nothing I can do about it. There is somebody—a daddy's boy—a real nuisance if you want to know my honest opinion, who wants her all to himself."

Florence freezes upon hearing the phrase "daddy's boy." The countess conducts a short meeting with Nihoul in the hallway. I overhear the words "she said," several times, as Nihoul shakes his head. It makes me wonder if Mama called the countess when we got home from Christmas shopping this afternoon, after the waiter ignored her and was friendly to me, and if she set this up behind Nihoul's back, just to get her revenge on me. Mostly I wonder why, for heaven's sake, I was feeling sorry for Mama.

Florence's brother smiles with a comical look of disappointment, then hurries into the crowded living room. The baron casts a superior glance down at me, which I take to mean he doesn't care whether or not I am available. Florence stands nailed to the floor, shell-shocked. I feel sorry for her.

"Don't worry," I whisper. "Patrick and I don't even have sex."

For a second, as she stares, Florence looks just like her mother. Soon, a sardonic half grin forms on her face.

"So, what do you do? Talk?"

There is a semi-private den at the end of an L-shaped living room, lit by the tiny flame bulbs on the candles of a tall Christmas tree. I sit on top of a console against the wall and trace its carvings. Some newly-formed couples use the large settee in front of the Christmas tree to make out. When men approach me, an aggravated Nihoul intercepts them to inform them of my current "untouchable" status. At this party, there don't seem to be any other children like myself, whose parents are not in the network, and Florence is by far the youngest aristocrat. I have never observed businessmen bringing their own children to the orgies, but aristocrats consider sex with children as part of their culture, and have no qualms exposing their young to their depraved rites.

Florence appears hand in hand with an aristocratic politician—a fixture at the orgies—and laughingly leads him to the settee, where they waste no time in sufficiently undressing and then go at it, full force. Florence makes delighted noises. The sounds attract other men, who form a line. The man finishes; Florence groans and, blushing, thrusts her hips up, opens her legs, flashes me, and so invites the next man.

How stupid of me to tell her Patrick wasn't having sex with me, I think, realizing Florence is trying to make me understand just how stupid it was. And I wonder why I felt sorry for her.

The line of men gets longer, and Count d'Auriac, Florence's father, joins the line. When it is his turn, he stands over his daughter, and smiles the biggest smile ever.

During a fraction of a second, I see Florence, a little girl, hurt, scared, and ashamed. At the very instant that I see it, she covers it with a smile that mirrors her father's, but her eyes briefly seek mine to confirm what I saw, and I know that she will never forgive me.

The count has left his jacket and tie behind and his white shirt is unbuttoned. His hair is wild and unkempt. He looks sexy, virile, and free. He and Florence look at each other in the exact same manner: with wicked pleasure in their darkened eyes, grinning like only the two of them could possibly know how good this feels, like no one else can have what they have together.

Later that night I suddenly catch a glimpse of what seems to be Patrick and Florence passing by an open doorway giving out into the living room. I assume Patrick is on his way to me, but don't see him for another hour or so. He leads me upstairs.

"Were you with Florence just now?" I ask weakly.

"Nope."

I conclude I must have seen her with someone else, but the blood drains from my head all the same, as though my very existence were endangered. Patrick pulls a key out of his jean pocket and unlocks the door to a stuffy square room with a soft mattress on a bare frame and a single shuttered window. I wonder how Patrick knows this room, and why he has the key, but can't bring myself to speak.

Patrick observes me as he leans against the door and casually crosses his arms and feet, and I remember him watching me in this way the first time we were together, when he implied that whatever we would do was up to me. It suddenly dawns on me that he only meant sex.

"Let's get out of here," Patrick says, unlocking the door again.

I hurry after him, and minutes later we are speeding towards Brussels on the brightly lit expressway in a red Porsche 911.

"You should lie down," he says, "We wouldn't want anyone to think I'm a kidnapper."

As I lean over to put my head in his lap, I wonder if he means that he wants me to satisfy him orally.

"Come," he says, putting a reassuring hand on my shoulder. "Just put your head on my lap."

Haemers Residence,
Greater Brussels, Belgium, December 1973

Patrick's single bed is a messy heap of sheets and blankets. Little triangle soccer flags and purple and white ribbons of his favorite team adorn the walls of his bedroom. Socks and soccer shirts cover the carpet. In the red light of a lava lamp, Patrick puts his favorite new album on the record player, putting the needle down on the beginning of the song which he says makes him think of me. Joining me on the bed, he sings the lyrics, or at least what he makes of them, something about seeing flashes in the girl's eyes, and I hear him saying *"like hypnotized."*

He tries to make up for his ridiculously strong French accent by pronouncing the words with an over-the-top twang, *"Feel my cock, babe, that's for sure..."*

I'm sure those are not the lyrics, and he makes me laugh, nervously, because the melodic music, though super-cool, is also slow and romantic, about a girl having the singer's heart and his soul.

Patrick laughs intermittently to put me at ease, but stares intently into my eyes. His tucked-in jean shirt is unbuttoned almost all the way down; his skin looks milky soft, his face beautiful. The music intensifies, the song reaches its climax in the singers' passionate voice, but Patrick mouths the words silently, his body still.

I hear Patrick singing to me, "*You got your love just keep you blind. But I don't care*" and gather that he means that I am naïve, since I have not gotten sexual with him, and that, to his surprise, he does not mind. We lie on the bed holding hands and I enjoy the sweetness that runs through my body like a cool, soft whisper. During the finale of the next song, after we've heard the same line about not always getting what you want repeated at least ten times, Patrick leans over, and winks.

CHAPTER FOUR

Domain "Kattenhof" Castle,
s-Gravenwezel, Belgium,
late winter-early spring, 1974

As soon as I arrive at the orgies, Michel Nihoul finds an out-of-the-way place for me to sit, as my untouchable status endures. Sometimes I spend the whole night in one spot. Patrick's protection has officially separated me from the other children, but I was already lonely. Ever since I lost my little friend Wouter two years ago, I have made sure to never get close to another child. The networkers only use the love we children feel for each other to hurt us. I don't want another child getting harmed on my account. Patrick seems to be my only hope for love, but I fight it. Girls in love with perpetrators are bound to be dropped; and, heartbroken, they are considered worthless to the network. And that is one way for child sex slaves to get themselves killed.

On this property, network events occur inside a greenhouse on the castle grounds. Florence, sitting on the arm of a chair, whispers something in the ear of a pale, skinny girl. They both look over at me and share laughs. Pimps arrive with more children, and soon, a little group of seven or so girls, from about nine to thirteen years old, forms around Florence. Sometimes they glance at me; sometimes they sneer. The pale girl seems to be especially full of spiteful glee. *She must be new,* I think; *she is more obvious.* With her emaciated, pallid face, cracked swollen lips, skimpy figure, and very long, dark blonde hair with two braids rolled up on her head, she looks like a sickly fairy.

More children arrive: boys, girls, some as young as maybe five, some teenagers, North African immigrant children. Hours pass. It is not a big party and there are more children than grown-ups. The adults are all men, all aristocrats, and they waste no time in flirting. Instead, they talk to Nihoul, point out certain children, and some do advance and take them out with them, and others don't. The children, except for the few titled ones, stand or sit bravely, demurely, heads bowed. The little aristocrats, whose families seem to be going through the motions of having a party to cover up the strange business Nihoul is conducting, act as hostesses, with Florence as their leader.

I recognize one stocky redhead, an aristocrat whom I once overheard as he asked Polo for me, but Polo refused, mumbling that he wanted to keep the pretty ones a bit longer. That is how I learned that children don't make it through the night in this man's hands. This was after I had been singled out by Polo's idol, the global Big Shot, because before that event, I was never considered pretty. During my first three years in the network I was expendable, and had been in situations which had made this abundantly clear. I am not ugly, but I'm also not that pretty.

A bronze-skinned boy with big shoulder-length curls, maybe twelve years old, keeps looking over. I presume he is from Moroccan descent, since most immigrant families in Belgium come from that country. I would like to look back at him but adhere to my rule to keep distant from other children. Suddenly, Patrick appears. As I hurry off hand-in-hand with Patrick, I feel bad that I did not respond to the boy, and my eyes seek his, if only to say goodbye. He averts his face, and, feeling rejected, I send him a contemptuous glare. Patrick smiles sweetly.

Florence, in conversation with one of the men, stops talking as her eyes follow Patrick and me. Michel Nihoul is smooching up a dark-haired teenage girl. He swings his head around to catch Patrick's eye and jokes,

"So, *le grand blond* is in love, huh? Okay, we all understand, but when are you going to start sharing?"

Patrick stops and lets go of my hand. Standing still, he calmly waits until Nihoul's face falls. Florence and a few others make up the attentive audience. Nihoul loosens his hold of the girl, trying to overcome his discomfort with apologetic huffs, squeezing his face into a forced smile. Once he has Nihoul's undivided attention, Patrick says, "If you ever dare touch her, or I find out that somebody else has, I'm going to kill you."

On the way out, I shoot Florence a look, answered by a tight-lipped smile. I realize that Patrick was serious when he told Nihoul he would kill him, and, from the way he said it, he made it sound easy.

Patrick drives, not to the exit, but up to the castle, speeding up until he screeches to a halt by the façade, skidding. A silent, grave butler who seems completely in the know guides us to our quarters upstairs, a large room with simple furniture. Patrick pulls a wad of bills out of his wallet and stuffs them in the butler's breast pocket. He does not try to be discreet, and the pokerfaced butler widens his eyes just a tad. I cover my laughing face. Patrick flashes me a mischievous smile as he joins me on the sofa.

"Here, I want to show you something," he says, searching a blue Adidas weekend bag he has brought along.

He pulls out a gun, and, laying it flat on his hands with the loop pointing away, shows me. Here is the answer to all my questions concerning Patrick's power in the network.

"It's a Browning," he says with obvious pride, and as if *Browning* were a French word.

He gives it to me to hold. I am surprised by the weight. He nods excitedly. I indulge Patrick and run my finger over the diamond-patterned handle, then look as if waiting for an explanation. He intensifies his gaze, like he wants me to understand that this is real, and dangerous.

"Have you ever seen a dead body?" Patrick asks, frustration creeping in his voice.

"Several times."

He raises his eyebrows, sighs, relaxes into the pillows, puts his hand on my neck and massages it. He leans in closer.

"Tell me."

I frown and shake my head. He puts both his arms around me.

"No, no, I didn't mean it like that. What I meant is that I forget what you've been through. And I forget who you are. You're very strong, you know that?"

"That's why it happened," I answer. "Because I was bold. It came to mind the first time I met you. Remember, when you said I was a whore who likes her job?"

My recall of his insult seems to revive all the love I saw then in Patrick's eyes, bringing awareness and acceptance to my defiant streak.

"Usually, when someone insults me, they never know that I noticed. But when I was first brought here, around my sixth birthday, I didn't hide it. I had been on some kind of a stage, used for some kind of a sick show, I can't even tell you, but by the end of it, I was furious. I was alone on the stage, so I stood up and shouted, 'You can't do this to me. This is not okay. I'm going to tell my father. He's the mayor and he's not going to let you get away with this. He'll make sure you'll all be punished.'"

The sympathy and sadness in Patrick's gaze tell me that, whether my stepfather consciously or unconsciously closes his eyes to my mother's nocturnal activities, a real father would protect me from them. But I don't believe it. *Papa would protect me if he knew—I just never told him.*

"Most of the people there were so high they didn't even hear me, like this was just another part of the show. There was one man who looked like he pitied me, but he disappeared and I never saw him again. I don't think Nihoul was there yet, but an old handler with an enormous paunch came over, a smile on his face. 'Come along,' he said, like a friend. He took my hand and we went for a walk. I was very scared, but he was friendly. I can't remember how we got from one place to the next. We ended up in a large basement and he said, 'You know, we really like you here. We'd hate to lose you,' and I wanted to believe that whoever 'they' are, they really do like me, because I was a nice girl and only six years old—why shouldn't they like me? And I wanted to believe that he liked me too, even though I didn't like him. And as we went deeper into this cellar—it was dark—I started to smell something. A faint but unmistakably sick odor, very specific. I would recognize it right away. Then I think he turned on a light that was maybe just a bare bulb, and there was a bath made of cement at the far end of this cellar, and he led me to the other side of it. He still had this easygoing attitude, like this is just something that happens if you talk, but there's no need to worry if you don't. So, at that moment, I completely got on his wavelength. The first thing I did was tell myself that this was not a human being, just a dead body, and there was nothing to be afraid of. I looked at her in the same way I felt that he did: like old leftovers. She was a young woman, and I remember thinking she looked working-class, maybe had been a prostitute, and then I thought it was strange that I should have such a thought about a dead person. I did not feel horrified; and still don't. She had a round, soft body, very, very white, all cut up. The deepest cut was this slash in her belly, horizontal, and it was open, like a purse. I stayed on the handler's wavelength for as long as he kept me in there, which seemed much longer than necessary. I got the message right away. I didn't plan on telling my stepfather about what had happened. At least not in so many words."

Now, Patrick, who has had his arms around me with his head leaning against my shoulder, again looks up with such pity, and—I don't know—I don't want to call it love.

"Did you say anything?" Patrick asks.

"Not to my father."

"Then who? Who did you tell?"

"My mother."

Patrick knows that I don't have a pimp and that Mama brings me to the orgies herself. I have a vague notion that I brought this on myself, by trying to tell Mama about what had happened the first time, when I had been taken by a couple with whom I was staying the weekend. Patrick observes my shameful reaction and seems to juggle several responses. Then, without relaxing the frown on his brow, with one short exhale that is sort of a chuckle, he expresses that he sees the irony.

"But she already knew!" he cries out. "Tell me, did anything change after you told your mother?"

"No, a few weeks later she gave me back to the couple, and they took me back to an orgy. The woman cleans our house every Thursday. I'd told my mother that bad things had happened. The next time the cleaning lady was at our house, she offered my mom to babysit for free, and I threw a tantrum. My mom sent me off with her again, but it seemed that was only because I had misbehaved. I also thought I had not expressed myself clearly enough about what had happened. I was too afraid because of the dead body and too ashamed, and I didn't know all the words. But when my mother started driving me to the orgies herself, I thought that I had given her the idea by trying to tell her, and therefore it was all my fault."

Patrick stares me squarely in the eye, frowning sternly. I get from him that there is nothing wrong with me, but that something is wrong with my thinking. Even as I talk about Mama, I hear my confusion reaching Patrick's consciousness, whereas he reflects back his clarity, which says that Mama knew all along, and nothing I could have said or done could have changed anything. I get it, but I cannot accept it. *She is my mother. I love her, and she must love me, if only a little bit.* Patrick puts his arms around me and rocks me.

"*Ma petite Annie,*" Patrick mumbles. "My little Annie. You're so sweet. You went and told your mother. Of course. "*Que je t'aime, ma chérie.*" (How I love you, sweetheart.)

I sleep on top of Patrick in a nice wooden bed with white starched sheets in a very neat bedroom. Everything is simple and clean, and I also feel cleaner than ever.

A loud shot jolts me out of a deep slumber. A bright morning sunbeam pours in the window, parading particles of dust floating through the room and highlighting a stain on the carpet that looked so clean last night. A second shot is fired.

When Patrick has left the room, I wonder if Mama is waiting for me in her car by the greenhouse where she dropped me last night. Before Patrick, I would meet her at dawn wherever she dropped me, but since he has been showing up, I sometimes don't come out until noon. Patrick returns with a copious breakfast on a tray, which he carefully sets on the table.

"Is there a hunt going on?" I ask.

"It certainly sounds like it, doesn't it?" he answers lightly.

I don't know why I haven't already peeked through the window, which looks out over the park. The woods look bleak, almost as they would in late fall. The lawn grass is green, but the trees are bare. There is one hunter, walking through the woods, carrying his rifle. How strange, I think, that there is not a group of them, combing the woods with dogs. What is he hunting? Patrick drinks his coffee, and also looks out the window. We hear a third shot. I see the lone hunter, still walking, holding his rifle.

"I wonder if my mom is waiting in her car, and if she might be in danger," I venture out loud, wondering why I say this to Patrick rather than keep it to myself.

"Your mother is no good," Patrick says casually.

I believed I wiped the honey out of my eyes as soon as I went into network mode, but this hurts so much. I know that Patrick is right, and yet, I am angry. I don't mind believing everything is my fault so that Mama can be better. I don't want to see her clearly. *It is Patrick who is no good, not my mother!*

Patrick approaches, this time intently looking me in the eyes.

"Your mother doesn't love you."

Bang. Another shot, embedding the truth.

But who will love me then? I think. Patrick wipes my tears and takes me in his arms. I glide into his embrace with terrific ease. The loud nearby shots fail to rupture a great sense of peace that quiets everything. As though I were a virtuoso musician and Patrick my exquisite, perfectly tuned instrument, every slightest move, slightest thought in Patrick's arms is responded to with perfect synchronicity. When I look up into his face I want to kiss him. I reach up; Patrick responds fiercely, swooping down to lift me. Looking into his eyes, I first see sadness, then...never have I seen such love.

Our lips almost meet. Another shot. There is a flash of something outside—moving fast. I pull out of Patrick's embrace, rush to the window. There is a boy, still far, approaching, running. *The children last night!*

I recognize the bronze skin and dark curls flowing around his sensuous face, the boy who kept trying to catch my eye last night, the one I rejected. Another shot rings out. The boy falls forward, arms spread out, shot in the back. I half expect that in a second, he will get up and start running again, but he lies on the grass, completely still.

I recoil in horror. Like a boiling geyser breaking through layers of rock, the sweet possibilities I warded off last night when he was trying to get my attention spout from my depths, and the guilt for not having responded is so overwhelming, it seems as though I killed him with my own hands.

"I want to go home."

Patrick munches on red grapes and nonchalantly observes the body of his rival. I suddenly remember the question Patrick asked last night, "Have you ever seen a dead body?" Continuing to look out the window, Patrick pulls his mouth open wide and pushes his tongue between the bottom row of his teeth and his cheek.

Don't you care at all? I think. As if in answer, Patrick spits a pit onto the floor.

"You don't even want breakfast?" he asks casually.

"No," I answer, indignant.

In driving me back to the greenhouse, Patrick pulls the same stunt as last night, pulling up really fast, magnifying my extreme tension and irritability. When Mama's car appears in view at the end of the lane, Patrick speeds up straight towards her, and comes to an extremely abrupt halt, missing her car by inches. An involuntary chuckle escapes me. Patrick winks, leans over and puts his arms around me. I turn my back to him and get out of the car, shutting the door without another look.

When we drive off in her boxy Dutch Daf, Mama cackles, "That was a very handsome young man. With really blonde hair, and a Porsche...so, is he the reason why you've been staying out so much?"

"Let's not talk."

After a short silence, Mama says, in an ultra-innocent little girl voice, "Yes, so I asked the dentist if there was a special toothpaste for you, so we could get your teeth whiter, but since they got yellow from the antibiotics that you got for your asthma when you were a baby, there's nothing to do about it. The yellow affects all the bones, so you'll just have to learn to live with your yellow teeth."

Instead of reflecting as usual on my listed imperfections, I am annoyed, and observe that Mama's eyes scan my features for signs of pain.

"You're no good, Mama."

"What?"

Mama keeps turning her head to me in disbelief, and passes a crossroads without stopping for a car coming in from the right. For the second time in a few minutes, Mama's car is nearly hit, as the other car screeches to a halt, missing us by inches, followed by a long, furious honk. Mama swerves and continues on the road.

"The next time I'm taking you there," she says, "I'm going to leave you there."

CHAPTER FIVE

Family home, Belgium,
a Saturday evening, March 1974

"**A**re you ready?"

"Almost."

"Hurry!" Mama hisses as quietly as possible.

I get out of bed, dressed and ready to go. My cue when my stepfather is home, is that Mama gives me a significant look when she tells me it's time for bed. When that happens, instead of putting on pajamas, I get in bed wearing my clothes, never sleeping a wink, waiting for the sounds of my parents getting into bed in the room next to mine, and turning out their bedside lamps. When my stepfather is asleep, my mother comes to get me.

Once the car has rolled silently down the driveway, Mama turns the key. After we pass the windmill, we turn left towards the church in the center of the village. Left again. To the Brussels highway, to some event where Patrick is likely to show up.

I breathe a sigh of relief. When we reach the church of the next village, Mama turns left, a trajectory leading to a vacant mansion. My relief was short-lived; it is as if an armored fist squeezes the blood out of my heart.

I haven't been back to the mansion since I met Patrick! It's been over six months! I know that Patrick's protection won't work in this mansion; these are not orgies but some type of secret club meetings which Nihoul or Patrick would never attend. A narrow bridge leads to the cobblestone driveway, the entrance of the mansion property. The fist clenches inside my chest.

"Mama," I whimper.

I notice how pleased Mama looks, and want to smile with her, as if we have had our joke, and she won.

"Can I come back home with you?" I ask, smiling feebly.

Mama laughs a single "ha," the sound of which hurts my ears. Opening the car door and standing requires much more effort than it should.

"I'll see you around dawn?"

Mama pushes her upper lip down, suppressing involuntary laughter. I hold the door handle, only releasing it when Mama stares angrily, and I don't close the door. Mama reaches over, pulls the door shut, locks it, and drives away.

An invisible cloud envelops my head, irritating my eyes. I enter through the unlocked front door, into a real cloud of cigar and cigarette smoke. A rumble of deep voices seeps into the lobby from the closed meeting hall. I head sideways, to the room where I have spent many lonely nights on a bare, stained mattress, waiting for dawn to color the curtains blue. The room seems even smaller than I remember. Maybe I am bigger. I sink down on the dirty mattress, thinking I am back where I belong.

Somewhere in Europe,
between the fall of 1972 and spring of 1974

I abruptly awake when the door opens, and jump up. The black outline of the figure in the doorway looks like a gorilla. In the faint light of a small lamp, I see a barrel of a man with thick black hair, no neck, a broad face and narrow, slanting eyes. He looks surprised when he sees me, and I hope that he will turn on his heels, because I look my age, small and skinny, without as much as a hint of breasts.

The man angrily motions for me to undress, and unbuttons his shirt. He does not seem to speak Flemish or French, and his mute grunts make him all the more a gorilla. Not only his chest, but his back too is covered with dark bushy hair. Naked now, he threateningly widens his eyes at me, seeing I am still dressed. My mind draws a blank. Then, finally, my training kicks in; I make eye contact and connect to where I am supposed to be. Now our energetic bodies are one. I feel a thousand chilled knives in my stomach, the hollow no one can live with. I feel all his fear, called violence once it is ejected into another.

He advances physically; I receive the entire charge of impending violence, and in utter panic, pull my t-shirt over my head, getting stuck with my arms up and eyes covered. It is too overwhelming. A loud roar. *He's attacking! He's going to eat me! I am sinking....*

I am looking up into a beautiful, sadly smiling face, and realize the sound I heard was the man's laughter as he pulled my shirt over my head. My near-saint part awakened, I am now guilty for having had negative thoughts about one who was only trying to help. I attune myself to find the unloved child in the man. I look behind the bags under his eyes, the heavy slanting lids that hide most of the iris. There, right there in his pupils; I see his sorrow. I embrace him, and hold him as though he were a sweet little child, even though my arms don't reach around his torso. I put my body against his; he pulls me closer. I feel his erection. He rubs my back, hard, and lays me down on the mattress.

The near-saint disappears; my bouncer emerges. The man's smell, his body, his anger; the bouncer can reject it all. He grabs hold of his short fat penis. That is all I can take. As my bouncer rids me of the perpetrator, it bounces me out as well, and the empty vessel takes over. Nimbly, automatically, with no intentional act of will, my whole consciousness withdraws out of my body. I don't see ugly genitalia, I don't hear fast, heavy breathing;

the faint whiff of manure in his sweat is gone. My nerves are switched off; I don't feel the pain from an adult penis. The man is gone and so am I, while the empty vessel does everything it needs, functioning as effortlessly as any peristaltic muscle.

I find my consciousness right by an ivory-colored woven cloth lampshade and thoroughly examine every tiniest fiber, tinier than my eye could see if I were to get up off the mattress and press my nose onto the shade. Then I begin to revert to another reality.

As the man nears his climax, my senses remain switched off, but my consciousness is present, like a coldly detached witness, observing, anticipating his ejaculation. I may switch between different parts; the perpetrators metamorphose at least as much as I do, especially at this point. Their release is usually fraught with terrible expressions, which I would rather never witness in any human being, let alone from this vantage point.

This one looks like he's choking on something, pulling his head back and doing something strange with his tongue; his eyes roll around. He shivers and relaxes, on top of me. My cheek is buried in the hollow of his hairy chest. I push his shoulders up to make him aware that there is a little person underneath him.

He reacts with a laugh, and says something that sounds Russian. As he gets dressed, he smiles and tries to make conversation, in broken English, and Russian. He strikes me as too foolishly happy to be dangerous, and I consider my options. Something about his mouth tells me that he is a silly man, that he was teased a lot as a child, and that he felt stupid. My task is to soothe his most deep-seated fears, those he has worked his entire life to cover, to prove to himself and to the world that he is the opposite of unintelligent and silly. At this moment, after his orgasm, he is off guard. I always need to be careful, but decide I do not need to placate him, and I just stare coldly.

Mansion, Belgium,
a Saturday night, March 1974

As the interminable night wears on, I become more and more confused. I realize in horror that it has been too long. I am not desensitized anymore to the horrors that had been normalized previously. In the past months, under Patrick's protection, I had gotten used to looking at people with ten-year old eyes instead of putting every pervert in the most favorable possible light. During the first rapes of this night, to avoid feeling the terror and physical pain, I automatically fracture into many different parts, most of whom are not even present. However, at some point, a brand-new part seems to appear out of my unconscious drive to survive, which allows me to remain in my body. Only, I find myself not having sex with an adult rapist. No; I am with a tall, slender, blonde youth with milky soft skin and hardly any chest hair. Patrick loves me, and I love him. He loves no one but me, and I love no one but him. Because he loves me so much, he is as good, as strong, and as pure as love itself. And I love him the same.

In between visits, which last until deep into the night, I keep checking my little pile of clothes, painstakingly going over the items, convinced each time that something is missing. Panicked, I count. *One: panties. Two: t-shirt. Three: cardigan. Four: jeans. Five: knee socks. Six: Kickers boots. Seven: anorak.* Often, I count less than seven, or believe I've counted the boots or the socks as two instead of one; then I start again, and then again. *Where did I leave off? What did I lose? Did somebody steal something? My jeans, where are they? I can't go home without pants! Who stole them?*

Tiny points of blue begin to peak through the roughly woven curtains and soon, faint daylight filters through them, laying the room bare in all its drab neglect. I dress and enter the lobby, where the stale smell of smoke lingers. All is quiet. I pull open the front door. Mama is not there, and it is too cold to wait outside. A bright sun rises on this early spring day. I venture through the parlor floor meeting hall with columns, wood paneling, sofas and emptied ashtrays—through to the kitchen, where I find a fridge. Empty.

I return to the lobby, sit down cross-legged and look through a window pane of the front door.

Now that the men are gone, so are the different parts of me that make me good. I feel dirty and ashamed. I would like to brush my teeth and wash up, but I sit by the door like a puppy dog waiting for its master, because I can't believe that Mama will leave me here. *She has to come, any minute now.* I can't wait to get home, lock myself in the bathroom and have my purification ritual. Studying my face in the mirror, I then consciously perform every cleansing act, every brush stroke, untangling the knots, washing away all the badness. The need to refresh is so great that I get up and step into the chilly morning air, but after a few steps I begin to worry: *What if someone sees me leaving this house? What if someone asks what I was doing here?* My deepest shame and fear are that I am a "whore," which I have been called more times than I can count. How could I answer questions about what I was doing here? There is no one to be seen in the front area or farther down the street. There are a small red brick building and abandoned stables on either side of the entrance to the property. Hiding by the brick building I can't be spotted from the street, and with pounding heart, I observe the small bridge that leads to the road. As I remain frozen in place, I imagine being stopped by an upstanding citizen who will look disapprovingly at my ruffled exterior and ask me why I am out by myself. *What would I say? That my mother didn't pick me up? That my mother took me to that empty mansion and she was supposed to get me at dawn? That I was working all night? As a prostitute?*

Under a blanket of panicky thoughts lies a vague memory of Mama's voice saying, "I'm going to leave you there." *Which means that she wants me to stay here, and that I cannot go home. Besides, I don't know if I would remember the way....*

The mansion has a toilet stall on the ground floor, with a small sink. No soap. The bathroom upstairs is just as bare. With all my might I try to pull apart the knots in my hair; it hurts my scalp and cuts into my fingers— and it doesn't work. When I look into the mirror, I feel ashamed of the way I look. I anxiously remember the past week, and imagine myself not being irritable with Mama, not saying anything to get on her nerves. *If only I had not said she was no good. If only I hadn't hurt her feelings.* I go back to the subtlest spoken and unspoken interactions between us, in which it seems I could have acted better.

I watch the light change; the sunlight that shone in the front windows in the morning now beautifully illumines the lane with the open road in view. Then the sun sets. Now it gets dark. I feel slightly dizzy and see points of light before my eyes. The families who live in the houses in this street must be sitting down to their dinners. I picture myself stepping out and ringing their doorbell. *I am dirty. What would they think of me? I don't look like I'm starving. My clothes aren't rags. What would I tell them I was doing here?*

My shameful thoughts are interspersed with bits of memories of various threats from Polo and other network regulars, reminding me that no matter where I might turn, if I were to even think about saying anything to anybody, it would always get back to them, because they have friends everywhere. Not only would I be punished or killed, but whomever I would talk to would also be punished or killed, and whatever happened to them would be my fault.

I push and pull, and manage to lift the dirty mattress in the little room up on its side, slide it through the doorway and push it to the front door, positioning it so that when I lay on it on my side, I see the driveway through a large window pane on the bottom of the door. As I lie there waiting, my guilt-laden thoughts flow again towards Mama. *I'm sure she doesn't know what happens after she drops me off—she's naïve like a child, proud of me for mixing with the most elite crowd in the country—aristocrats, famous politicians, doctors, judges, lawyers, top businessmen.... How could I expect her to think anything is wrong?*

Goading myself back into the box in which Mama can do no wrong and I love her completely, I feel nausea rise. Sitting up, cross-legged, I close my eyes and ride it out. A whitish point of light appears, with a golden rim. The light expands, shines like a sun both bright and subtle, whether my eyes are opened or closed. For whatever reason, this light looks familiar and it is comforting. It is steady and brings steadiness to me. I try more and more to get absorbed in it, and the more I do, the better I feel. All worries fall away. The great shifts in perception of myself and of Mama level out into detached clarity.

There is nothing in this universe as enticing as this light. It seems to be a sign that there is more to life than food and family. I do not have a sense how much time passes, but my body is still, my mind is still. I feel entirely at peace, and don't know why. I don't care why. There is comfort pouring from the light.

And then the night gives way to a new dawn. I wonder if Mama will come. She does not. This is Monday, a school day. My thoughts, dormant all night, anxiously flow out, focused and fastened—in her absence—on The Mother.

I have lost weight; my pants are looser. I put my hands on my hips and feel the bones more sharply. My ribcage is showing. I walk to the kitchen and automatically open the fridge, to once again find nothing. My stomach has stopped growling. My belly hurts. I get dizzy, so I sit, breathe, get up, and continue walking, slower.

Funny that this should be the place to be so hungry, I think. *This is the Hungry House.*

I remember the man whom I had told I was hungry in the little room in this mansion. Having seen him eight or so times in a row, he tried to make conversation in a sensitive way, and I thought I might confide in him. A while later, on an overcast afternoon, Mama dropped me at a white villa in Rhode-Saint-Genese. Michel Nihoul wrung his hands with glee when he saw me. There were five or six other children, mostly girls, and we were made to sit down at a table set up outside, in a circular, red brick courtyard where French windows opened to the back of the home. Nihoul gave a mock speech.

"Children, there is one among you—her...."

He said it casually, as if it barely mattered, but pointing at me, so all the others looked.

"...Who has complained to one of our guests that she gets hungry. Do you hear? She gets hungry. So, since I don't want any of you to ever feel deprived or neglected, I thought of a way to address the situation, which, I hope, will satisfy your cravings once and for all; that you never again will feel the need to bother our guests with trifles such as these. Dear children, I have prepared a meal. I hope that it will be to your liking."

Nihoul entered the house through the French doors. After a few minutes he returned wearing oven mitts, carrying an enormous metal baking sheet. I could smell meat, but not what kind. It smelled bad. He set it down. A rump. Nearly black with red bloody stuff—horrific.

"Here," said Nihoul, "I'm going to try to put it back together for you."

He ran back in and came out with a second tray that he lined up with the first in the middle of the rectangular table. The second tray had the head and shoulders. Of a boy. With sunken cheeks and shrunken skin, charred except for a few patches of stubbly blonde hair. Piece by piece, Nihoul put the puzzle together, until the whole corpse was laid out, with skinny blackened limbs. Nihoul seemed to be having a great time. He has always loved his own jokes.

Why did I tell that man I was hungry? Why did I tell my mother she was no good? Why can't I keep quiet? Why am I always so bad?

I was sitting near the head of the body. Nihoul had begun cutting up the shoulders, asking who wanted a nice fleshy part, saying this was the best meat. As he was carving, I saw that a tooth fell out of the boy's open mouth onto the tray, and Nihoul did not notice. As Nihoul put a piece of flesh on somebody's plate with his back turned to me, I snatched the tooth from the tray and hid it inside my palm. Heart pounding, not looking to see if the other children saw me, I stuffed the tooth in my pocket.

Nihoul served me last: a chunk of thigh meat, grayish brown. He jokingly offered salt and pepper. I took the salt shaker and doused my plate with salt, tore off a piece of flesh, put it in my mouth and tried to swallow without chewing. Meanwhile, Nihoul kept jabbering, talking about the importance of chewing your food well for good digestion. I hurriedly ate everything off my plate without thinking. The meat was slightly rotten, but so overcooked I tried to focus on the burned taste.

The morning after that afternoon in the brick courtyard with Nihoul, I had stayed home from school and ended up alone all afternoon. I dug a hole two-fists deep by a low bush next to the narrow dirt path that leads alongside the house, right outside my bedroom window, and placed the tooth inside. I sat there for a long time, figuring it wasn't much, the burial for that boy. Then I put the dirt back in the hole, patted it over and over so it looked nice and smooth, and sat there some more. I thought I might cry, but no tears came. I took a walk to the woods. It was a gorgeous day, and I thought about the boy, who could not smell the air and enjoy the beauty of the trees and the sky. I wanted to find forget-me-nots, but not knowing what they look like, I picked five wildflowers with tiny blue petals, walked home and placed them on the grave.

I now rise from that memory and adjust myself on the dirty mattress, look out the bottom window pane again, and think about Wouter, my little friend whom I witnessed tortured to death. He also had blonde stubbly hair. He was also a victim of the network. I think about the young woman's body I was shown in the cellar after the first time I was brought to an orgy. I think about the Moroccan boy who was shot and killed during the recent hunt, his body splayed out on the grass, arms open.

I ascend the stairs, stopping when I get too dizzy, and go back to the bathroom. I feel and smell filthy. I finger brush my teeth, but they still don't feel smooth. I try scratching off the plaque, to no avail. I finger comb my hair. The knots won't come undone. My hair looks ratty and greasy. I splash water on my face and a bit over my hair, but I just get cold and wet, no cleaner. I don't like the way my face looks: sallow and narrow.

I think of Patrick, and how good it felt last time I saw him. *But then I rejected him and I'm sure I hurt his feelings. I'm sure I've lost his love.*

I resume my position by the front door window, and the next thing I know, I am waking up after what seems like a long nap. I try to sit up, but as I rise, black spots appear and expand before my eyes and I faint. I wake up again, sit up and cross my legs, closing my eyes, hoping that I will see the light again, but it is uncomfortable sitting cross-legged at this moment. My mind wanders here and there, and I let it. The worries come. I let them pass. My anxious thoughts about Mama come. I let them pass. After a while my mind and body do quiet down, and though I can't see the light, I feel better.

Later in the day, on another futile round looking for something to eat or drink or cover myself with, the light suddenly appears before my eyes again. I stand still and put my hands over my eyes to see it better. It stays, so I go back to the mattress by the front door window, and sit down, and then it gets smaller and goes away. Still, the comfort lingers, and I just sit, with my coat over my cardigan for warmth, as if the light were there.

I am sitting cross-legged on the mattress by the window next to the front door. I have been here five days. I am not hungry or thirsty anymore. After three days, my stomach gave up. My system is shutting down. I don't have to use the bathroom anymore. The body is wasting away. Bones stick out from underneath the skin. My teeth and hair are not so different from day two. My lips are swollen and cracked. I amuse myself by running my fingertips over the rough surface and picking at the loose ends of hard skin. I smell myself and don't mind; it is only my body. I am preparing to let it go, not waiting anymore. I spend more time bathing in the comfort of the light than bothering about externals. The light teaches me that it is important to prepare for death, because death is the only certainty of life. It tells me that there is a way of dying, to let go of the body before the body lets go of you. I haven't found out how yet, but I think that I might; I think that I will.

Here comes Mama's car, rattling up the driveway, moving slowly past the door and coming to a stop a little further ahead. I am not inclined to move. Mama turns off the ignition, and does not move either.

If I remain sitting, I can hold on to my truth; one of rapes through the first night and starvation the four following days—brought here and then left by Mama, just as she had promised.

After several minutes, the motor starts up again, and, gripped with the panic of being left behind again, of having to stay here and die alone, I bolt upright. Black spots converge into a black hole before my eyes, sucking in consciousness. I pry my eyes open, steady myself, remain standing on pure willpower, and walk to the car at an agonizing pace. I open the door and plop down in the passenger seat, giving up, exhausted. We take off; I am lightheaded, and close my eyes.

"Why didn't you come home?" asks Mama. "We were worried sick about you."

Was I supposed to walk home? Did she tell me, and did I forget? Is it not that long a walk? Did I get it all wrong?

I hear my thoughts, and stop the anxious flow. I am too tired. I remind myself of my truth, wondering if it even matters. Plain facts are ignored rebels in this totalitarian state of Being Good where my mother rules. It would be so much easier if I could accept that I made my family worry—that would be better for everyone. I lean my head against the door and turn to look out the window, averting Mama's critical gaze, which says that my appearance proves what she has always known: that I am rotten to the core.

The first person I see when I enter the front door of our house is the cleaning lady who initially introduced me to the network. It is Thursday, of course—the day she cleans the house. Her small, scheming eyes flicker coldly as I cross the freshly mopped slate tiles of the lobby. I head to the kitchen. Odors enter my nostrils like voluptuous promises. There is a pan on the stove with browned melted butter that must have been used as sauce for some meat dish, and a pot with some leftover boiled potatoes. This is my stepfather's fare. Papa is often abroad for work, sometimes months at a time, but he was home during my time away and will most likely be back for dinner. I mash a quartered potato in the pan and take a small bite. The browned butter tastes too strong; too meaty and salty, but the potato abounds with subtle, nurturing flavor. After my small meal, which is all I can eat, I am overcome with acute exhaustion and lay down on the sofa in the living room. Less than a minute later, the cleaning woman runs the vacuum noisily around the sofa while Mama stands by the kitchen door, arms crossed, looking on disapprovingly.

I take a bath and wash my hair. The knots are so tight I can't comb them out by the time dinner is ready at five.

My stepfather's bald crown is the first thing I see when I enter the dining area. As I approach him, I imagine that when he sees me, he will be shocked and ask me what happened. But when I sit down, he greets me as if I had been there all week, and as if nothing were amiss. He squeezes his eyes shut, bows his head and folds his hands. Loudly and slowly, he utters a prayer. When he concludes with "Amen," Mama and my brother chime in. Mama serves a long sausage that she cuts into pieces in the pan. Mashed potatoes. Boiled endives. Spinach for me.

Mama goes to the kitchen. I anxiously look at Papa, hoping he will notice my weight, my pallor, maybe the knots in my hair. Mama's senior by twenty years, he is fifty-four, with white fuzz, purple veins running across his big nose, and bloodshot eyes that avoid me. He gets up slowly, picks a tulip-shaped glass and a half-empty bottle of red wine from a cabinet, and pours, looking intently at the liquid. Holding up the glass, he teaches his two children, "You see? See the rich brown tones in this Burgundy? That's how you can tell that it's old."

As he looks up at the wineglass, his thin lips curl into a tight smile, while his little blue eyes remain unsmiling. He swirls the liquid, takes a deliberate sip and swallows audibly.

"Papa?" I begin.

He looks at me. His gaze is so devoid of recognition of my state that I doubt myself.

"I haven't been home," I stammer.

"Yes, I've heard about your fancy exploits," he jokes. "Too busy mingling in the higher circles to give any time to your poor father at home!"

"Don't you see anything different about me?"

I say the last words very quietly, because Mama returns from the kitchen with a bottle of orangeade and glasses for my brother and me, and then serves Papa's food. I put my hands around my waist, touching my middle fingers to show him. He can see, but he does not look.

I mix the spinach with potatoes, spoon some melted butter on top and take a bite. My mouth muscles must have lost their tone; it takes effort to chew and swallow. The spinach tastes like the cardboard out of which it came. After the chocolate puddings are finished and Mama begins to clear the table, Papa stays behind, savoring his second glass of wine.

"Papa, I was very hungry while I was away," I venture nervously.

Papa throws a sideways glance over my body as he drinks. When he puts his glass down, he says, "I can see that you've lost weight. Didn't they give you enough caviar?"

After pronouncing "caviar" in an exaggerated dialect accent, he forces out a big, fake laugh, betraying his envy of the elusive elite to which he would so love to belong.

"Seriously," he goes on, "make sure you don't get too thin."

Papa's eyes glide over my body as if I were a good bottle of wine.

"Papa, I'm trying to tell you something," I continue, nervously eyeing the kitchen doorway through which Mama may appear any second.

My little brother gets up from the table and goes over to the television area, asking his father if he can watch TV. Papa picks up his glass, stands, and stretches self-consciously. Adding a little audible yawn for effect, he follows my brother. I jump up.

"Papa!" I plead.

"What do you want now?"

Papa laughs as if I were conniving to get something from him, as if he humorously condoned my shrewdness. As he turns on the television for my brother, I clutch his arm. *It's real, Papa,* I am trying to say. *I really need you.* He finally drops the pretense and looks at me, and I see that watery, alcohol-induced softness in his eyes through which his love lights up, mixed with desire, and a melancholic smile appears on his face.

"Papa, listen, I didn't eat; there was no one there."

Mama enters and eyes us suspiciously. Suddenly, it seems as if she just caught me trying to seduce Papa. Her cold stare turns towards her husband. He stiffens and pulls his arm loose, as if he just got caught too.

"What stories are you trying to tell me?" he mumbles.

His eyes once again become dim and he makes his way to the table to help Mama clean up. I feel that they are a nice couple and I was trying to disturb their peace. *I'm even too lazy to help them clear the dishes,* I think. *I was too lazy to walk home from that house in the next village. They were worried about me.*

The next day, Mama keeps me out of school. The doctor arrives later that morning. He does a perfunctory exam on me while chatting with Mama, decides I am getting over a flu, writes a note for school, backdates it to the beginning of the week, and tells me to get some rest. After the doctor has left, Mama gets a comb and scissors. She tells me to sit straight up on the chair and not to move. I hear the scissors cut, once, twice. Mama pulls out a chunk of hair, a knot with a lot of long hair attached.

"You're cutting it all off!" I exclaim in horror, touching the back of my head.

"That's the only way to get it out," Mama retorts. "That'll teach you for running away from home!"

Another big strand of my hair is being pulled. *No! Stop it, please! Okay, I ran away from home and stayed with rich people who fed me caviar. That's what you told papa and that's the truth.*

Snip.

Okay, I tried to seduce papa.

Snip.

Mama! Don't cut off my hair!

CHAPTER SIX

Belgium, a Wednesday evening, April 1974

Ever since the Christmas party, Florence has been steadfast in her spite, whereas I have been through too much to care. When she calls me up to meet with her, her words barely register—I respond automatically and bike over to meet her on a quiet lane in the open fields.

"There are some friends waiting for us, over there on the path, by the crossing. We're meeting Danny and some of his friends; I think they came all the way from Schoten."

Danny is Florence's sixteen-year old, blue-collar boyfriend, with a fuzzy mustache, an earring, and strong Antwerp dialect twang. Florence is still a child, only eleven. We turn onto a dirt path and see Danny and three other boys waiting for us with their arms crossed. Danny takes Florence by the hand, and they hurry off along a hedge, into a muddy, freshly plowed field.

"Bye!" Florence laughs with a nasal snicker, waving as Danny pulls her along.

It's getting dark. The three big boys encircle me, laughing quietly.

"Do you have weapons?" I ask, businesslike.

One of them rubs his genitals and laughs.

"Yeah, baby, we got weapons."

"Nothing else?"

The two others laugh. The boy who touched his genitals whips out a penknife, flips it open and sticks the blade in my left nostril, guiding my head up with the knife until we look each other in the eye.

"Oh, you mean this kind of weapon, whore?"

I blink to answer yes.

"You're not going to nod? Afraid I'm gonna cut up that little nose of yours?"

I blink again, and keep looking at him in the same way.

"She's not even scared of you," one of them laughs.

My assaulter lifts my head up higher with the help of his penknife, and I widen my eyes and stiffen my head and neck muscles to look scared, even though I'm not. These are just boys. Even if they are up to no good, I don't sense any of the sick energy their adult counterparts emanate. He lowers the knife, but doesn't fold it back up.

"Where can we go around here? We can't fuck her in the middle of the road, or can we, guys?" the boy asks his friends.

He looks sternly at me.

"You're from around here. Where to?"

"I don't know. I've never had this happen before."

"Just shut up," shouts one of the boys as he grabs me by the back of my anorak and roughly pushes me ahead on the path.

"Hey," says one of them. "Look."

He nods to an empty construction site coming into view, and the two other boys smirk. My assaulter is the biggest bully of the trio. The smallest and thinnest of the three, with sand-colored hair, hasn't said a word. The building on the site is erect, a frame of cinder bricks, but the windows and doors have not been put in. One of the boys pushes me across a four-by-four plastered in dried mud, and through the dark doorway.

"I guess we're not gonna find a bed here," jokes one of them.

They seem brand new at this, I suspect, and notice that I still don't feel fear—likely a result of my training in Germany two years ago. The most organized and thought-out torture methods had taught me, among other things, to derive detailed information from taking just one look at males, to assess their danger level.

Close to an open rectangular frame for a window stands a workbench covered with tools. I systematically begin to take the instruments off the table and place them on the hard mud floor. The boys seem puzzled at first, but when they understand, they laugh.

"What did you say again," laughs one, "That you've never done this before? Seems to me like you're a pro!"

Another volley of laughter. Ashamed, I stare into the ground. The boy with sand-colored hair quickly approaches, saying, "She's making it easy for us, and for herself."

His voice is high and clear; he sounds compassionate. His Flemish is pronounced softly, without the strong Antwerp accent of the other two. A wide grin animates his face; his eyes dance with joy.

"Peter's a real charmer," teases one of the older boys.

"You'd better come and help," Peter retorts, catching my eye.

The expanse of Peter's eyes is such that his gaze seems ready to spread out across the universe, but a serious, almost disciplinary brow reins it in. When the other two dutifully come to his aid, Peter's playful smile says: *See? They were laughing at you for doing this, but now they're doing it themselves.* When the table is clear, two boys retreat. Peter stays.

"Here, why don't you just sit down? This table seems just right. Here's my jacket, you can sit on that. You want help with your jeans?"

His hands seem to be everywhere at once. Though he is aggressive in his assertiveness, his gestures are caressing. Peter looks me in the eye, one hand cupping my face, while the other unzips his jeans. He puts an arm around my hips and pulls me closer.

"Here, there's no need to be afraid. It's not going to bite."

I can see what Peter is doing, but I don't mind; I am just observing, still unafraid. Peter also observes as he rubs his penis between my legs. My arousal seems to correspond to his. I put my hands inside his shirt, touch the skin on his lower back, and pull him closer. I close my eyes. My lips touch his face.

"It feels so soft and good," he whispers.

When he penetrates, he slightly trembles, and then smiles. He's not too big, not like a grown-up. I experience no fear, no dissociation, no distance. Peter stops; the moonlight illumines a beautiful smile. Absorbed in sensual pleasure, in a sense of togetherness, nothing else exists. We hold each other, becoming so still we barely need to breathe. Peter whispers, "I don't want to give the others a turn."

Peter directs me to sit higher up on the workbench, turns me sideways, and climbs up while he calls one of the boys out of the dark, "I'm staying here, better make it quick."

Peter lays me down on his jacket so my legs hang off the end of the table, while he stands by my head.

"It's gonna be over soon. Just pretend it's me. It *is* me," he whispers in my ear.

I am ashamed as the other boy unzips and lowers his pants, suddenly afraid that Peter is someone who always charms his victims. I keep my legs closed. Peter maneuvers his hand inside my legs and as I mentally give in. My thighs relax. The other boy takes his turn. It hurts.

"It's gonna be okay, you'll see," Peter whispers.

As if we were boyfriend and girlfriend trying this weird new thing, Peter kisses me. The other boy finishes; Peter kicks him and jumps on top of me. We make love until the thought of the other boy fades away. As soon as I think of the third boy, Peter calls him and stays with me throughout his turn. Then Peter lifts me off the table and swoops me up in his arms. As he carries me, it is as though I am being given all the comfort I have needed after every rape. His solid grip and serious look impart the tenderness for which I have always yearned. He takes me to a spot on the floor where the mud is sort of even, carefully arranges his jacket on the floor and puts me down. Our caresses are barely physical; our attunement has woven a cocoon of intimacy around us.

"Hey, Peter, aren't you being a bit selfish?" we hear one of the other boys' feeble voices calling in the dark.

"Fuck off!" Peter shouts. "And get out. I need some fucking privacy."

As we see the shadows of the two boys disappear, Peter yells after them, "I'm going to be a long time."

I don't know how long we make love on his jacket on the dried mud floor, but I keep wishing for it to go on. It is as if all the nerves and nerve ends are showing off, trying to surpass each other in just what they can do, and how effortlessly they can do it, forming an electrified field of pleasure. Afterwards, as we lie in each other's arms, Peter whispers, "This was my first time."

Though it is completely dark, our eyes have become used to it, and he sees me staring at him in disbelief.

"It's true. This was supposed to be my initiation. The others have done it before; they were going to show me."

"But you're in charge!"

"No, Danny's in charge, he's the oldest. I'm thirteen, I'm the youngest, but I take care of myself, you know. The others, they can't tell me what to do."

"But you were so sure of yourself, and so quick!"

"I was really nervous; I just pretended I knew what I was doing, but I didn't have a clue."

"It's hard to believe this was your first time."

"I can't believe it myself. But it's because it's you, I think. I mean...."

When he cocks his head sideways, my heart leaps. We remain close and still, like halves of a whole, put back together for a little while.

"I want to see you again," Peter whispers.

"Yes...." I think out loud.

"Only if you want to," he adds quickly. "But how?"

"I could come back here," I say. "We could meet here again."

"Yes, maybe on Saturday?"

"I don't think I'll be able to get away on Saturday."

"Maybe your friend can cover for you," Peter proposes. "You can tell your parents you're with her."

"Yes, but not Saturday. How about next week, Wednesday?"

"Okay. I'll be here at five. And it's just us from now on," Peter quietly adds.

He looks at me nervously, lowers his head and gestures.

"I'm sorry about that," he says, shuffling one foot in the dirt. "I was just told about the sex part, like you already knew, and then when we got here...and I went along anyway because I thought you're so pretty, but...I'm sorry."

He slowly shakes his head. We walk out with our arms around each other, and find the other boys and Danny and Florence waiting. After many goodbye kisses, Danny's promise to get Peter back next week, and Florence's promise that she'll cover for me, Peter and I finally let go of each other. As I pass Florence, she nods respectfully. I wonder if her scheme was yet another answer to my telling her Patrick wasn't having sex with me, making me feel what I was missing.

As I bike home, I think about Patrick. Over the past month, Mama has taken me to the mansion one or two nights a week, and not to any other network events. Believing in Patrick's true love has gotten me through many rapes. But I did not think of him at all with Peter.

Papa opens the front door as soon as I reach the driveway. When I enter, he says, "Where have you been? We've been looking all over for you. Your mother is worried sick."

Mama is in the living room. Her messed-up mascara has formed black circles around her eyes, and she clutches a balled-up hanky, screaming, "Where have you been! It's ten o'clock! I've been on the phone with Countess d'Auriac; we were so worried, we called the police! Where have you been!"

"Florence took me to see some friends of hers. It's her fault."

"We're going to forbid you to see Florence for three weeks!" she yells. "I'm going to call the countess to make sure that it happens."

I marvel at Mama's ability to always find just what will hurt me, but I am not worried. Girls like myself, whose parents give them to the network, usually don't survive their teens. But if someone from outside the network cares about me, who knows.... I go to bed full of hope and happiness, thinking that maybe there is a chance for me.

CHAPTER SEVEN

Family home, Belgium,
a Saturday evening, April 1974

"**A**re you ready?"

Mama whispers, leaning over me. I'm in bed—stiff, awake, dressed. I pull an anorak from the coat rack and loosely throw it on before following Mama to the front door and to her car parked in the driveway. I get in the passenger's seat, shivering. Mama releases the hand brake and lets the car roll slowly down the driveway. She turns the key, maneuvers backwards and brusquely turns the car around, driving off. When we reach the church, we turn left. Then we pass the center of the next village, and I expect Mama will turn left, towards a lane leading to the vacant mansion, where she has been taking me lately, but instead she goes straight, towards the Brussels highway.

Patrick!

A handler opens the front door of a villa with an enormous lawn. I follow the noise through a large lobby, so afraid I tremble. My heart bonks wildly in my chest; my mouth is parched. I hope and pray that Patrick is not here, but as I enter the salon through a large open doorway, I spot him talking to the tall wrinkly man whom I saw sitting with the bosses on the night I met him. Patrick does not seem to notice me. I can't stop trembling. Patrick turns his head and looks at me. Not knowing what else to do, I make a beeline for him through the crowd and jump into his embrace. I kiss his face, covering my feelings of guilt and fear, sensing an amused, sarcastic smile from the bystander. Then Patrick smiles his own ironic smile that looks almost exactly like the other man's, except that the silent spectator is more caustic and mocking than Patrick.

What's going on with you? Patrick asks by way of a smiling nod. *Yes, I'm happy to see you too.* I can't calmly reply, so I look intently into Patrick's eyes thinking, *I love you.*

I love you, too, says his twinkling gaze, and I bury my face against his shoulder to hide the tears, because I feel unworthy. Holding me, Patrick tells the other man he'll be off.

"Is that your father?" I ask as Patrick carries me out of the room.

"Yes. He had to be there for you to kiss me? You should have told me; I would have gotten him over a lot sooner."

"He doesn't mind?"

Climbing the stairs holding me, Patrick's breath becomes belabored; he frowns, shaking his head.

"He's more like a good friend," he concludes.

I raise my brow thinking: *What kind of a good friend is that?* Patrick averts his eyes and opens the door to a room under the slanted roof, with two quaint single beds.

"So, here we are. You still want to kiss me now?"

He gives me that look, ardent desire burning through his incredibly clear eyes. I lower my gaze, but not my face.

Though this is to be the very first time I am sexual with Patrick, I am on exceedingly familiar terrain. When we, mind-controlled sex slaves, tortured with tried and tested techniques to draw out exact results, are doing what we were created to do, our entire psychology is applied to the task. The Belgians are a local chapter of the global network, and Polo and his friends differ from the big leaguers in that they generally don't read my mind. I can freely have my private, critical thoughts about them, whereas it would instantly endanger my life to have an unflattering thought about the most powerful global networkers in their presence. Not allowed my own thoughts, I become the materialization of their projection, complete with the thoughts and feelings they want from me. I have been trained to be a "wild French sex machine," utterly and animalistically abandoned to the experience. Patrick reads my mind, and this activates my training, but I also find him attractive and I like him, and he seems to also genuinely like me—all unwelcome complications to an impossible situation.

Patrick brings his lips close to mine, only very slowly. His desire is tangible, but he restrains, which rouses my desire, and I also hold back, savoring the game. Patrick carefully puts his lips on my face, relishing every tiniest touch as the treasure he has been longing for these past six months. I don't know why, but my thoughts flow to Peter: how easy it was, how nice not to have to think, and how happy that made me. The thought: *I liked it better with him*, springs up.

Patrick breaks contact, pulls back and looks at me. I stare him frankly in the eye. Suddenly he kisses me passionately.

"*Que je t'aime, mon trésor,*" he whispers. (How I love you, my treasure.)

All through the kiss, I am aware of some distance on my part; a wish to do away with all this intensity and mind power and passion. This distance and these thoughts may be part of my unconscious seduction, an automatic response from the training in Germany. Mind control induces trauma in a slave to push the mind beyond thought, open up intuition and psychic abilities, and then put all of these abilities in service to the slave's owner. For example, the global Big Shot who was my owner sent me to spend weekends with a top German politician. He then had me report on the man's weakness to give him an advantage in his business and government dealings with him. But last year, I had painfully rejected the global Big Shot's plans for me, and, after days of intense punishment, I was returned to Belgium. Ever since, I have only been used by the Belgians, and here I am, with Patrick.

Without wanting to, I notice that my response to Patrick is stronger than with Peter. I may seem more passionate, but I am less involved. Once undressed, my mental distance increases with the fear of getting hurt.

"I'm not going to hurt you," Patrick says, but his smile seems to be saying that he might very well hurt me; that my fear is the very thing that turns him on.

My breathing turns shallow while the adrenaline whooshes through my body. He stands and holds me up with his hands, so I have no physical control. Without warning, he pushes himself inside, and I experience a powerful sexual sensation, fully in correlation with the raw fear. All I can do is cling to him, to surrender entirely or I will suffer tremendous pain. His fingertips send powerful erotic signals up my spine, which is so arched that my head hangs upside down. Giving up any and all resistance, I surrender, allowing in the extreme pleasure, until I find myself crying, I don't know why. We enter into a state of wild ecstasy, and keep the ripples going, willing the ultimate bodily bliss to linger, playing the game again; opponents united by sensations that seem at once too subtle and too powerful to be experienced with anyone else.

I am lying on one of the beds, hands behind my head, feeling extremely relaxed, and entirely free of guilt. I shoot Patrick a look of resentment.

He is much too pleased with himself. I did not want to lose it like that. What choice did I have? Physically I don't stand a chance. I'm too small. I still prefer Peter.

"*Mon amour,* how beautiful you are like this," says Patrick as he strokes my face, teasing.

It does feel good to be so connected, and to feel beautiful, but I don't like that I seem as grown-up as he.

"You are not ten years old, you know," says Patrick.

"It's true, I'm not. I'm eleven."

"You had your birthday?"

He comes to sit on the bed, happily putting a hand through my hair. He kisses me.

"Happy birthday."

He kisses me again. A big long kiss that soon becomes intensely sexual and could easily escalate into another round, but he stops.

"Still, you're not eleven, either."

"Then what would you say I was?"

"Eighteen, at least. Or you can be twenty. One year younger than me. That's your age, okay?"

"I'm eleven. I have a lot of growing to do before I'll be twenty."

Suddenly perturbed, Patrick stares out ahead, unfocused. Dropping his head in his hands, he repetitively combs his hair back with his fingers. Unlike other men in the network, he seems at least to have a sense that there is something off about having sex with a child, that maybe there is something else going on besides what the networkers all seem to have agreed upon: they are not pedophiles—no—pedophiles are those dirty guys who *only* have sex with children.

"But you're not a child."

"But I am."

Patrick smiles as if I were teasing him. I did mimic him: it was such a grown-up answer, though I did not intend it. It is as if Patrick transferred his adulthood onto me through the sex, as if he were the sex slave. Now I am the one who is detached, ironic, feeling free, and I even lie on the bed in the same relaxed way he usually does, with my hands behind my head, while he is sitting nearby, nervously trying to please me. Patrick leans over and caresses me. When he touches the mons, a wide smile spreads across his face.

"Okay, yes, it's true. And what a nice thing, too. It's the nicest thing ever, so soft, without the hair."

Patrick laughs as I blush fiercely.

"I've had a hard time getting you back. What happened to you in the last month? Where were you?"

I tell Patrick about the nights in the mansion, and about being left to starve by my mother for five whole days before she came to get me, implying that he was right when he told me that she was no good, and that I now understand and am completely on the same page as he. Patrick promises that he will arrange things, so I will never have to return.

Villa, Brussels region, Belgium,
a Sunday morning, April 1974

As soon as Patrick has jumped into his clothes and left the attic room, I climb on the nightstand and push open the skylight window to smell the fresh morning breeze on this bright sunny morning. I stick my head out, feel the wind and see the endless, perfectly mown lawn, the driveway, and Mama's car, parked below. Then I notice Patrick's white-blonde head of hair. He heads out the front door, marching quickly and assuredly, so his limp is not noticeable. He approaches Mama's car and starts a conversation. They talk for quite some time, laugh sometimes. Then she hands him something that he stuffs in the pocket of his tight jeans. Mama starts the car and drives off. Patrick returns to the front door. I jump down from the nightstand.

"Are you ready? Let's go," says Patrick as the door swings open.

I throw on my clothes and hurry after him. When we drive off in his Porsche down the long driveway, I look at him questioningly. *Should I duck?*

"Don't bother," Patrick laughs grandly as he turns onto the road.

It is as though flamboyancy and recklessness have replaced the power that he gave up during sex. We drive to the road that borders the forest and arrive in Fort-Jaco, a part of Brussels where the Porsche does not stand out in the least. We park in front of a bakery.

"They had absolutely nothing to eat in that place," he clarifies.

Upon hearing his lie, I freeze. Patrick looks at me, puzzled, waiting.

"Come on, what's wrong?"

"You want me to come with you?"

"If you want."

As I hesitate, I notice Patrick freeze as well. I jump out of the car. Sunday mornings are the busiest in the Belgian bakeries. We join the line of people in their Sunday best with hats to match—the post-mass crowd. Patrick grins.

"*Bonjour mesdames, messieurs.*" (Ladies, gentlemen.)

Some people nod, others mutter *bonjours*, but those filing past us on their way back from the counter glance apprehensively. Patrick moves as if to put his arm over my shoulder, then changes his mind. He puts his fingertips in his jean pockets. I wonder what he has buried in there that Mama gave him, and feel very uncomfortable. My private crisis seems to make Patrick even more shaky, and when it is our turn to order he anxiously looks on as I try to tell him with my eyes, *just order something, whatever,* because my French doesn't bear a trace of the local accent and I fear it would instantly betray that we are not related.

"So, what do you want?" asks the lady behind the counter.

Patrick's voice slips, like a teenager's. He tries to recover with a forced cough.

"Just a croissant," I answer as quietly as possible, but the lady's gaze glides from me to him, and him to me.

"And for the gentleman?" she asks, stiffly.

Patrick, his fingertips still in his pockets, trembles. His shoulders arch forward awkwardly, which makes his stance look rigid and unnatural. His sensitive mouth quivers into a tight smile.

"Me too, a croissant," he says self-consciously.

The baker's woman stuffs two croissants in a bag, all the while staring coolly at him. Patrick shakes when he pays, drops a coin, hobbles when we leave, limping worse than ever, past the line of customers waiting outside, all of whose eyes are glued on us.

With a deafening engine roar and screeching tires, we tear down the road at breakneck speed towards Waterloo. A few, or maybe many miles ahead, Patrick abruptly halts by a small cluster of modest red brick row houses, the first one of which has a large chicken coop next to it. Frightened by the noise, the brown chickens scatter and squawk at the far end of the coop. Patrick gets out of the car, pulls the croissants out of the bag and, as though they were stones, hurls them over the wire fence, and ostentatiously brushes the crumbs off his hands with big up and down arm movements and loud slaps. He jumps back in the car and accelerates at an insane speed. After a number of interminable seconds, we slow down, park, and enter a small restaurant, rather dark inside, and empty. A middle-aged man comes out to greet us, wiping his hands on a short white apron.

"What are you serving today, *mon cher?*" Patrick asks. He acts super confident and grandiose, while his gestures are brusque and his transparent eyes look frozen.

"I'm preparing rabbit at the moment. If you're willing to wait, I can serve it to you in about, let's say half an hour, with an asparagus cream soup to start?"

"Lovely, perfect. As long as you can bring us a coffee first, with warm milk on the side, and a hot chocolate, with some bread and butter."

The man, who has his hands on his hips, raises his brows. Coffee *before* lunch?

"We're having the menu," Patrick promises. "I just want the coffee and the bread first, while we wait."

Patrick's definitive manner clearly indicates that the chef should now turn on his heel, but the man purses his lips and cocks his head sideways, looking every bit the patient food expert. Patrick's nostrils widen, and that deadened look in his eyes frightens me.

"I don't know if you'll be able to properly taste the food if you're going to have strong and sweet flavors crossing your palate before the meal. But I don't mind; I'll give you some coffee and hot chocolate. I have a nice country loaf, too, very crusty."

"Well that's great," Patrick revels with patronizing sarcasm quite thrown away upon the chef. "I realize we're turning things on their head. We're trying to fit everything in one sitting, to give my niece a sampling of everything here, since she's visiting for the day from Antwerp. She's Flemish, you see."

The man asks me, in Flemish, where in Antwerp I am from and informs me, in Flemish, that he grew up in a neighboring suburb. He asks me if I know the street, which I don't. I start to feel very uncomfortable having a conversation which Patrick cannot understand. The man asks, in Flemish, if I like asparagus. I quickly shake my head. Patrick shifts nervously in his seat. The man promises, in Flemish, that he will heat up some leftover spinach cream soup for me. I feel terrible for not being able to put a halt to his blabbering, and look at Patrick, pleading for understanding. He winks. I continue looking at Patrick, ignoring the chef, and Patrick's eyes twinkle back to life.

"Okay, let me get your hot chocolate, young lady," says the man, finally reverting to French, "and your coffee, monsieur, and your bread, and I will get back to the stove or you'll be waiting a whole hour for your main course."

About ten minutes later, Patrick and I are having breakfast. Patrick eats with great relish. He is just as exuberant as before the incident in the bakery. The chef appears and asks, in French, if we are satisfied, and though Patrick answers, the chef smiles at me. When the chef returns to his kitchen, Patrick looks at me, and his eyes are once again glazed over. Uncomfortable, I smile. Patrick observes me, gets up, picks up his blue Adidas bag and with a nudge lets me know I should follow; I quickly jump up. He guides me to a small bathroom in the back and locks the door once we are inside. He closes the wooden toilet seat cover and sits.

"Come here, *chérie*."

He takes me on his lap. I cross my legs around his body. His dead eyes make him look like a drunkard, and I wonder how I can feel close to him again.

"When I see you smile, I just have to do this. You're so sweet. *Que je t'aime, ma petite Annie*." (I love you so much, my little Annie.)

Patrick is aroused, and pulls me against him so I can feel it. He puts me down, stands, orders me to take my jeans off and lowers his own to his knees.

"No, not here. What if the man came? What if he hears us?"

"I thought of that," Patrick answers. "Take off your pants, quick."

Patrick takes his Browning handgun out of his sports bag, holds it in his left hand, arm stretched, as if to shoot into the floor, then puts his right hand over the gun, doing something, cocking it, I guess. It makes me infinitely sad, and my feeling is instantly reflected in Patrick's eyes, as the ruffian transforms into a deeply sensitive soul, expressing all the sorrow over his compulsion to play his part in this ineluctable drama.

Quick as lightning, he grabs me, peels off my pants, pulls me on his lap, and rubs himself against my lower back. I am frightened to death that the man will come knocking. Patrick orders me to put my feet on the sink in front of us. He lifts me up and begins to have sex. Naked, I feel extremely vulnerable. When Patrick lowers me, I feel the cold metal of his gun against the skin on the back of my thigh. My tremendous fear, either of the gun going off through my leg, or of witnessing a murder, or both—lulls me into a trance. My nervous system is highly charged and I find myself in a state of extreme intoxication, shared by Patrick. Afterwards, Patrick sits still, pulls me against him, his lips on my neck, his gun still below my thigh. We hold our breaths, listening for sounds outside the door. We do not hear anything, but can tell from the silence that the man is there, that he has returned from the kitchen, noticed us missing, and realized we are in the bathroom. Maybe he has guessed we were having sex. Patrick carefully removes his lips from my skin and moves his mouth to my ear to whisper, "Make like you're sick."

I shake my head.

"Make a sound as if you're throwing up."

I shake my head. I don't want to act my way through the restaurant, past the owner.

Sitting on this loaded gun in this impossible situation, I curse my compulsion to kiss Patrick yesterday. Now he acts like the slave, trying with all his might to break out of his chains and liberate himself from his self-created chaos.

I look up at the window, a twenty-inch wide sliver of sky under the roof, which opens inward from the top, coming down to a slant, leaving an opening of about fifteen inches from the ceiling. I turn my head back to check with Patrick. He remains still for several more seconds, then gets up, turns on the tap to drown out the noise, makes me stand on the toilet seat, and supports me as I climb up to stand on his hands. I grab the top of the opened window, swing my leg up and clamber through with surprising ease. I drop down into a small backyard onto tall weeds without hurting myself. There is no one in sight. I run through empty backyards and find an alleyway leading back to the road, where I head towards Patrick's car driving towards me. I hop in, and as we tear away, I finally relax, relieved that I did not hear a shot and can assume the restaurateur is alive and well. Maybe the bill has even been paid, and Patrick has found some easy, good excuse to get himself out of that place without making trouble.

CHAPTER EIGHT

Construction site, Belgium,
a Wednesday evening, April 1974

It is surely five o'clock by now, and Peter is not here. I got to the construction site ten minutes early, with an excuse other than going to see Florence, which I am not allowed. I told Mama that Patrick wanted to see me and that he was picking me up down the street. She had that bewildered look, like when she believes I am torturing her, but nodded.

I picture myself with Peter on the beach in the South of France, like so many teenagers each summer doing seasonal work. I have heard much about the Côte d'Azur in the network. To get jobs for the summer, it seems reasonable to arrive in May, which is next week, and Peter does not know about the plan yet. I don't even know if he speaks French, but I thought of that; he could be a dishwasher in one of the boardwalk restaurants. I could sell ice cream or something, and after the summer we can travel to the Beaujolais or the Bordeaux region to pick grapes, like so many do each fall. I rehearse telling Peter about my situation, and then the entire solution. Peter will have to get us there. But he is not here.

I don't know Peter—I have trouble remembering what he looks like—but when we were together, I had this powerful sense that he is one who could love me; that he already did, and that I could reach out to him and he would understand and want to do anything for me. As the minutes roll by and the sky darkens, I am reminded of last week when we met, and that sense remains. He is supposed to be here now and he is not, but I cannot believe that he would not want to be here. I know that he came to rape me and that he did; and that it is strange that I should trust him. But intuition about a man's—and in this case a boy's—feelings for me is my best survival tool. This skill was sharpened during the training in Germany, when I was taught to recognize what a man really wants, regardless of what he says. The confidence in the veracity of my intuition is what gives me the strength to keep on going.

Someone approaches! Wishful thinking stalls the obvious: the outlined figure in the near dark is an adult. I stand by the hedge next to my parked bike, hands stuffed in my pockets. He frowns as he walks past. Worried as I was that he would ask what I was doing here by myself, it is a little disappointing that he did not, as I always hope and expect that someone out there will be concerned enough to ask questions.

Peter is not here, and I carefully consider the possibility that I was wrong about him. As soon as my mind begins to go in that direction, I feel nauseous. Hurrying to the site, I sit down on an open window ledge, feeling sick. If Peter just used me to get off, and is dropping me, and if I was wrong about this powerful sense I followed without thinking, it seems that I must be wrong about everything. This nausea comes with unbearable fear, which was evoked countless times during the training in Germany. Whenever I got anything wrong, the punishments were so cruel they were sometimes worse than death. In spite of the torture, the training was highly effective. I am supposed to know exactly how males feel about me. Essence, truth, love—everything substantial exists on a plane other than the physical, and the underlying laws of nature and human actions determine life from that invisible realm. The training had me forcibly connect through the ether so as to read men's deepest desires, to detect their deepest fear and nurture their emotional wounds. Peter is only two years older than myself. If I was wrong about him, if I have lost my survival skill, I don't see any point in going on.

I hear a voice in my head, screaming that if my man left me, I might as well kill myself, and I look around to see what tools are available so I can end my life. Then a vague question arises in my mind, wondering about this voice.

The suicidal message in my head in connection to feeling rejected romantically would haunt me long after the message was instilled, until the full memory of the source of these self-destructive thoughts would finally surface. I would be taken back to a lab-like setting in 1972 with the Belgian network boss Polo. He had just picked me up from a small European airport where I had been flown in on the private jet of the Big Shot networker whom Polo had tried to befriend by gifting me to him. Exceeding Polo's expectations, the Big Shot had taken a particular interest in me, and had brought me with him overseas for nearly a month. Only, Polo probably had never counted on also having to drive me around like a lowly handler for the Big Shot, and he was in a terrible mood as he took me to this lab.

I had been strapped to a medical table. Polo had screamed into my right ear that if my man leaves me, my life would be completely worthless and I might as well kill myself. At the foot-end of the table were two younger men, maybe in their thirties, in white lab coats. One was holding a clipboard, making notes, while the other sexually manipulated me, acting completely detached, as if this had been a simple medical routine.

Polo had loudly repeated the message in my ear. When the memory of his torturous indoctrination would finally surface from beneath thick layers of shame, it would include the strong sense that this had not been Polo's own idea, but that he had been following instructions, which he hated. By linking the idea of suicide to my presumed sexual attachment to "my man," those men, especially the Big Shot, would be assured that if they tired of me, or if something didn't go according to plan, they would not even need to take care of the dirty work of eliminating me; I would be doing it for them. Only, Polo had been so annoyed that, though he did scream loudly in my ear, because he had thought this was stupid, his resistance and resentment had also seeped into my consciousness, and I now wonder about the voice in my head.

This evening, less than two years after the indoctrination at Polo's hands, and about one year after the Big Shot's plans for me were indeed thwarted and I did not consequently commit suicide as I should have, here I am, waiting for a boy who failed to show up at our appointment, and I am once again ignoring the voice in my head urging me to kill myself.

The only place I could possibly find out whether or not I'm mistaken about Peter is at Florence's. She might know more, through Danny. I hop on my bike and ride over to her home. The manor looks cozy, with its lit windows on all floors. I am aware of a strong need for warmth and security.

I ring the bell. Countess d'Auriac opens the door, raising her brow.

"Is Florence home?" I ask sheepishly.

The countess calls Florence, all the while staring at me. I know she knows that I am not supposed to be here; and she knows that I know that she knows it.

"What brings you here?"

"I have to ask Florence something."

It takes the countess two sharp seconds to decide.

"I guess I'm going to have to call your mother and tell her you're here. She'll be worried about you again."

My mother worried! Said by the mother who pimps her daughter out to, among others, her husband. So much for the warm atmosphere emanating from this home; it is a good front, but, like everything else about this family, a lie. The countess, her gaze steady as the north, saunters gracefully down the lobby towards a small table with a telephone.

"Did you hear from Danny?" I timidly ask Florence. "Peter didn't come."

Florence's mouth curls into a blatantly mocking grin, and her eyes light up in triumph.

"I guess he wasn't serious," she says with a little nasal laugh.

I must have been wrong about Peter, and am losing faith in any reality beyond the horror of the reality of my life.

Maybe I will find a victim, and pass along all the malice I have had directed at me. No one seems to be able to own evil; it gets tossed around like a volleyball on fire. I don't want to fool myself; if this is all there is, and this is all I am, then maybe I should be evil too. Maybe I should become a part of the other force: the repulsion from truth and love, pushing everything down into its black vortex of chaos, bewilderment and death.

Castle Van Revelingen,
Rhode-Saint-Genese, Belgium,
a Saturday night, May 1974

Mama has dropped me off at the same small castle where I met Patrick last fall. How different things were back then. Mama now seems to be close to Patrick. When I had returned home from my failed date with Peter, she commented, "I knew you were lying, because Patrick didn't tell me that he was picking you up tonight."

As the handler on duty opens the doors to the salon, I notice the too-thin girl whom I think of as the sickly fairy, with ash blonde hair down to her buttocks and two thin braids rolled up on top of her head. I have not seen her since the strange party in the greenhouse, and half wondered if she had been in that hunt the following morning, and if she had survived.

She is standing by a banquet table, near an enormous smoked fish platter, decorated with colorful vegetables and small pieces of toasted baguette. The sickly fairy studies everything, as if she is choosing, except she can't seem to make up her mind. I head over, pick up a slice of toast and put it in my mouth. Patrick joins us at the table. The fairy suddenly looks longingly at a slice of bread that Patrick picks up.

"Would you like to have this one?" Patrick offers, with his characteristic subtle sarcasm, as there are about fifty identical pieces on the platter.

The fairy nods. When Patrick asks if she would like some butter, she nods again. While Patrick butters the fairy's toast, she sneers triumphantly at me.

She is not going to last long, I think. When Patrick hands her the piece of toast, she is too happy, and when he leaves with me, she looks stunned and spiteful. I wish that she could figure out which men favor which girls, and learn to maneuver her way through the web, attracting the men who are more or less safe, avoiding the dangerous ones, and leaving alone the indifferent ones. Surviving is a skill, like any other, sharpened by intuition, which I am losing.

Patrick takes me up to the same room where we were last fall, with picture windows and a nice bed with white linens. This is the place where Patrick let me know that whatever we would do would be up to me.

As if, I think, irritated.

"You didn't like our sex?" Patrick asks.

I sigh, and look at Patrick.

"I've never liked it as much," I say coldly.

"So, what didn't you like?"

"The fear."

Patrick, who is still by the entrance, takes the Adidas sports bag slung over his shoulder, which presumably has his gun inside, holds it out, and carefully deposits it on the console table. He comes over, caresses my face, and kisses me gently on the lips.

"Do you like this?"

I shake my head. Patrick mock frowns, lifts me in his arms, carries me to the bed, lays me down, kisses me again, more intently.

"This?"

I shake my head. He undresses me, seems moved, caresses me. He lies down against me, kisses my face.

"This?"

I guess that Patrick and I are playing the game again, and that he's showing me he can do the no fear thing.

"No, I don't like it," I answer.

He gauges my response and cocks his head to the side. *Of course, I'm not just playing,* say his warm eyes. When he touches me, I melt. Every time he does something new, he asks if I like it, exactly when I most enjoy it. I keep answering no, and feel such lightness, a joyous sensation, pure. It makes me feel clean, somehow, and clear.

"Are you still afraid?"

As much as I enjoy what I feel, I consider the gun in his bag, the network, the sex. However much I can face my challenges and surrender to circumstances, all that does nothing to change the fact that I am utterly powerless.

"Yes."

Patrick lies still for a long time. We don't move, or even breathe much.

"I want to take you back to my place tonight," Patrick finally says. "It's not that far. My parents and my brother will be there, but we'll just be quiet. I'll sneak you out tomorrow; it won't be a problem."

The warmth emanating from Patrick's eyes has never been expressed with such clarity and simplicity. It's unlike him to explain his plans; usually I am just going along and finding out in the moment. By telling me what to expect, he makes me feel safe. Warmth and security. Just what I had longed for.

Patrick has to talk to someone before we leave, and I find myself back at the banquet table inspecting the various comestibles, and notice the sickly fairy sidling up to a dark-haired baron, a frightful man who was the main executioner during the ritual murder of my little friend Wouter.

Really, she has all the wrong instincts; she could not have picked a worse one. The baron walks away, and when the fairy follows alongside, he throws her a condescending, what-are-you-still-doing-here look that finally stops her in her tracks. She looks sad as she makes her way over to the banquet table, where I am eating a slice of toast. The sickly fairy throws me a hateful glance.

"You know, that guy you were just with, that baron? He's dangerous," I volunteer between bites. "Better stay away from him."

"Or, maybe he just doesn't like *you*," she snaps. "Because you're so *fat!*"

Haemers residence, greater Brussels,
a Saturday night, May 1974

It turns out Patrick's family is not home yet, as we enter the townhouse through the front door. We ascend the stairs, covered with thick royal blue carpet. There is a lot of blue and white everywhere. Patrick also often wears sailor's shirts, or a jean shirt in white pants, or a navy-blue training jacket with white stripes on the arms, and he has blue and white Adidas gym shoes. Only his soccer polos are in different colors. Up in his room, a purple Jimi Hendrix poster adorns the wall. Patrick pulls an album out of its sleeve and puts it on the record player. The song he wants to hear begins with a sniff, which he finds hilarious, so he moves the needle back several times to hear it again and again.

It almost sounds like a children's song, happy, with an easy rhythm and pleasant guitar, and yet it is about cocaine. I know English from watching subtitled American television shows and spending time with the Big Shot networker. And I know cocaine, of course, from the orgies.

"So, you like cocaine?" I query, half expecting the song is a prelude to a drug party.

Patrick tries to pull me off the bed to dance, but I'm too shy and just watch him, his body soft except for the stiff right leg. Then he picks me up and wildly twirls me around, singing that he is trouble and is heading in my direction.

Patrick puts me down on the bed, puffing.

"All right, I need something slower. I'm exhausted."

He flips through his albums.

"Aha! Here. This is my dream for you and me."

He puts the record on, stands me up on the bed, and we embrace as I listen to a beautiful, soulful story of a man's rescue by an angel, who promises to return to be with him in the future. In the song, the man needs to release her, and wait for the day she will come back.

Patrick mouths the lyrics, looking at me with great sadness.

In the final verse, the angel returns to take him with her, and they fly off, together at last.

We hear sounds. Patrick whispers it's his parents arriving, and that we should keep quiet, because their bedroom is on the same floor. We lay down. Keeping silent is a fun game.

"I will have to let you fly away, you know?" he says softly. "We can't be a regular couple for a long time to come."

Grateful, I press my body into his.

"But I would like to really be with you, when you're old enough. You'll be such a beautiful woman, too; I can't wait."

"How are you planning to let me fly away?" I murmur, thinking of the South of France.

"I don't know yet," Patrick whispers. "But it's going to be the only way, because we can't spend five years like this."

I consider telling Patrick about the South of France. I wonder if he would drive me there, to drop me off. *Five years...would he even remember me?*

"I want you to give me something," Patrick says in a low voice as he gets up from the bed. "Something so I can always remember you, no matter what happens."

He takes a penknife off the chest of drawers and pulls the blade out. Back on the bed, he opens his left hand and rubs his right pointing finger over the cushiony part of his palm, under the left thumb.

"Here. You should stab me here, so all I will have to do is look down at my hand, and I'll think of you."

"You can do that without a scar," I whisper nervously.

"No, I want something real. A blood tie. Nothing is stronger."

"But I don't want to stab you. I don't want to hurt you," I whisper hoarsely.

"I want you to," Patrick persists. "Anyway, it's not hard to do, you just have to be quick."

He holds the penknife in his fist, lifts it and with a firm, quick movement brings it down, to show me. I don't need to see it; I know it all too well. I know it from the training in Germany, but the Belgians also force us children to do repulsive things to make sure we will never know we are their victims, but are convinced we are perpetrators, just as bad as they are. Which is exactly how I feel at this moment.

"I don't want to do that again. I killed a rabbit with a knife once. I don't want to do that again," I gasp.

"It's okay," Patrick laughs. "I'm not a rabbit, and you're not killing me...but tell me...."

"No!"

"Was it at one of the orgies?" Patrick queries.

"No!"

Images flood my brain. I see the large dark empty space, like a small hangar, maybe at a farm. A metal kind of long table. Polo was there, with one of his friends. There was a crate full of little rabbits. And at least ten children. We were each given a rabbit. Then we had to choose: our life, or the rabbit's.

The other children valiantly chose the rabbit. As I had already experienced exactly what happens to the intended target when I had refused to follow an order to kill during the training in Germany, I could never put myself through that again. From that moment forward, every killing had been a mercy killing. The Belgians forced the same horrendous training on the child slaves, but without high-tech facilities, special equipment, or a doctor in charge. Polo mostly did it himself. It was clear that the baby rabbits were not going to be spared. We children were being trained, and if we could not take the training, we would be marked as weak, and perhaps killed along with the rabbits.

When I was asked, "Who lives, the rabbit or you?" I did not want to waste my energy, and quietly said, "Me." Polo responded, in his flat, ironic voice, "That is why we like you, because you always give the right answer."

Since I was the first to choose correctly, I had to go first. I did not want to look at the little rabbit, though holding it, I saw that it was black. I held it by the skin of its neck, trying not to think about how soft its fur felt. Instead I focused on the rigidity of its little body, vibrating with terror.

I'll quickly end that, I thought. I looked down to see where to hit, pulled its head back and stuck the knife hard in its throat. As soon as the blade made contact, I looked up and away, not wanting to see the blood or the body. I let go of the dead animal, dropped the knife and backed away, refusing to look at it again, or at any of the other children or animals. But I heard. The rabbits cried and squealed until the waking nightmare was over.

Polo and his friend praised me and showed me off like a great example to the other children.

"You know," Patrick offers after I've silently let the images roll by, "those rabbits would have been killed anyway, for food."

"They were too little to be eaten. They were babies."

"So, if you kill a cute, innocent creature, does that mean you end up feeling that you're not so innocent yourself?"

I grab the penknife out of Patrick's hand, push his left hand down onto the bed, lift the knife and quickly, hard, lower the blade into his hand. He flinches. The hand stiffens. I grab a t-shirt off the floor and wrap it around the hand. The white cloth immediately stains bright red. *Do you understand now?* I look at Patrick. *I am not innocent at all.*

"You're really good at this," Patrick exclaims admiringly.

"Don't say that!" I whisper furiously.

Patrick smiles in a way I have never seen before. He gets up, leaves the room and heads for the bathroom, where I hear him turn on the tap. It becomes clear to me that all my fear is for the evil inside of me rather than outside. Patrick returns, pressing gauze on the bleeding wound. He still has this smile on his face, both sweet and mischievous.

"Now I know why you're my mate," he says.

CHAPTER NINE

Family home, Belgium,
a school day morning, June 1974

My favorite bell bottoms are too short, I observe with dismay. I pack my book bag, a leather briefcase with back straps. Not often do I get to do my homework, but last night my little brother went to bed early, Mama left and was gone the whole evening, and I was able to study for a big grammar exam we have today. I put my book bag on the kitchen bench and butter some bread as Mama places a cup of hot cocoa on the gray Formica kitchen table.

"You're not going to school today," Mama announces with an excited smile.

I stare. It's never good when Mama keeps me out of school.

"Patrick is picking you up in half an hour," she states proudly, adding, "You better put some extra clothes and *underwear* in your book bag."

Mama lifts her brow. My head is crammed with grammatical rules. I don't even want to see Patrick.

"You'll be gone a few days," she adds.

Half an hour later, Mama's eager cries inform me of Patrick's arrival.

"Ann, look at that car! He's come in a different one! A BMW!"

I wonder if this is a trick, if there is someone else getting me for something dangerous.

"Hurry," Mama urges me on in a very friendly way.

At the front door, she puts both her hands on my shoulders so she looks straight at me. Her eyes are moist.

"You go and have a nice time, now."

As I throw my book bag onto the back seat of the black BMW, Patrick says,

"I hope your bikini's in there."

"I don't have a bikini."

I pull the passenger door shut. Patrick immediately leans over and slips his hands under my t-shirt. It is early in the morning, I am ready for school, and it seems really weird to do this, let alone in front of my mother. Patrick, supremely confident of my reciprocity, kisses me.

As we drive off, a flash of suspicion hits, fast and sharp as the falling blade of a guillotine. I put my head in Patrick's lap. His fingers run through my hair. As he drives steadily at 130 km an hour, I initiate oral sex. Suddenly, the thought of biting springs to mind. There is a slight pause. Then, with the idea that I might bite hanging between us, Patrick's fear intensifies the experience.

We arrive in Knokke-le-Zoute, a resort on the Belgian coast by the North Sea. Patrick parks in front of a Normandy-style mansion. One of the network regulars opens the door and, after a jovial exchange of greetings between the men, leads us up the stairs to a darkened room with two twin beds and stone floors. I push the shutters open, revealing the busy coastal tram route outside.

"I don't think I want to stay here, do you?" Patrick rattles, making sure to catch our guide on his way out.

Patrick disappears with the network regular. The door is open, so I walk out and peek over the railing, and notice Patrick meeting up with the aristocratic politician, a fixture at the orgies of the Belgian network. Patrick won't let the politician finish a single sentence. A while later, we drive to a large villa on the beach. The person who opens the door takes us past a sitting area with bay windows overlooking the ocean, where we interrupt a meeting of several more network regulars, male and female, dressed rather formally. I feel very much out of place and stare into the floor as Patrick goes over to shake hands. Some stern, threatening looks are directed at me; I turn away. When Patrick is finally done, I hurry after him up the stairs into a bedroom looking out over the dunes, the beach and the silver sea resting under a pearly haze.

"They hate me," Patrick says.

"Why? Are you too bold?"

"It's a good thing they're scared of me," he retorts with a grin. "They're so stuck up. So typically Belgian. All hypocrites. I much prefer Americans. They're practical and open, just the opposite of here. They don't look down on you if you're not super-educated; they look at your intelligence and what you can do. I would love to go to New York."

"Why don't you?"

"Nah...things are supposed to happen here. There are plans. They'll need me. I'll never be able to leave."

Patrick looks thoughtfully at me; I wonder if he'll say more. He begins to touch and kiss.

"I'd like to go to the South of France."

Patrick regards me with a curious smile. The blood rushes to my cheeks.

"Run away," I clarify.

"You want to run away from me?"

"No, from everything else."

Patrick stops sliding his hands over my body and seems to think things over.

"You can't go to the South of France without a bikini."

He resumes stroking me, which soon turns sexual, but something bothers me. Patrick looks worried.

"You're not in the mood?"

"It's not that...it's just that...." I put my hand on my genitals and feel my cheeks heat up. "It's hurting."

"Let me see."

"No!"

With the other networkers, I was mostly absent when my body was used, but under Patrick's gaze, I am intensely present, so I keep my legs stiffly closed. He playfully tries to force his hand in between my thighs. I refuse to give in. Finally, he promises not to look, and touches me very softly. Only his fingers move. Patrick scoots down with a beseeching look, promises he will close his eyes. I give in, submitting to my body's reaction, to find myself inside a cloud of incredible softness. The pleasurable sensations amplify to a level almost too much to bear. Transported, I mumble, *"Je vais mourir. Je vais mourir. Patrick, je vais mourir."* (I am going to die.)

My murmurs emerge as from out of a dream. Patrick is uncharacteristically agitated. He abruptly brings his face back next to mine.

"I have to...do you think it'll be all right?"

I nod once. A look of terror stirs Patrick's slightly widened eyes.

"Does it hurt?" he asks.

I shake my head, once more surrendered. We enter into a state of exultation. Patrick clings tightly to me, groans, begins to cry, and continues sobbing in my arms long after our bodies have returned to a condition of relative normality.

When he has quieted down, lying on me, he looks up, harried, eyes dim, skin ashen, all allure drained from his features. The features themselves are slackened, as if the jawbone gave up. He looks like a little boy, afraid I do not love him. Getting steadily worse, his sensuality is sucked out of him together with all of life, leaving a sickly, dull creature behind, weakly imploring me, certain of one thing only: that he is utterly unlovable.

As he averts his gaze, I put my hand through his hair and caress him quietly, steadily. Under my caresses, Patrick blooms. Even his hair, turned limp and colorless, seems to brighten, thicken and bounce back to life. My impulse to touch lessens as our state of relaxation deepens. After a while, I barely move anymore, yet we are wide awake, alert, attuned. This, it seems, is as close as I will ever be to anyone. Once in a while, Patrick looks up at me, and expresses, in his understated way, gratitude and sweetness I have never known.

We walk over the dunes to the beach, holding hands. Each particle of mist reflects the sun, creating magical light that surrounds us like an enormous halo. Patrick looks happy. Completely transformed, he is gorgeous, glowing with contained, contagious joy. He greets a passer-by who waves and, noticing his golden retriever's attraction to Patrick, initiates a brief, pleasant exchange. The dog loves Patrick, doesn't want to leave him, and as it reluctantly follows its master, keeps turning its head to find Patrick's eyes.

Patrick's mother is the pristine beach who gave him his color and beauty, his father the North Sea who gave him his eyes and his depth; and in this moment that seems to transcend space and time, I am not eleven years old or a child slave, but his ageless, eternal friend. As we stroll along in the sheer golden light and I turn to look at him, I am struck by a powerful thought: *This is who Patrick really is, this extremely beautiful, joyous youth. This is the closest he's ever come to being his true self. That is why he is happy.*

We clamber up the steep granite dam to the wide, somewhat crowded yellow brick boardwalk lined with cafés, fish restaurants and beach shops. Patrick smiles and rests his arm over my shoulder. People, especially women, greet us with friendly smiles. I put an arm around Patrick's hip, then both arms, pull myself closer and lean my head on him, sheltering from the strong wind that blows my hair in my face. Women respond all the more. They all smile, like how cute I am, and flirt with Patrick. Teenage girls giggle. We, or at least he, is causing a sensation. Yes, he is captivating, with his tall, strong but soft body, wavy blonde hair, radiant skin, square jaw and piercing blue eyes. But this is crazy. Whenever a woman gives Patrick a lewd glance, I give him a squeeze. He squeezes me back. After many squeezes, a darkly tanned, bejeweled woman in a billowing white skirt and white bikini top that barely reins in her full breasts, raises her brows over eyes of stone with a bawdy smirk at Patrick, who responds with a smirk of his own. She considers me with a harsh stare. I remove my arm from Patrick's waist.

"That..." Patrick says without trying to keep his voice down, "...is a whore."

The woman freezes behind us. Once she is out of earshot, Patrick says, "You will never be that. No matter what you do, you could never be a whore. Not even if you tried."

Patrick leads me into a large upscale children's clothing store. We check the tables for swimwear and are met by a polite sales lady with gently crossed arms and a cardigan hanging over her shoulders. With friendly smiles, she informs Patrick there are bathing suits in baskets towards the back. Patrick finds a bikini in navy stripes with rings holding the tiny pieces of cloth in place. I am shown into a changing booth, and when I come out, both Patrick and the sales lady inundate me with compliments. My cheeks are burning. Never before have I felt like such a whore.

"Now you are ready for the South of France, darling," Patrick says in a rather loud voice, with a wink at the sales lady, who smiles as if she understands everything.

"Let's look at some pants for you, too, sweetheart," Patrick goes on, indicating my too-short corduroys. "Those have obviously had their day."

I find a pair of bell bottoms that everyone agrees suits me splendidly, and as Patrick is about to pay, he picks up a polo shirt, several t-shirts, plus a sailor sweater roughly my size, and throws them on the counter too.

"Where in the South of France are you going?" asks the lady as she adds up the bill.

"Not far from Nice," answers Patrick, as if he's thought everything out already. "Do you know the area?"

"Sure," answers the sales lady. "Where exactly?"

"We have a house on the Cap Ferrat."

"You have a lovely time out there," says the enthused lady to both of us as she hands him the shopping bag. "And come and see us again."

As soon as we step out of the store—so the sales lady can get a good look at us through the window—Patrick lifts me up and kisses me on the mouth. When we move on, the sales lady waves goodbye. Patrick waves back.

Once we are back in our room, I ask, "You don't really have a house there, do you?"

Patrick smiles mysteriously as I try on the new shirts.

"They all look really good on you."

"They fit," I shrug dismissively.

Patrick's smile turns sad.

"Thank you, for all those clothes."

"What would you do by yourself on the Riviera?"

"Sell ice cream?"

"You're not old enough."

"I can pretend to be fourteen or fifteen."

"If you could pass for an older teenager, you wouldn't have to go any-where. Then I could get a flat in Brussels and you could just move in with me. But you don't look a day older than your age."

"But I'll say that I'm older, and it will work."

Patrick sighs as he lies down on the bed and puts his arms behind his head.

"Yeah, going to France and getting a job would work, but moving in with me wouldn't, huh?"

I stare at Patrick, throw off the new sweater and pull on my old t-shirt.

"Right," Patrick puffs. "What did I expect?"

"You think I don't love you because I want to get away from here?" I argue.

"That's right. You said it!" Patrick yells.

The pain in Patrick's voice cuts through my defiance. I sit on the bed and gauge his expression.

"It's just that it's still hurting."

Humor returns to Patrick's eyes. He slides up to me and puts his head on my lap. He lifts his left hand and rubs the cut in the cushiony part under his thumb.

"What hurts me is the thought of giving you up. But I know that I'll have to, because you're no good as a slave."

I take his hand and rub the healing stab wound. There is a raw pink eyelet gash, surrounded by several layers of scar tissue.

"Is it itching?"

He nods. "Soon this is all I'll have of you. It's hard to let you go, you know? What I have with you, I'll never have that with anyone else. And the sex; I know I'll not have that with anyone else either. That only comes around once in a lifetime."

"I wish I could stay with you forever."

Patrick looks tenderly at me.

"You're so pure. You don't say much, and when you speak, it's simple and sincere. That's probably why I love you so much. No, I don't really know why. I just don't know."

"But don't you think, when I'm old enough, that we could be together then?"

"You won't even remember me," he laughs wistfully.

"Don't be silly. Of course I will!"

"How? The clothes I got you will be too small soon. Any object, you can lose. Unless...."

I know Patrick is thinking of the scar I gave him, and considering giving me one. It is as if the great waves of the North Sea are crashing through the window.

"No, I'll remember you. I promise. And I'll come and find you, wherever you are."

Patrick gets up from the bed and rummages through his Adidas bag, while I cower against the wall by the door. He finds the penknife.

"Please, Patrick. I don't want you to stab me. I don't need a scar. Really, I don't. I love you; that's enough for me. Don't hurt me."

"Sweetheart, you're much too worried. It's not even going to hurt."

Patrick flips the knife open and advances towards me.

"Look at it this way," he goes on. "You're not out of the network yet. Who knows, maybe you'll be tortured before you can leave. Could you stand it?"

"I was prepared for that," I gasp. "But you, don't torture me!"

Patrick looks at the blade and puts it down on the side table.

"But I'm scaring you. Come here, let's sit on the bed together and talk."

"But not about that!"

"Come on," Patrick laughs. "You're being slow."

I sit stiffly on the back edge of the bed. Patrick indicates his left hand.

"When you did this, it never even hurt me. The little bit of discomfort I had afterwards just made me think of you, and I enjoyed it. If I did it to you, it would be the same. I would do it so you wouldn't even feel it, just give you a mark. Just something to cherish the bond that we have. Because we love each other. Don't you love me?"

I throw him an exasperated look. He goes on.

"And if, I'm just saying if you ever would be tortured, if for some reason I was unable to prevent it—you never know with these guys—then, if I puncture the most vulnerable spot on your body and teach you not to even feel it, then there is nothing anyone can do to you after that."

"You wouldn't stab me in the hand?"

Patrick touches the back of his knee, which he once said is the most vulnerable spot on the body. I spontaneously break into tears.

"But how will I walk?"

"But, my angel, *I* walk," Patrick says. "And what I'd do to you is nothing compared to what was done to me. A prick; no more."

I can't stop crying, and lie down. Patrick pulls off my new pants, then my shirt. He caresses my back, and comforts me, muttering, "*Allez, ma petite,*" (Come on, little one), as I sob for a long time, all the while expecting to feel the knife. Once Patrick's steady caresses have calmed me down, after I've stopped crying completely, he rubs the back of my right knee and says, "Okay, now just breathe. You'll just feel a little prick, that's all."

What I feel is like a kitchen knife boring all the way into my knee, cutting through skin, flesh and tendons before being pulled out. My leg stiffens instantaneously. This is it. I'll never be able to walk normally again. My leg begins to shake violently. Patrick puts a cold wet towel over the wound. There is blood everywhere. *I'm going to die.* I can't stop shaking. I'm in shock. Patrick, piling towels over his arm, lifts me so my knee rests on the towels. He kisses me all over my face and whispers, "*Que je t'aime, ma petite.* You'll never know how much I love you. Keep your eyes open. Don't go to sleep. I love you, sweetheart."

Nothing is harder than to keep my eyes open. They just want to close. They need to close. All goes black. I keep slipping, losing consciousness. I'm way down there in the darkness, sinking lower and lower, to where all is quiet and still. Patrick's fervent whispers, his protestations of love, reach me, keep pulling me back out. Each time I descend into the abyss, Patrick's whispers increase in urgency and, it seems, in feeling.

"Come back, little one. Don't leave. Come now, you have to stay here. *Ma chérie.* Don't go. *Je t'aime.* Please. Annie. *Ma petite Annie.* Don't leave me."

I feel that I'm going to faint again, but it seems that if I really want to, like Patrick says, I can prevent it. It makes no sense, but his words of love sound true. I believe him. I find the will power to lift up my arm and throw it around Patrick's neck. If I cling to him, it seems, if I let in his love and let myself know just how much I love him, then I can stay.

Suddenly, I am freezing cold, shivering; my teeth clatter. I notice that my skin has turned a bluish ashen. I cling to Patrick. *I love you, Patrick. I love you so much.* I feel Patrick respond. He lifts me higher, holds me tighter. The next thing I know we are in a bathroom. Patrick lowers me onto the bathmat. Tells me he'll be quick. Assures that I'll be alright. A refreshing feeling. A wet towel against the wound. Another towel wrapped around the knee to hold the first one in place. A bath sheet wrapped around my body. Patrick lifts me up again. I hang onto him, bury my face into his chest. How can I get closer? He kisses my hair, my face. Holds me. Strokes me. Whispers of love. I relax, stop shivering. He lays me down. Props up the pillow. He keeps caressing me. That is what I need. *Don't stop, Patrick.* Now I can go to sleep.

CHAPTER TEN

On the road, June 1974

T he side of my face is buried in a soft pillow. I lie on my stomach, a towel over my back. My cradle jiggles softly. It stops. I wake up. There is a shooting pain on the inside of my right heel. I try to shake it out. *My knee.* I remember. I want to go back to sleep. I hear a muffled cacophony of metallic sounds very close to my head, men's voices—Patrick's—little bells, and there's a smell—of gasoline. I open my eyes. Black leather. Of a car seat. I would like to get up. I would like to take a look at the back of my right knee. I pull off the towel and raise myself on my hands, twist my torso, notice my panties, make out the cut, right below the knee crease, towards the inside of the leg, surrounded by a bruise. It is dark red, dry, hard to see.

Patrick must be taking me home. *What am I going to tell Mama? How am I going to get through exam week? I already missed half. I can't go to school like this. I'll have to stay home, study, and do make-ups.*

I slowly sit up, maneuvering my leg so the wound won't touch the seat. When I open the door, I am met by a warm gust of wind. I wind a towel round my waist, put my left foot down on the asphalt. Where are we? What is this hilly countryside, with endless fields of sunflowers beside the express-way? Patrick concludes his business with the attendant on the other side of the car and comes around. When our eyes meet, Patrick smiles sheepishly.

Where are we? Patrick slides his hands under my armpits for support as I carefully drag my right leg out of the car.

"You've had a good long sleep."

I put my right foot on the ground, try to put weight on it. It is as though an iron rod were being pushed into the wound, down through the calf to the heel. I can stand though, and push Patrick away. Hopping on my left foot, the right drags behind.

"I can't believe you're walking. It hasn't even been twelve hours. You have an amazingly strong body."

"I've needed it."

Very slowly, I walk, refusing to give the pain power over me.

"But this is impressive! Last night I thought you might have to lose the leg, or die, and now you're walking on it!"

I stop to scan Patrick's face for traces of self-awareness, and find none.

"You really scared me," he rattles on. "It was just supposed to be a prick. I never expected you'd react like that...I must have used too much force...I didn't mean to...."

I explode into a fit of laughter. Can't stop. I'm in such pain. Patrick rejoins me with an occasional guffaw and self-conscious grimaces. When I want to head towards the passenger seat, I realize I cannot walk without his help, which gets me going again, laughing and crying at once. Once I am calm and sitting, Patrick disappears into the gas station store and returns with snacks, soft drinks and a little skirt for me, with stylized yellow flowers in a Provençal pattern. We really are in the South of France.

We drive into the town of Aix-en-Provence. As I lean heavily on Patrick's arm in narrow streets, I wonder if anyone notices that we both limp. Patrick helps me sit down at a sleepy outside terrace where we have lunch. Sounds of peace flow from the steady trickle of a fountain, soft chatter, twittering sparrows and leaves rustling in the canopy of plane trees.

"After you eat garlic," Patrick comments as he carefully places his espresso cup back on its saucer, "coffee tastes exceptionally good."

He takes a moment to savor the flavor. I wait, pick up his cup and dump the espresso in my hot cocoa, taking a taste from my mug, mimicking him, savoring, carefully placing the mug back down. Not bad. I'm struck by the look in Patrick's translucent eyes: so brilliant, sweet, and full of love. I fill his cup back up with the mixture from my mug. He tastes it. Not bad.

Cap Ferrat, France, June 1974

The road turns onto the peninsula of the Cap Ferrat, winding through paradisiacal gardens to a small house in the shade of pine trees on a seaside bluff. Patrick opens the shutters, deposits me on a sofa, flips through a stack of records and puts a French album on the turntable. While he takes a shower upstairs, I listen to a cool baritone with angelic voices in the background. The languid song is an exact reflection of my dreamy state, about being somewhere on the seashore in the sun. The singer wonders if this is an erotic dream, or if it is real.

There is a fulfillment happening during this song, lying on this sofa, in this home on the French Riviera, more meaningful even than the promise of escape. These words about finding oneself in an idyllic spot transport me to the past, when the Big Shot networker who owned me had described what was to be my glamorous destiny. He had spared no resources in meticulously preparing me to become his future celebrity slave, who would break the hearts of the world's most powerful men, all while spying on them for him. Without a platform of my own, those powerful men would never notice me, so I was to become known in France as an actress and singer. He had described my future life of luxury in great detail. I would own the best cars and yachts, and live in the best locations—in Paris and on the sunny seashores of the South of France.

These promises were to be sealed with an induction ceremony that began with my performance for my owner and a select group of politicians, royals, billionaires and celebrities—the top tier of the global network. There, I sang Edith Piaf's *"Je Ne Regrette Rien,"* singing away all that came before, to be ready for my new life, while focusing my seductive powers individually on the audience members. This part was no problem; I had acquired those quick-fire skills in my previous training. However, the performance was only the beginning. The latter part of the event confronted me with the horrific price I would have to pay for said celebrity; an action to cement my place into the secret cult of the world's elite. Even though I was not quite ten years old, and even though I'd had no choice but to perform the action, I realized that it was too high a price to pay.

The next time I saw my Big Shot owner, I went against him, and got angry, which I knew was taboo and even potentially deadly. The glamorous future for which I had been so fastidiously trained and prepared was the only one, apart from death, which I had ever imagined. While the course of my destiny was drastically altered during those few seconds, the trinkets that had been dangled before my eyes were still floating around my consciousness in the form of unfulfilled desires. As I now lie on this sofa in this house on the Mediterranean coast, I enjoy the fulfillment of this one dream with all my being. *I am in the South of France.*

Patrick returns to the room in clean pants, no shirt, with a wet washcloth and towels. He undresses me and washes my back, as I become suffused with the elfin melody of the next song, about a girl whose lollipops flavor her kisses with anise.

"Do you understand the words?" asks Patrick as he washes the back of my right knee, painstakingly cleaning off dried blood around the cut.

The man sings that the girl's eyes are the color of anise, of happy days. I nod.

"I guess it's alright for him," Patrick says.

It is certainly not the first time that I hear a comment justifying pedophilia in the network, but never before have I been indifferent to such a remark. Lulled by the dreamy ambiance, I take pleasure in the slow strokes of cool washcloth on my back, shoulders and neck.

"Do you like lollipops?" Patrick asks as he gently turns me over onto my back.

I reach my arms up to embrace him, experience a thrill upon feeling the soft, cool skin of his back, pull him close. A kiss. Does he understand? Not yet. Another kiss. He gets it.

This dream seems to be more real than reality. Lying on this couch with Patrick, feeling the Mediterranean breeze and his skin, my lips tremble, and my body, with a slight shudder, awakens.

Patrick puts on a '45 record; the electronic opening notes set the stage for a playful ambiance for an over-the-top, sexual duet.

"You sound just like her," he says as he rejoins me on the sofa. The woman's voice sounds high and childlike.

"No."

When the woman sings "*I love you*," Patrick comments, "Here you can tell she's lying."

Than the male voice answers something about this not being real love, implying it is all about the sex.

I laugh, "No wonder."

Patrick whispers, "I love you."

"Me too."

The woman goes into the refrain in her breathy, falsetto voice.

"I don't sound anything like this," I remark.

"It's near the end, the breathing, you'll hear; that's when she sounds like you."

Our lovemaking lasts long after the song has finished. I make sure not to breathe audibly; that is the game, and part of this re-awakening to the realm of lightness, where the weight of the world is not felt, suspended on a cloud of romantic love, dissociated from reality in an atmosphere of physical comfort. This is the high I have been trying to ward off for the entire time I have known Patrick, because I have been to this addictive place before. I have felt this high on hope when I believed in real love—and should know better than to assume that this can last, or possibly end well.

I was never in love with the network Big Shot; it was rather that he created the persona who is currently waking up. The initial part of my education had taken place early in the summer of 1972, in his luxurious homes, where he had introduced me to his world of privilege and lifted me onto his cloud above the rest of the world, where everything was good and beautiful, cradled in sensual comfort and carefully curated peace. No darkness or negatives existed on this cloud. I was the materialization of his pleasant projection that fit perfectly onto that cloud—light, airy, and sexy. He loved to have control behind the scenes. He would have loved to secretly own the French celebrity I was to become under his guidance. I had to exist entirely for him, without a thought of my own. Nevertheless, while I had been under his tutelage receiving his attention, I had been just as high on hope for true love as I am now. Only, less than a year after the start of that story, after I had angrily said no to the price for belonging in the Big Shot's material heaven, I had been pushed off that cloud, and the fall had been steep and hard.

Cap Ferrat, France, June 1974

Every morning, Patrick drives me to a café in the harbor village for breakfast. Afterwards, we buy a baguette and charcuterie to take home for lunch. Back at the house, Patrick carries me down the stairs hewn into the rocky slope, to a small pebble beach on the quiet ocean inlet where we sunbathe and he swims.

To aid with my healing process, Patrick insists I eat red meat. For dinner we drive back to the village, where we sit looking out at the fishing boats, yachts and sailboats. Because of the pain in my knee, my actions are more deliberate, and because I feel loved, my every move and every word are perfectly timed, perfectly received. Everything seems perfect.

After a week or so, heading to the harbor café for an afternoon drink, I ask Patrick to let me try to walk by myself. I concentrate on not limping, and though it slows me down even more, I succeed. I give him a look: *There, I'm not limping. You didn't get me to be like you.* He nods.

Sitting on a café terrace overlooking the harbor of Saint-Jean, listening to buoy bells and the relaxing water flow of a single spout fountain, Patrick sips an anise liquor.

"Your eyes are like those of the girl in the song, like anise" I say to Patrick. But when he sings that they are the color of happy days, those days seem to be in the past."

"You want a taste?"

He offers me his drink. I try it. Not bad. Indicating our set-up with a sweeping hand motion, Patrick states, "This, too, will be in the past."

"This, yes. Some of it, of course."

Patrick smiles a slightly sour, sad smile, like here we are, faced with this thing that I won't understand.

"You know," he ventures, "there is one element that will definitely be different in the future. You know what that is?"

"No, what is that?" I respond flatly.

"The element of choice. Now, because of your age, this is not your choice."

"Isn't that why you didn't touch me for so long?"

"Yes, I thought I'd leave it up to you, and I believed that would make the choice yours, but I was wrong. I don't know why you decided to get physical with me, but I know you well enough to know that it wasn't just because you felt like it."

I bow my head in acute shame.

"Oh, it's all right," Patrick continues. "It's your duty, in a way, to always think of your survival first. You can't really do anything freely. Freedom of choice is reserved for adults."

"I love you."

Patrick looks disarmed, and frowns like he wants to say something he might not have sufficiently thought through.

"When I look at you, I see this incredible pride in your eyes...." he begins.

His remark throws me in a state of confusion and panic.

"No, no, it's a good thing. It's the quality that gives you all your strength. It's defiance, yes. But with pride. It's because of that, I doubt once you'll be a grown woman, once you'll have the choice, you will choose to be with me, because I'm no good."

"I know that. But I love you anyway. It's not going to go away."

"I'm a crook. I rob banks, money transports, post offices, anything. Sometimes I kill people. I like it. You'd make a great Bonnie, because you're a killer too—don't kid yourself—but when I see this fierce pride in your eyes, like just then when you were walking, without a limp, and the way you look at me, it makes me know that you'll never want to be sidekick to any Clyde. Or any millionaire for that matter."

"Why do you like to kill?"

Patrick leans back to ponder the question.

"You know, most of life, everything we see on the surface—it's all lies. When you confront somebody with their death, then you see the truth about them. You have no idea what I've seen: best friends trying to get each other killed, just to save their own skin, and that's just the beginning."

"And what makes you pull the trigger?"

"Weakness. Not just weakness, but cowardice, like in the form of disloyalty. Like those guys, as soon as you put a gun to their heads, they try to bargain with you, and the stuff that comes out of their mouths...."

Patrick shakes his head in disgust.

"I hold the gun against their forehead. That's the moment they reveal themselves. And when I have myself a real piece of shit, and he's pretty damn pleased with himself because he thinks I'm going to kill his best friend and not him, and then I shoot his brains out, the quiet that follows the blast, it fills me with a sense of...deep...wellbeing. Peace."

"So, you wipe out the lies...and the dirt underneath the lies?"

"Yes, it's exactly that, because this sense afterwards...I feel clean, like the dirt has been cleansed. It's specific. And it feels good."

I nod.

"And you do this out of free choice?"

Patrick regards me with a flicker of distrust.

"I don't know. I guess it's something that I have to do, because there's this...desire in me."

"You said that being with me gives you peace."

"That's true. I do feel it with you. There's something real about you, and being together. And in fact, I haven't done anything lately, because I haven't really had the need."

"You know, I've felt, with you sometimes, I've suddenly felt clean also. Cleansed. Sort of like the feeling you were describing."

Patrick nods.

"Do you think that, if we could be together in the future, as a couple, that you might not want to kill? Or rob?"

"If anyone can change me, I'm sure it's you. But you're putting the cart before the horse. You can't be with me just to change me, and you probably won't want to be with me before I'll change, so...."

"So, we don't know."

"Right, we can't know. Anyway, having a regular relationship, that's if you'd want one, living together, is very different from what we have now. I would have to provide for you somehow, and I'm really good at just one thing. But also, there's the excitement now, because it's illegal. You're the forbidden fruit."

"So maybe you don't really love me."

"You know, there's a lot of little girls at the parties, and I can have all of them if I want, like your friend Florence. She's been trying, believe me, but I don't love her, or anybody else. Yeah, I guess it's not a choice, I love you; who the hell knows why?"

I blush and stare into the table. Patrick puts a consoling arm around me and pulls me closer.

"Don't worry, you'll always be exciting to me. No one's ever put me in a state of arousal that lasted six months straight. That's what happened. I was aroused thinking about you, but I think about you all the time. I can't believe that I had this much self-control. I didn't think I had it in me. Your beauty just turns me on; it's something incredible."

"For me, it's also your beauty that excites me," I admit.

I look at Patrick, observe his handsome tanned face, the gold chains around his neck, his gold bracelets (amulets, he calls them), his beautiful hair, his jeans tight in the crotch, his broad shoulders, rippling arms, bronzed skin, his white rib tank top covering his strong, lean body that is yet soft, his eyes the color of anise lollipops, and I enter the purely physical world. Whereas until this moment, I primarily saw the ethereal beauty of the light inside Patrick, I currently focus on the external, on the impermanent attributes, buying into the lies, objectifying him as I have been objectified, thinking: *He is such a thug. He is so sexy.*

"But not before we had sex," Patrick clarifies.

"No. I saw it; it just didn't have the same effect, physically. I never had that before. Maybe I was too young. But now it's all changed."

Patrick leans over and looks me directly in the eye. I move in, sharply concentrated, ready to listen.

"I really want to fuck you right now," he says. "Long. And hard."

Patrick pulls me close and kisses my face, then my mouth. There are some other people on the terrace, and for the first time since we arrived in the South of France there are looks, as in what is going on? Patrick leaves money to pay the bill, puts his arm around me, and as quickly as my bad knee allows, gleefully, like naughty kids, we hurry off.

CHAPTER ELEVEN

Haemers residence,
Cap Ferrat, France, June 1974

Except for some meals, we don't leave the house anymore. We don't even make it down to the little beach. We spend all our time in the bedroom, having sex. Once self-respect is substituted for the idea of sexual power over a man, purity becomes burdensome, and its release freeing—but what is freedom inside the cycle of romance? I cut a piece of baguette open, butter it, and slice a local cheese, leaving some end cuts on the kitchen counter.

"You have no idea how many thousands of breadcrumbs I've cleaned up after you since we've been here," Patrick says. "Do me a favor, sit at the table."

When I do, Patrick sits down across from me. Some crumbs fall on my lap.

"Sit up! Sit up!" he cries.

He comes over and brushes the crumbs off my pants into his hand and carries them to the trash.

"Just try to sit up properly at the table, so you don't spill. I know it's not your fault," Patrick says. "But you've got to learn sometime."

He sits back down with a sigh.

"I'm just having a snack!"

"But it's nice to have meals together. That's why I'm sitting with you, to make it into a meal."

"But lunch is bread and cheese also," I laugh.

"That's only because you can't cook. I know it's not your fault, but it's getting expensive, taking you out to dinner every night."

"It's true. I can't cook," I confirm, tipping my chair back as I take another bite out of the sandwich.

A small piece of cheese drops onto the floor. Patrick jumps up, grabs me by the shirt and pulls me out of the chair.

"Now you're going to pick up that piece of cheese, get a cloth, wet it, and clean the floor before you do anything else, you understand! My parents are coming soon. I don't want the house to be a pigsty when they get here. And you're not helping. You understand? YOU'RE NOT HELPING!"

"Let me go."

When I am kneeled down to wash the floor, I feel humiliated, and dirty. Then I sense Patrick's sensual gaze on my exposed lower back. He touches my skin with strong, sensual strokes, and takes the cloth out of my hands.

"I'm sorry, I didn't mean to. I don't know why I got so mad."

He lifts me in his arms and kisses my face.

"It's not your fault, you understand? I'm sorry."

Holding me in his hands and kissing me, Patrick walks us up the stairs, to the bedroom.

Mediterranean at Cap Ferrat,
June 1974

We are on a small sailboat, anchored at the inlet near the house, which we reached minutes after setting sail. I want to try swimming—the wound has healed nicely—and jump into the water. When my head pops back up I find myself looking straight into Patrick's pale blue eyes. His long lashes look darker and longer when wet. I stare in awe. Patrick, barely moving his lips, grins derisively.

"Does it sting?" he asks.

In response to his sarcasm, I observe Patrick's eyes like a critic. Now his smile turns bashful.

"Okay, ready?" he says.

He takes in a big gulp of air, so I do the same, and he plunges down, kissing me as I tumble backwards underwater with him attached. When I am completely out of breath, he stays under a little more. Then we come up. The next time we go under, he fondles me. When I think I absolutely need to breathe, he keeps me down. I nearly faint, sinking back into the state of extreme relaxation I experienced during my torturous time in Germany. There, I was held inside a sensory-deprivation saltwater tank. Extended periods of weightlessness apparently release one's psychic abilities, which I needed in order to bypass logic and infer truths about men, so as to better fulfil their sexual desires. Underneath my deep relaxation in sex rests a volcano of fear and resistance, but there won't be any explosions of that kind as long as I believe that the love between Patrick and me is the best there is and ever will be—the true love I have been seeking forever.

The combination of the weightlessness and lightheadedness turns the sex into something of an erotic dream, in which the pleasure buried under the weight of life is released and felt in a pure, raw way. When we go under again, I do the same to him. With my hands on his shoulders to keep him under, I suck in a huge gulp of air, then put my feet on his torso to push him farther down. I slide my legs around his hips and restart the sex. Patrick's head drifts back, then his spine curves as he relaxes completely, then all his muscles flex awkwardly. I pull him up.

When Patrick watches me climb back aboard the sailboat, he comments, "I guess you don't need help."

We dry off on deck, and he offers me a brown bottle of suntan lotion. I give him a look; he pours the oil in his hand and massages it into my arms and chest.

"You're so amazingly athletic. Do you do any sports?" he asks.

"Gymnastics. And horseback riding."

"Oh really? With the life you lead, I didn't think you had time for anything else. Where do you ride?"

"I ride when I can on weekends at the stable and do horse camps a few weeks in the year, and then I also used to ride with Florence. Sometimes she got horses from her parents' friends. It was a lot of fun to ride with her, in the woods around the castles, or galloping through the lanes."

I remember the thrill of racing the horses in the gorgeous surrounds of the castles; these were the best times I had with Florence; maybe the best times of my life.

"It made me feel free," I admit.

"So, you definitely won't limp, then," Patrick concludes, "The riding made your legs really strong. You are amazingly strong anyway."

Patrick slowly massages the suntan oil into my legs.

"See, that's something I don't have," Patrick says wistfully.

"What?"

"That physical prowess."

"You're very strong," I laugh.

"No, but not like that. You're wispy, and you look soft, but when you move, you see these little flickers of muscle shooting into action, like you could do anything. I don't have that. I limp."

I catch a glimpse of Patrick's sad eyes as I turn onto my stomach.

"That's something you can't understand," Patrick continues as he rubs the suntan oil into my back.

"What?"

"What it's like to live with a limp."

I turn my head to look him in the eye.

"I'm just as lonely."

Patrick searches my gaze and concludes, "No, it's different. You couldn't understand."

The soft lapping of the waves against the hull, the gentle rocking of the boat, the warmth of the sun; these trappings are instantaneously as bare as prison walls. As Patrick isolates the muscles of my back with his fingers to massage the oil into my skin, I feel bad for being strong, and making him feel insecure. I take the bottle from Patrick and begin to massage the oil into his back, moving quickly down to his legs, to look at the scar at the back of his right knee. It is covered with raised scar tissue.

"That is a big scar," I say, gently massaging it. "How did you get it?"

Patrick looks very sad and self-conscious, as if the scar made him unattractive. I look at the back of his knee. Years of practice have made me an expert in making men with a tortured self-image feel better, and as I am drawn to find him ugly, I focus on letting my love for Patrick flow through my fingers. *All of his vulnerability is concentrated in this scar. And he is so terribly vulnerable. That is why he is so sensitive, so insecure. I love him. I love him so much.*

"Stabbed," Patrick says, with a slight nod.

In a rush of explosive anger, I imagine, with lustful pleasure, causing a blood bath. *I'll stab you too! You did it to me! What do you want from me? Sympathy?*

As Patrick cringes under my murderous glare, an eruption of love melts away my anger. *Look at him!* I think. *He's just like a sweet little boy. Scared.*

I put my own body over his, as his skin suddenly seems too white, too exposed, and I kiss him tenderly in the neck. Patrick turns on his back and begins to respond to my kisses, very tentatively, like a child. I look at his face: it is lit up with angelic beauty. The look in his eyes is completely trusting, completely pure. Quite overwhelmed by his ethereal beauty and the innocence shining from Patrick's clear round eyes, I reach down to touch his face, and he arches up to meet my touch, but instead of caressing his cheek, which I thought I was going to do, I push against his forehead, and the back of his head hits the hard deck.

I run my fingers through his golden locks, rub the scalp, grab the hair in my fists, pulling harder than I intended. I kiss him; his lips are exceptionally tender. I rub my loins against his; it is as though I am spoiling an immaculate being—as though Patrick is in the role of a young victim, and I am in the role of an adult perpetrator. When I feel his response, I become high. Power detached from responsibility creates the idea of freedom. Every instant is so dense that my internal timer slows to a near halt. I have no idea what the next nanosecond will bring, or what I might do. I have no idea who I really am or what I am capable of, nor do I care. Spontaneously, I look at Patrick's erect penis as if I were a feline observing a little bird. Patrick ejaculates, and laughs, embarrassed.

He lifts me up and sets me on a raised casing on the deck and begins to make out. His clumsy caresses, shallow breathing, his painful attempts to regain his manliness drive me crazy. *What's his problem?* I think, irritated.

I know what to do when a man has trouble getting aroused. I raise my right leg up so the skin around the wound stretches tighter, tighter. Patrick puts his hand on the back of my thigh, and sure enough, glancing at the wound agitates him. Stretching my leg, I feel the crust behind my knee rip. The blood begins to flow, trickling down. Patrick, licks, sucks off the blood, vigorously, ardently.

A yacht slowly glides into view, pretty close-by. I drop, fall onto Patrick, who gives me a questioning look; I respond with a panicked nudge. The yacht stops. There are at least ten people on deck, all looking at us. I can see them clearly: their faces, hair color, their bathing suits. They are all adults, so they must see that I am not.

"Come on, we'll give them some entertainment," Patrick says.

Patrick lays me down on the casing. With fresh blood all around his mouth, he looks like a vampire. I laugh; he grins, kisses my neck, nibbles, bites. Here we are, in the world of appearances, proving that the man is a man and the woman is a child. We have our attentive audience, endorsing and encouraging us. After Patrick orgasms again, he continues the sex, if only just because he can. He has no problem anymore. When we simultaneously turn our heads to see what has become of our audience, the placid scene on the yacht has transformed into the beginning stages of an orgy, with several couples kissing wildly.

"Another good deed done," Patrick concludes.

He regards me with a curious look.

"I'm going to wash up," he announces, and runs off, jumping overboard, leaving me exposed on deck.

I hurry after him, but climbing the railing, I become apprehensive.

"What, are you scared?" Patrick taunts me.

I jump in. As soon as my knee hits the water, a sharp pain tenses my whole body. I paddle my way over to Patrick. He swims away.

"Hey, don't come to me. You did this to yourself."

The pain becomes unbearable.

"You really liked that, didn't you?" Patrick continues, meaning sex in front of strangers.

"I didn't have a choice," I snap.

Patrick stares and blinks, then his eyes narrow.

"No, but that's something I didn't know about you. You're an exhibitionist."

"So are you!"

Back on board, I hide in the dark cabin to put my bikini on, because the yacht is still there, even if most of its occupants have disappeared from the deck. I pour water over the wound and wrap a towel around my knee.

Patrick enters without a word. There are narrow benches on either side. Patrick lies down; I sit as far from him as possible. After what seems like a long pause, in a nasal, authoritative voice, Patrick says, "You're going to have to go home soon. I can take you back tomorrow."

"Never!"

Patrick's fiery gaze expresses the hurt and sadness of all the victims in the world.

"If I take you back tomorrow," he says deliberately, "you will be able to make up your exams and make it to the next year. You won't have to double."

"I'm not going back to my mother. Never," I repeat.

"My parents will be here soon. What will they say when they find there's a girl living in their summer home. You expect they'll adopt you?"

"Your father saw us together. Just tell him I'm your girlfriend."

"Leave my father out of this!" Patrick yells.

"Why? Isn't he the one who brought you to the orgies? Why would you have to hide anything from him?"

"Stop it!"

Patrick covers his eyes with balled fists.

"I never meant to stay at the house anyway," I say softly. "Maybe if you could buy me a small tent and take me to another town, I'll find a job. I'll be alright."

"And supposing you got away with that, which most likely you wouldn't," Patrick scoffs, "then what would you do once the summer is over?"

"Go pick grapes in the Beaujolais, for example."

Patrick begins to snigger, but he refrains.

"You're too young to live on your own. If I leave you here, your mother is going to go to the police, and I will have to go to prison for kidnapping you."

"My mother doesn't want me. All she does is try to get rid of me. If you told her I had died, it would make her happy."

Patrick's fists relax. He lets his hands slide back behind his head and mulls things over several minutes. When he looks up, he smiles sweetly and conspiratorially.

"You really think so? Alright. I'll try to go talk to your mother. Maybe I can put you up in a small apartment around here. There's a lot to figure out, but we'll try."

Cap Ferrat, France, June 1974

We don't leave the bedroom, not even for breakfast. We don't eat. Like two drops that became one, we are nurtured, engulfed in a never-ending wave of pleasantness, floating in a flowing, tangible stream of sex-induced euphoria, which I fully believe to be love.

"I really should go," Patrick confesses. "Get in the car and start driving. Take care of things. But I just can't bring myself to leave."

He stays one more day, two more days. Sometimes, he seems overwhelmed by grief so deep that it makes me cry. When we have sex, Patrick whispers, "This is all I want to do. I just want to be inside of you for the rest of my life. This is the only way I can be happy."

On the third day, lying in my arms, Patrick whispers, "It was my father."

I look at Patrick, see a mental image of him as a boy, his knee all bloody, an enormous kitchen knife.

It was your father who stabbed you?

Patrick nods. I hold him for a long, long time. We fall asleep.

I wake up alone. Descending the stairs, I notice Patrick sitting on the sofa, feet on the salon table, watching a soccer match on TV, the volume so low the fans' cheers are barely audible. I observe Patrick and wonder if he, like all Belgian boys, used to play. After his father stabbed him, Patrick would not have been able to play anymore, or at least not like before, but Patrick still loves soccer, and I see a sweet boy infinitely loyal to his father. Thinking back to our day on the sailboat, I consider that Patrick may be right, that I don't really understand what it is like for him. Surely, he is reminded of the fateful moment his father stabbed him with every step he takes. He must always be conscious of it, always wondering if or when strangers will see it, finely attuned to how they then might perceive him differently: as an invalid, broken, or an outcast. I place my hand on Patrick's shoulder, which suddenly appears unnaturally large.

"Oh, I didn't see you."

When the match is finished, Patrick says, "I really should get going. If I don't leave now, I never will."

He packs his Adidas bag, gives me money, tells me he'll be gone for two or three days, and hugs me, holds me. He clings to me. I cling to him. The kisses don't end. Patrick carries me to the couch. We make love with great emotion, as if we were never going to see each other again. Transported, Patrick mumbles, repeats, "*Restes avec moi. Ne me laisse pas tomber. Restes avec moi.*" (Stay with me. Don't drop me.)

His words emerge as if from behind mind and matter, as if he is asking me to never let go of him, to love him always, no matter what, well beyond death.

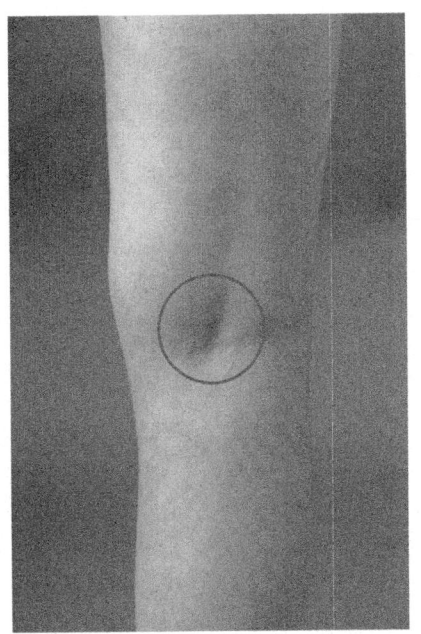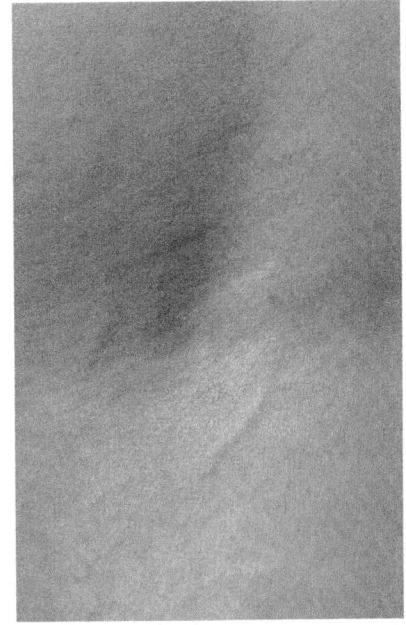

Back of my right leg and close-up of back of my knee, on photos taken in
2022, 48 years after the wounding. Left: Notice the depression and darkened
skin around the scar. Right: the dash-shaped scar from penknife wound,
moved over the years. (The smaller, vertical scar touching the bottom of the
dash-shaped scar, is from another assault, described later in this book.)

CHAPTER TWELVE

Haemers Residence,

Cap Ferrat, France, June 1974

It must be a week since Patrick left, and still there is no sign of him. The money he left has been spent. The baker gives me leftover baguette before closing time, and a lollipop. The butcher, too, passes along snacks: salami, carrot salad; and one day I get half of a roast chicken. The people in this town are friendly. And they worry about me, and about what might have happened to "my cousin." I tell them not to worry, I am fine. And I wonder how I will do once Patrick will really be gone, because I have already had to dissuade the waiter at the café (who gave me an ice cream) from warning the police, because I am so young, and they can all tell.

Back at the house, I try to clean up. I wash the kitchen and living room floors with a small sponge and hot water. It takes a long time, but I think it looks cleaner. I use the same sponge to wipe the dust off the cabinets, dressers and the salon table, and to wash the kitchen counter and sink. I make the bed. I sleep a lot.

At night, I am overtaken by fear that something is terribly wrong. I try to imagine Patrick meeting Mama, informing her that I have died, and I try to imagine Mama's reaction, but nothing comes. I think about the morning Patrick took me to the Belgian seaside, the last time I saw Mama, how nice she was. I wonder why, and I panic. The only thought that soothes these fears is that it was Patrick who showed me that my love for Mama was misplaced. It was Patrick who told me that my mother was no good.

A thud abruptly awakes me from a morning nap on the living room sofa. Patrick is back, throwing down his Adidas bag. Instantly, I feel as though I never moved from this spot all week, and I am completely without initiative, dependent on him to make every move, even to get off the couch.

I did get off the couch, I remind myself as I get up.

My impulse to embrace him is checked by a cold glare. Two sheets of ice cover his irises, and his face is red from the chill. He looks older, harsher, as if he has been having tons of sex and drugs. Without a word, Patrick runs up the stairs. I hear him shower. Ten minutes later he returns with my school bag stuffed with my clothes.

"I cleaned upstairs. You check the kitchen, get all your stuff out of the fridge and throw out the garbage. We're leaving."

Once we are driving in the Porsche, I want to ask where we are going, but Patrick is so distant that I can't bring myself to do that much. He seems furious. We are stuck in morning traffic on the road along the boardwalks of Nice, half an hour at least. Patrick curses at the other motorists. Past Nice, we hop onto the autoroute, towards Marseilles.

"Where are we going?"

No answer. His eyes, which used to be the most attractive thing about him, have a scary glazed-over emptiness. I am too afraid to speak, until Patrick turns onto the road for Paris instead of following the signs for Marseilles, when I finally manage to utter, "I'm not going home, you know."

I feel absolutely ridiculous, as if I am a pretentious brat, trying her little game with someone with real authority, who sees right through her petty manipulations. The idea of Belgium and of Mama reminds me that I am not a brat. I am not trying to manipulate anybody. But I would rather die than go home.

"Just drop me off at the side of the road, that's good enough. Just stop the car," I say, in a state of great agitation.

Patrick has finally noticed me, and throws me a sideways glance with some interest, but it is negative, as in I could become a problem.

"Stop the car!" I yell.

Panicked, in a confused gesture, I put my hands on Patrick's forearms, something to make him stop the car. While steering with his left hand, Patrick wrings his right arm free and swings it out, hitting my face with the back of his hand. Black spots dance before my eyes, becoming larger. For a moment, the shock is greater than my panic. I am about to faint, but the fearful prospect of being returned to mama after losing Patrick's affection causes a fierce adrenaline rush.

"I'm not going back!"

Patrick ignores me. I wonder if he will drive straight through. *No, he'll have to stop for gas. I will run away,* I decide. After some time, as we get on the ramp leading to a rest stop, my heart pounds. The Porsche rolls towards a pump. Highly concentrated, I wait for the right moment, but before we have slowed down enough, Patrick grabs my upper arm. He stops by the pump, opens the door and pulls me across the driver's seat out of the car, bruising my side, hip and thigh. He puts me in front of him, gripping my arms behind my back. The attendant arrives; he doesn't seem to notice anything amiss.

"I'm going to get her something to eat," Patrick informs the attendant.

He pushes me in front of him, keeping my arms tied behind my back. Just as no one seemed to think twice about seeing us together as a couple, no one seems to think twice about my being taken hostage. *Isn't my face black and blue from that slap?* I wonder. *Isn't it obvious that something is wrong here?* If I pull the slightest bit, Patrick squeezes my arms so hard it makes me want to cry. *I will cry,* I think.

"Ow, let me go," I say, loud enough so that a couple of tourists who are just exiting the store look at us.

"No, you have to eat. Just come in with me to see if there isn't anything that looks appetizing. You've gone too long without food, I just won't have it," Patrick says, with exaggerated concern in his voice.

The couple sends Patrick sad smiles and supportive looks. Inside the store, Patrick buys a baguette with ham and cheese, and holds it before my eyes as if to tempt me. When he finally releases my arm to pay, I run for the exit, but Patrick is on me like a hawk, and in front of at least six customers and the cashier, grabs me and pulls me back to the register.

"Children just will not listen to their uncle," he announces as he pays, and with a glance at me, "Even when their parents made it very clear that they should."

"He's not my uncle!" I blurt out.

I expect that Patrick is going to pull out his gun and start shooting, or that the crowd is going to move in on him, but nothing happens. I search the customers' faces. Everyone looks baffled. No one moves a muscle, except Patrick. With speedy expertise, he swipes his change off the counter and pushes me out, gripping my arms so I can't escape.

"She has been this difficult all day long," Patrick calls out as he pushes me out of the door, as if he has finally had it with this behavior of mine.

Before anyone in the store moves, Patrick rushes me to the car, pushes me inside and tears off. I see one of the customers open the store door and stick his head out, his face a question mark. We are off.

Back on route, I sense Patrick's gaze, and meet his eye. He looks hurt. In a flash, I am reminded of the last time we made love, just before he left for Belgium, just after he had revealed that his father had stabbed him in the knee, and I remember his plea, "Don't drop me. Don't let me down." I feel very guilty.

Patrick places the ham and cheese sandwich on my lap.

"Here, I did get that for you."

I stare at the food.

"Well, are you going to eat it?"

"I'm not hungry."

"You're not hungry?"

I look at him, puzzled.

"You're not hungry?" he repeats.

I shake my head. Patrick opens the sunroof, mumbling, "Ungrateful brat."

Patrick grabs the sandwich from my lap and throws it out. A few seconds later his arm reaches back; he feels for my leather book bag on the backseat, searches for the metal clasps, pushes down on one, then the other, flips the cover open, grabs my clothes and throws them up and out. The striped sweater, pants and shirts he bought me all systematically disappear through the sunroof. Last to go is the striped bikini. *My bikini!* I begin to cry, covering my face with my hands in shame. Patrick pulls over onto the shoulder and stops the car. He places his hands on my shoulders, so I face him directly.

"And now you're going to stop your bawling. I've had enough of your antics. This is the last time I'm telling you this."

Patrick seems so perfectly in control, so upper class, and such a stranger; it makes me feel as if I am a vulgar, pretentious brat. I am used to taking on shame—it is in fact my specialty—but if I once had the emotional distance to make it a part of my game, I lack this distance from Patrick.

Clinging to the idea of love out of survivalist fear, I focus on Patrick, the scary object of my affection who absolutely needs to be made whole so he can become the person who loves me once more. *If only I could understand....* I remember not showing gratitude when he bought me those clothes, and how it hurt him. Right afterwards he got the idea to stab me, and it makes me wonder if Patrick had perhaps felt like a lowlife and an ingrate right before he was stabbed. *What happened, that Patrick's father stabbed him?*

Patrick drives so fast that we turn onto the driveway of my family's house before dark. Mama waits outside by the front door. Patrick gets out of the car, stretches, and I notice that he exchanges a look with Mama. I try to catch his eye; he nods coldly.

Mama is exceptionally cheerful when I walk into the house, minutes after Patrick has backed up and driven off. When Mama notices my slight limp she turns cold, and I instantly receive an entire script: I am faking the limp to try to look like I am in pain, so as to make her feel guilty, to manipulate her into taking care of me, to attract her attention. Attracting attention is evil. I am evil.

"So, you've been traveling quite a bit, haven't you? Knokke, the South of France...and it's not finished. Papa called from Greece, and he's taking us to a five-star hotel on Rhodes in a few weeks. That's some summer you're having."

Family home, Belgium, June 1974

When I fail to show interest in food several days in a row, Mama stops offering. She is chipper these days, and likes to take me along on her errands. Vivacious, flirtatious yet contained, she is at her most charming to the men she runs into, and casually invites them to stop by our house for afternoon coffee. Her offers are met with enthusiastic acceptance. After accompanying Mama to the pharmacy one day, I plop onto a chair as soon as we are home. Mama opens a small bottle and hands me three large pills.

"Here, take these."

"No thanks."

Mama laughs and shakes her head, as if I've got the wrong idea completely.

"These will make you feel better. You're not looking good."

"No thanks."

"You have to take them," Mama says quietly.

"I don't *have* to take them," I counter.

Mama begins to quiver, as if to lash out, but instead says, "Here, you have to. It's for your own good."

She pours two more pills into her hand.

"Those are sleeping pills," I point out with the help of the label. "What are you trying to do?"

Mama shakes, jerks, and drops the bottle as she lunges, grabs my head in an arm grip and tries to stuff all five pills in my mouth. She shoves in a lot of bitter, dry, powdery stuff, and I spit and fight. Some of the goo is going down my throat. I wrestle my head free and stand, like a wobbly, bloody bull in the arena, facing her. Mama grabs the bottle and shakes more pills into her hand. I run, but my injured knee slows me down. She catches me and lowers her pointed elbow into my shoulder.

"Open!" she screams.

Tears fill my eyes from the pain. Another handful of pills is shoved into my mouth. Mama sticks her thumb and index finger down my throat. I convulse. Pointing at my mouth, I plead with Mama through stuck tears. *Don't you understand?*

Mama runs off, returns with water, pulls my head back and puts the glass to my lips. I spit the water out together with much of the incredibly bitter slime. Mama grabs my head in a tight grip.

"Now don't spit!" she screams "Or I'll have to start all over again!"

She pours water into my mouth, much of which runs down my face and body. Mama puts her hand over my mouth.

"Now swallow it! SWALLOW IT!" she shrieks.

Again and again, I swallow, seven tablets at least. I fall down, exhausted. Mama drags me to my bedroom and puts me on my bed. Lying on my stomach, I don't want to sleep; I want to know why she needs me to be asleep. I concentrate on listening for sounds, forcing myself to stay conscious. Being the last of three on a gravel road, our house only gets traffic from visitors. Occasional gusts of wind rustle the foliage, a bird calls, and after a half hour or so the first car arrives, one that sounds exceedingly familiar, like a Porsche 911.

For the first time since Patrick dropped me off and exchanged that look with Mama, I feel a spark of hope. He must have come for me, or Mama wouldn't have drugged me.

I want to get up but can't move. Facing the wall, I hear their voices coming in my direction, though I can't make out what they are saying. They are in my room and stop talking. I try to move, at least my head, and can't. Finally, Patrick's voice pricks through the silence.

"You drugged her, didn't you?

"Nooooooo," Mama answers in a sing-song voice.

Mama does have childish excitement in her voice, but for the first time, she seems to be mocking her own tone, like she has self-awareness and a sense of humor about her evil character.

"You're so bad," Patrick comments.

That was a compliment.

Long silence. Then they leave my room. No matter how hard I try, I cannot lift my head. I cannot move at all. *No, wait!* I move my fingertips. Then my hands. I practice until I can crawl my fingers to the edge of the bed. With a Herculean effort, I manage to crawl to the hallway towards Mama and Papa's bedroom, at the agonizing pace of at least a minute per foot. I hear vague noises. I feel sick. One hand on the ledge. Two. I raise myself up. With my hands on the door handle, I push it down with all my weight; the door opens. There they are, doing it, she naked, he dressed. He stops moving.

Mama calls out in triumph, "You thought you could have them all, didn't you?"

Everything stops. The couple looks as if they are endlessly far away. A beam of light starts where I am, expanding to throw light on them there in the distance. For a moment, tension seems to intensify the light. Patrick, now returned to full size, turns his head back so as to meet my gaze, and from that almost upside-down position shoots me an ice-cold glance that says, *"You trying to make me feel guilty?"*

His glute muscles tense as he thrusts himself inside my mother, who makes a happy, moaning sound.

I turn, hold the undulating door stile, convulse, and push myself out of the room, believing I will faint. No! Leaning against the oscillating wall, I drag myself to my room, arms spread out, hands, face and chest against the wall. I stumble, sort of run, and fall onto my bed. The room spins madly, but steady is the memory of the look in Patrick's eyes.

Family home, Belgium, July 1974

I find the bottle of pills neatly stored in the medicine cabinet in the bathroom, and don't have the energy to analyze or resist the loud voice in my head which tells me I have nothing left to live for and need to end my wretched life. I take all the remaining tablets, wash them down with lots of orange soda, and go to bed. I lose consciousness, and, after a long and deep sleep, wake up. Disappointed, I stay in bed. Sleepy and slightly woozy, I don't have the energy to get up, and remain immobile for another day.

The men are starting to make good on their promise to visit Mama. The Catholic village priest has been by every afternoon for a cigar and cognac. I feel so invisible that it surprises me when one day he says he is glad I am looking pretty again, because he had noticed that I was looking sickly the last couple of days. He smiles with a familiar glint in his brown eyes. Immediately, Mama sends a suspicious glare my way. I scurry to the kitchen, suddenly afraid that I was attracting the priest's attention on purpose. The thought that I am evil is constantly confirmed.

I steal deviled eggs off a freshly prepared platter, overhearing Mama as she gushes to the guests about our upcoming trip to Greece, where Papa is currently working. We are to stay in a five-star hotel at an extremely reduced rate, what with the war on Cyprus. The Americans are supposedly involved. Most tourists are staying out of the area, but not us. Mama can't wait to go along on one of Papa's trips. Then she jokes that her husband abandons her all the time; that she needs the company. "The company" takes bawdy delight in her joke, and Mama soaks up the attention like the first rays of sun after a lifetime of overcast skies.

One evening, Mama directs me to the car, and I can tell from her silence that it is network business. She drops me at a villa an hour's drive from our house. To my surprise, Michel Nihoul opens the door. As I had not spotted him at any network events ever since last winter in the greenhouse, I had hoped to never set eyes on him again. The feeling seems mutual: his face turns sour when he sees me. I slip past him into the darkened space, crowded with partiers. A man stops me, someone I never noticed before but who seems perfectly comfortable in this setting. He offers me a drink. He is clearly not new—it's me; I have been out of the loop. I observe the man, tune in. *Nothing*. I don't know anymore. The blood drains from my head. I accept the drink. Nihoul hurries over, shoots me an irritated look, apologizes to the man, explaining that I am not available, and directs me off to the side.

"You can go over there and wait for your boyfriend."

Instantly, out of the depths of my soul, hope springs up. Soon, Patrick appears, nudges, and I run after him up the stairs to a bedroom.

Patrick sits down on a polyester cover over a too-soft mattress, elbows leaning on his spread-out knees. As hard as I can, I slap his face. He puts his hand on his cheek and looks up, rubbing his cheek and sort of smiling, like "that was hard, but I have a sense of humor about it." *Oh, you think it was funny?* I think, and spit. He slowly wipes the slime off his nose and cheek and wipes his hand on his jeans.

"What am I even doing here with you? You want to have sex? Is that it?"

He frowns. *Yeah, that's it. You have a problem with that?*

"Dirty pedophile."

Patrick laughs like he appreciates a good joke.

"Your breath stinks, just like hers. You're disgusting. I don't want to have sex with you."

"What are you making such a big deal about? I was just...." He slowly shakes his head looking down. "I was just satisfying some kind of scientific curiosity. It wasn't serious."

"Scientific?"

Patrick nods and smiles impishly.

"You know, since you're related."

"I heard you when you were in my room. I heard you when you said she drugged me. You knew that. And you went ahead anyway. And then when I saw you, you didn't stop. And afterwards you didn't come to me. You completely betrayed me."

"No, I didn't," Patrick replies humorlessly. "I'm not a traitor."

"That is all you are. A big, fat traitor. Traitor! Traitor!"

Patrick suddenly has me by the hair, pulling my head back, so I am looking up, staring into his face.

"You little brat, you're only alive because of my protection. If it weren't for that, they'd have gotten rid of you a long time ago. Everybody thinks you're a big pain in the ass. So don't start playing your little tricks and telling me lies, because I'll drop you just like that."

Patrick snaps his fingers hard, and releases my hair.

"Good. Good. Why don't you drop me? You betrayed me. Don't try to tell me it's not true. Don't lie. Drop me already, because you already dropped me. Be honest about it and really do it."

Patrick's balled fist hits my jawbone with such force that I fly backwards and hit the ground. He pulls me up, throws me on the bed and punches me again. My left eye closes and rapidly swells.

It is not the first time I have dramatically fallen out of favor with a perpetrator. When I got angry with the global network Big Shot, he did not simply reject me, but made sure that by the time he was done with me, I would feel sub-human. The stain of that shame, my sense of being bad and worthless for speaking up, is far from healed. To the Big Shot, my refusal to go along with his plan and the glamorous future he had in store for me meant that I was vulgar and lowly. He made sure to impress upon me that my low birth was the cause of my "profanity," and then created conditions in which my physical self was so desecrated that I would feel as worthless as he believed me to be. It would take many years to realize that my action, which proved to this Big Shot that I was inferior, in fact proved that I had integrity.

My defiance towards Patrick started out as an unconventional way to please him, but in the current situation, it is a shaky attempt to hold onto the few shards of self-respect I had gathered with his support. When I confronted the network Big Shot, I expected to be killed, knowing full well that he was never going to allow my outburst. With Patrick, however, I have this faint hope that I can challenge him, and that he can love me through it.

"Are you going to stop it, yes or no?" Patrick screams.

What do you want me to stop? He hits me again, in the ribs, undoes his belt and jumps on me, pins me down. I resist. After a short struggle he manages to rape me. I resist, but find myself pondering the meaning of Patrick's cry, "Are you going to stop it or what?" Suddenly, right there in the middle of the forced sex, it becomes clear: he needs me to stop being this person who hates him.

When I hesitantly put my arms around him, Patrick responds tenderly. Giving up my mental resistance, I return to the state of intoxication in which Patrick is my true love, soothing the physical pain of the beating, of the rape, and the mental agony of the betrayal. All my feelings do find their way in; I feel the pain in all its depth, and whisper, "No. No. No. No."

When after hours of sex Patrick finally relents, I begin to cry, and Patrick kisses my tears, wipes them, mumbling, "My love. How I love you. It's you I love, no one else. I only love you."

I believe him; it makes me cry harder.

"I hurt you," he says.

Patrick examines my black eye, whereas I thought he was referring to sleeping with my mother. He cocks his head to the side and smiles apologetically.

"I'll get some ice downstairs. It's a little late, probably, but it might make you feel better."

I shake my head.

"I don't need ice."

Patrick embraces me, holds me, and covers me with kisses. I feel grateful.

"I'm sorry," he says.

We make love all night long. When I see thin stripes of light shining through the shutters of the one window in the room, announcing the new day, I wonder if Mama is waiting for me on the driveway, and what Patrick is going to do.

"Oh, it's day," he comments lightly, and begins to make love again.

I wonder if his comment was innocent. Patrick stops, looks me in the eye. Don't I know him anymore? He gives me a blank stare, then winks. It is already dark again when we leave the stuffy room, having had sex the whole night and the whole day, without food or sleep. As Patrick finally opens the door of the room, I begin, "Did you...."

I falter. Patrick gives me an open, questioning look.

"Please tell me," I persist, even though my mouth is parched with fear, "Did you ever sleep with Florence?"

Patrick looks me straight in the eye, seriously, until I'm calm and receptive.

"No. I never slept with her."

At first, his answer refuses to register. Then I hear the words again in my head, and it is as if I understand them only then. Patrick drives me back to Mama's house. When we pull up on the driveway, I start to open the car door.

"Hey, you're not even going to say goodbye?"

He reaches over to stop my hand on the handle, kisses me, flipping the lever under my seat, so we flop down.

"You know, I don't really want to let you go," Patrick says. "It's that I have a dinner with my parents tonight. I promised I'd be there."

He smiles apologetically. When we get it going, I am uncomfortably aware that Mama must be watching from the window.

After Patrick and I have sex in the driveway for one hour, Mama opens the door to let me in the house. She is visibly relieved to see my swollen, bruised face.

"I'm hungry," I announce with an authoritative nudge.

She seems surprised. Wasn't Patrick beating me up just now?

"Oh, this," I say, casually indicating my cheek. "This is old. We made up."

Mama glares spitefully and rushes off towards her bedroom. I head to the kitchen and scour the fridge for leftovers, without success. There are a few slices of slightly old bread in the basket, so I make myself a chocolate spread sandwich.

When I see myself in the bathroom mirror a short while later, I am aghast to discover that half of my face is completely disfigured. In a fit of panic, the knowledge surfaces in my consciousness that Patrick did this, that Mama expressed pleasure over it, and that neither was the least bit shocked.

I don't exist in their eyes. I serve as an extension of one or the other to play the part of what they can't face in themselves! I'm already dead!

The following morning at the kitchen table, mama gives my brother toast with jam and hot chocolate.

"What about me?" I dare to inquire. I can't remember the last time I was offered a meal.

"We don't have enough bread this morning because somebody ate it last night," Mama announces.

"Then go buy some," I shrug.

My brother, seven years old, breaks a piece of his toast and hands it to me. Mama stops him.

"No, no. She will just have to learn not to have her breakfast late at night. That's all. It's her own fault."

"Oh, it's my fault now," I snap.

Mama winces, her eyes widen and fill with tears.

I angrily blurt out, "I never screamed that I thought *you* could have them all!"

"What are you talking about?" Mama cries.

"Hah! I've never seen you so happy. Is it only when you can steal my guy away that you can be that happy? Is that it?"

"Your guy; listen to that. She's eleven years old and she's calling a grown man her guy. And anyway, I never said that. You misunderstood. I wasn't even talking to you. I didn't even know you were there. I'm thirty-five years old, I think I know what I say. I don't need you to come and tell me what I said."

"Then what did you mean?" I ask, confused and deflated, badly wanting to believe whatever she says.

"I don't even remember what I was talking about, because it wasn't anything important. Oh yes, now I remember, I was talking about your school. You thought you could do all your school books, your lessons and everything, and go away during exams, and still pass. That's what I said."

"*Do your school books*," is all I can focus on until I realize that I had forgotten all about school.

What is going to happen next fall? Is Mama saying that I have to double? I can't conceive of the humiliation. I start to cry, cradle my head in my arms. *How could I forget about school? What is wrong with me?* Mama puts a consoling hand on my shoulder.

"But Ann, you don't have to cry for that. It's not so bad. Maybe Papa can do something about it. Maybe he could go talk to the nuns once he gets back from Greece."

I look up into Mama's friendly eyes.

"You think?"

"We'll see," Mama says with a little laugh. "We can always try."

"What happened to your face?" my brother asks.

Before I can think of a suitable reply, Mama interjects, "Ann was very silly. You know what she did?"

My brother smiles and shakes his head.

"She walked right into the swing, and it hit her eye."

That afternoon, the priest, leaning back in a comfortable armchair, feet up, cigar in the corner of his lips and cognac tumbler in hand, is so shocked when I enter the living room that he jerks forward.

"Ann, what has happened to you?" he exclaims.

"She walked right into the swing yesterday," Mama quickly volunteers.

"How did you do that?" he asks me. "How could you have hit your face like that?"

"Her brother was swinging, and Ann didn't look when she passed in front of him. Right, Ann?"

Mama smiles at me, like we're getting away with our little secret, and isn't it fun?

Later in the afternoon, a friend of Papa, a missionary to Congo back home on vacation in Belgium, walks up the driveway to join Mama and the priest. When I open the door, he shakes hands and comments that I've gotten big. He glances at the contusion as if it made him angry. Once Mama is pouring liqueur for the missionary he remarks, "And what pranks has that daughter of yours been up to, huh?"

"Ran right into the swing," the priest calls out. "In the backyard."

He points his thumb in the direction of the backyard and begins to laugh.

"That must have been quite a bang, when that hit," he goes on. "I hope you didn't scare the neighbors, Ann. It's always so quiet here; they might have thought the roof came crashing down."

Mama joins him in merry laughter, and so does the missionary.

"You sure made a mess of your face!" the missionary jokes.

In the following days, more visitors comment and joke about my bruise, which has turned a reddish brown. When my little brother is present, he does not deny that I walked into him when he was swinging, and the next day he talks about it as if he remembers it so, without being let in on the secret. At one point, I picture myself walking into the swing, an image that has been called and recalled in the past few days, and I'm suddenly confused. *Isn't this a real memory? Didn't I walk into the swing?* Wasn't I in the backyard, making my way over to one swing, passing in front of my brother, not judging his swing range, not paying attention where I was walking, and didn't I get hit by the wooden seat corner, as my brother swung forward? *Isn't that how I got this bruise?* It seems that way. When I undress later that night, observing all the other bruises on my body, I wonder if I got those from the fall, when the force of the swing knocked me to the ground.

Mama, completely in her element, has been busy spoiling the men with amuse-bouches, which I snack on excessively. The visitors are also served copious amounts of beer and liqueur; a bowl with various cigarette brands adorns the coffee table, and every afternoon the atmosphere in our house is that of a regular party den. With her newfound charm, Mama is less subservient and less eager to please, which makes her all the more pleasing. That is why it comes as a surprise when one day, alone with me, she reverts to her little girl behavior, acting oh-so-excited.

"Today," she announces with a conspiratorial giggle, "I'm going to go out for a while. I'm going to be gone the whole afternoon."

"Oh yes? Who are you going with?" I ask.

"A handsome young man, with blonde hair," Mama coos.

"Patrick!"

Mama stands before a mirror, puckers up her lips, and puts on red lipstick.

"He loves *me!*" I shout.

"But Ann," Mama says, "Why would he love you? You're just a child."

Grabbing a pack of cigarettes out of the bowl, I run out of the house, down the gravel road to the backyard of a nearby windmill, and climb up large packs of turf wrapped in yellow plastic, stacked like enormous playing blocks under a corrugated metal shelter. A half hour later Mama's car passes. As soon as I light up, I feel dizzy and sick. Still, I continue, deeply inhaling the smoke, the way Patrick does. My lungs burn. It hurts awfully. I immediately light up a new cigarette after the first and keep smoking. Focusing on the pain in my head and lungs, on the hand activity, the oral sensations, the sensations in the upper body—it all feels good; much better than the emotional pain over which I have no control.

The next day, Papa arrives home from Greece. Mama talks to him, and he goes to talk to the nuns at school, and it is arranged that I will start sixth grade next September without doing any make-up exams.

I don't see Patrick before leaving with the family to Rhodes, Greece. After one week, the five-star hotel where we are staying closes for lack of business due to the nearby war, and we have to move to a hotel with fewer stars. But not even that can dampen Mama's bubbly mood, or Papa's alcohol-induced cheerfulness.

CHAPTER THIRTEEN

Belgium, a Tuesday, August, 1974

I live on chocolate candy and orange ice pops, and avoid being in or near the house so that Mama won't have an opportunity to take me on another of her errands. There are no more parties at the house, not with Papa around, so she runs all the more errands. I hide around the neighborhood, in the wheat fields near the house, behind the windmill, or in the hidden dirt roads, smoking cigarettes.

One day I stray further from the house than usual, and run into Danny, Florence's boyfriend, smoking on his shiny blue 50cc Suzuki motorbike parked by a small chapel with a Mother Mary statue in a quiet country lane. When I approach, he recognizes me, and is clearly dismayed. I am scared to talk to him, but here's this little bubble of life dancing inside of me; if I don't do anything, that bubble will pop, and there will be no other.

"Hey. How's Peter?"

Danny frowns, so severely that the crease on his brow is clearly outlined behind the screen of blue curlicues of smoke he lets escape from his immobile open mouth.

"You really hurt his feelings," Danny states with the integrity and judgment of a real working-class boy.

"Me? I was waiting for him all night. I was really hurt."

"Is that true?" Danny asks.

"Of course it's true."

There comes Florence, walking towards us. Danny watches her, calmly smoking, knitting his brow. Florence kisses both my cheeks in a customary greeting, then kisses Danny on the mouth, perfectly nonchalant, as though Danny and I were not looking at her in the way that we are.

"So why did you tell me she wasn't interested in Peter?" Danny says to Florence, glaring.

"I told you, she has an older boyfriend," Florence answers without skipping a beat.

Florence smugly observes me.

"I waited there for hours, and then I came to your house and you said Peter wasn't interested in me," I say angrily.

For a split second, Florence shoots me an incredibly dirty look, and then turns to Danny.

"I don't remember her coming to my house, but what I told you is true. She's been dating an older guy for months."

"That's none of my business," Danny decides, flicking his cigarette butt all the way to the other side of the lane. He turns to me.

"So, you want to see him?"

Belgium, a Wednesday, August, 1974

The very next morning, Peter rides towards me on the lane with the chapel on a 50cc Suzuki motorcycle, shiny blue, just like Danny's. I don't recognize Peter, apart from his dark blonde, tousled hair, but when he smiles, his face brightens, his eyes light up, and everything we felt together comes flooding back. I remember his particular smile, with his beautiful mouth and widely spaced eyes, like two dancing lights. I've so lost the habit of smiling that it is as if my mouth is doing weird things.

"Nice bike," I say, trying hard to overcome this giddiness. "I thought you were too young to ride."

"I turned fourteen. So now I can ride."

"I thought you had to be sixteen. But oh, is this Danny's, maybe?"

"No, it's mine!" Peter says, a little offended.

He dismounts and parks the bike next to the monument of the Virgin Mary.

"Shall we walk?"

He places a hand tentatively over my shoulder, without putting any weight, waiting for my permission to touch, to walk. I nod, happy to be reminded of his gentle quality mixed with this peculiar authority.

"So, what is this I hear about a boyfriend?" Peter asks in a small voice.

"I think he's more my mother's boyfriend."

Peter looks at me, with his sweet smile, curious. I tell him that my mother drops me off at parties for grown-ups, where I sometimes see Florence because her parents are there. I check with Peter to see if I need to say more. I do.

"These parties, the grown-ups, they're nobles, and other important people, like politicians and doctors, and the children are there...I have to work there...you know...as a prostitute."

Peter stares wide-eyed.

"But I'm not a prostitute," I hasten to add.

Peter frowns and shakes his head.

"And this man—he's twenty-one—he liked me. And so, I had to think very hard, because the girls who are favored in this way, the way he favored me, they usually don't make it."

Once more, I check to see if I've said enough for Peter to understand. The lane ends, turns into a quiet country road, and we walk in the summer sun.

"First he made sure nobody else could have me, so that makes a lot of people mad, especially the other children."

"Like Florence."

"Yes, especially Florence. Because she likes him. So then afterwards, when you're dropped, they kill you."

Peter stops.

"They kill you?"

He turns to me. I nod. Peter's eyes fill with tears. As I explain to help Peter understand, the words and phrases flow from my mouth like a strong current releasing water into a liberating fall.

"And this man—Patrick is his name—he didn't even want sex for a half year, but he did protect me, so when my mother took me to the parties, I was there, but I didn't have to work. I think that's why Florence was so jealous, and I think that's why she made this arrangement with Danny, you know, how I met you. At that time, I'd not had sex with Patrick yet. It started afterwards. And then he went and had sex with my mother, but he didn't officially drop me yet. But I think this is going to happen very soon."

"You're saying very soon, you're going to be killed?" Peter asks in disbelief.

The feeling suddenly hits me. Everything I've said, what I live with every day, sounds so enormous, so extreme when I hear myself say it, that I need to remind myself that it is true. I never ran into the swing. Suddenly, my sight is clouded with tears. Peter looks on while I experience the emotions, then he takes me in his arms, and the same quiet, blissful feeling I experienced with him a few months ago at the construction site returns: I'm not thinking, not of the past or the future, just not thinking. There is nothing but stillness.

"I wish I could hold you like this forever, never let you go, so that nothing bad could ever happen to you again," Peter says.

After a little while, Peter asks, with an excited, charming smile, "You want to come with me?"

"To your house?"

"Around, anyway."

We turn to walk back towards the lane, where the bike is parked, tightly holding on to each other.

"What about you?" I ask. "What's your life like?"

"Nothing like yours," Peter laughs, self-deprecatingly.

"No? Is your mom nice?"

"No...or I don't know," Peter says with a frown, softly. "I haven't seen her in years. My parents broke up six years ago. That's when she left. I live with my father."

"She just left? You don't talk to her?"

"I don't want to."

Peter's face scrunches up with extreme, defensive anger. I pull him close. His face relaxes into a grateful smile before he slides into my arms.

"And Danny and those boys, they're your friends?"

"Sort of. I don't see them that much. I know a lot of kids from the neighborhood, but I don't really feel very close to anybody."

"Me neither," I chime in.

My anger over all the betrayals, recent and distant, is emphatically mirrored in Peter's eyes. I climb on the back of the motorcycle, feeling very close to Peter. We ride through the flat green countryside, past hamlets and pastures bordered with brooks and pollard willows on the way to the Antwerp suburb where Peter lives. After almost one hour, we pass a narrow bridge over a canal and enter a quiet residential neighborhood. Peter slows down to indicate a small red brick house as the one where he lives. At the end of the lane, Peter turns and drives up to the entrance of a wooded public area. We get off the bike, stretch our legs, stiff from the long ride, and walk along holding hands.

"Are you hungry?" Peter asks.

"I can't tell. I haven't been eating much, besides chocolate."

Peter protectively puts his arm around me.

"Really? Why?"

This kind invitation is all I need to tell Peter everything about Mama, who stopped offering meals recently; and about her leaving me to starve for five days in an empty mansion.

"The last time I asked for food, a few weeks ago, my mother wouldn't give me any. And it was just after Patrick was with me again, so, I guess I'm being punished again."

Peter's hurt laugh cuts through the woods. In a small glen where the canopy of tall spruces opens to let in the sun, he fluffs up dried needles.

"I'm going to get you a few things right now, and I'll be back very soon. Okay?"

I worry that I've chased him away, but Peter puts a reassuring arm around me.

"You're safe here, I promise. I just have to sort of inspect the grounds, you know—see if my father's home, my brothers, stuff like that—to see what we can do later on. But I'll bring food back, also."

Peter embraces me and we kiss, which immediately turns sexual. He stops, laughing.

"If we start that, I won't do anything else and we'll have to stay here in the woods all night without anything to eat. I'll be right back."

In spite of Peter's perfectly fine explanation, I still struggle with the worry that he does not want to have sex. Life has taught me that my entire value is based on my ability to get men to have sex with me.

Peter unglues himself and turns to go, but stops again.

"Umm, this Patrick, so he hasn't dropped you. Not yet, right? So, does that mean that you still, you know...that if, say tomorrow, he feels like, you know...."

I nod. A half hour later Peter is back with fresh food. He holds out a tomato. As I bite it, the juice trickles down my chin. Peter pulls out a napkin and eagerly wipes my mouth, looking like a caring doctor, with a slightly comical frown that turns one eyebrow up at the root, like a child imitating a grown-up. I feel so old.

He proceeds to feed me bite by bite. I tell Peter I rarely eat tomatoes, and that they never tasted this good. I tell Peter that before my chocolate diet, I ate spinach every day, because I had seen that it makes you strong in a Popeye cartoon, and I needed all the strength I could muster. I can't stop talking. Peter listens. After being fed a banana and orange for dessert, Peter reaches into his pocket and pulls out two chocolate candies. As we chew on the impossibly sticky bonbons, Peter sticks up his pointing finger and says, "Chocolate is good, as long as you have other things too, to balance it out."

I kiss Peter, push him down on the bed of dry needles. He gives me this smile. It looks like it's just for me, this impish joy over the pleasure I can give him.

"Have you been with other girls since the last time?"

"I don't want another girl," Peter answers with a high-pitched laugh.

With Peter, I seem to quickly switch from having far more mature to age-appropriate responses for my eleven years. With a look from his dancing eyes, Peter asks if he can lift my t-shirt and I am overcome with shyness. I would like to ask him to wait, but find myself frozen and incapable of expressing my needs. I nod, and then take the initiative, which makes me seem strong and mature. I pull him close and begin to make out. A blanket of sensual gratification quickly suffocates all awkwardness. Peter wants to slow down and I have fun playing with him, showing him the ropes. We spend the afternoon in the way we did at the construction site—delighting in the high of the togetherness and sharing the stillness.

Sometime during sex, I enter into a trance. Words emerge, escaping from the deepest, hidden part of my consciousness. To my own great surprise, I whisper, "I love you, Peter. I want to stay with you forever. I want to marry you."

Peter responds with perfect synchronicity, with perfect ardor, with perfect protective love, saying my words back.

Around four o'clock, Peter announces that it is time to go. I expect he is going to take me back home on the motorcycle, but the bike is gone from the entrance of the wood.

"Where is the motorbike? Are we walking?" I wonder.

"It's not far."

We walk to Peter's house, hand in hand. I look for the parked bike, but can't see it anywhere as we pass alongside the red brick house to the backyard and the backdoor. Peter lets me in and shows me to a small bathroom upstairs.

"This is my toothbrush. You can use it. You can just freshen up, or whatever, get ready for the night. You want my pajamas?"

My hand flies to my mouth. This laughing thing is all so new and awkward.

"I get to stay? Really?"

"I have a little tent in the backyard. It's all set up. In half an hour we have to be in there. And then we can spend the night. But tomorrow I'll have to take you back, otherwise it's going to start to look suspicious. Is there anything else you need in here?"

"A hairbrush?"

"My sister must have one somewhere. I'll find it."

In the next few hours, Peter busily comes and goes in the tiny tent in the backyard, making appearances with his family, getting reassurances no one will disturb him in the tent. Over our dinner of macaroni and cheese, Peter says, "You know how I said earlier that I didn't see Danny and those guys that much? Well in fact, I don't think I'll see them at all anymore. I mean I like Danny, but I don't want to go out and do stuff with those guys anymore like I used to. You know, like stealing and stuff. Whatever."

Peter shrugs and throws me a guilty look.

"You have enough bad stuff in your life without me making things hard for you too," he adds softly.

I give Peter a kiss.

"You're so sweet."

"Oh, but you make me."

Peter disappears to get dessert and returns with a plastic jar, proudly showing me the contents: ice cream with whipped cream. Later, with my head burrowed in his lap, Peter brushes my hair.

Castle, Rhode-Saint-Genese,
Belgium, a Friday, August 1974

Only a few hours ago I was with Peter, holding on for the long ride back to my village on the motorbike, and then the even longer, teary goodbye near my parents' house, knowing that we might not see each other again. Peter promised that he would not let it happen. He said he would try to take me back to his house again as soon as tomorrow, and that he was going to focus on finding a solution for me. He would have to talk to his father; he had to find a way to introduce the situation. It would not be easy, but there had to be a way, Peter had said, and he was determined to find one.

Mama was very upset that I had been gone the whole night, and now I realize why, as she drives me through the forest in Brussels to the small castle where I first met Patrick.

Mama drops me off by the entrance in broad daylight. There is nothing going on, certainly not an orgy, and I wonder why I am here. Patrick opens the door.

"Are you coming in?" he asks with a happy, sweet smile.

Instead of responding as I normally would, I freeze. Patrick's expression falls. He takes me straight up to the corner room in the back, flings himself on the bed, puts his hands behind his head and taps the mattress. I stare.

"Get over here!" he yells.

I move to the bed and sit down, stiffly facing away from him. Patrick caresses my back.

"Come on," Patrick says, trying to get through.

I turn my head and glance down at him. Patrick sits up and kisses my neck. I stiffen even more. Patrick kisses my cheek, my mouth. I fight it. Patrick strokes my body. I fight it. He touches me between the legs, rubs me through my jeans. *Oh sure, you think that's going to do it?* I think. Patrick chuckles, and continues to rub. His breathing accelerates. He gives me that look, ardent desire burning through his clear eyes. I avert my gaze.

Patrick lifts me off the bed so I sit on his hands, pushes his fingertips into my lower back. I concentrate on a point of the windowsill, stare, put all my concentration on a small chip in the paint. I feel Patrick's fingers, and remain cold. Patrick throws me on the bed and rips off my clothes. *Oh, he's going to rape me. That may have worked last time. Not again.* He sets me back on his hands and pushes himself inside. I feel it, and fight it.

"Come on, little one," Patrick pleads.

I fight it. Patrick stops. Sighs. A few silent seconds pass.

"You're not afraid anymore," Patrick observes.

My blank stare is met by an equally cold, equally defiant gaze from Patrick.

He pulls me off him, holds me out, and demonstratively opens his hands, so I drop down on the floor. He walks towards the door, rummages in his bag on a console table, and returns. From behind, he brusquely pulls me up by the shoulder of my t-shirt, so the neckline hem cuts into the flesh, and I feel a cold metal thing against my right temple. *Oh, he's putting his gun against my head,* I think, still indifferent.

Patrick puts his left hand under my chin and pulls my head back, keeping my head and the gun locked in place. I feel the metal warm up against my skin. I hear a metal spring bounce inside my head, and the loop pushes hard into my temple. A great rush whooshes through my brain and body; every nerve, every cell, every neutron seems to explode. *It's happening.*

The moment extends, seems to take forever, and then passes. The metal keeps pushing into my temple. He cocked the gun. I wait for another agitation. I keep waiting. I wait so long my thoughts begin to roam.

I guess this is real. I guess Patrick is really going to kill me.

It seems that I should be afraid, but now that the adrenaline has abated, I note with some surprise, I am still indifferent.

"Are you afraid now?" Patrick asks.

I become still in the knowledge that Patrick will pull the trigger if he doesn't like what I do or say next. In the silent tension, as I concentrate, I begin to relax. If the torturous mind control training prepared me for anything, it is a situation such as this one.

Patrick told me he uses his gun to break through the lies, that when you confront someone with their death, they reveal their truth. What is my truth? He wants me to drop the cold front and be the person who loves him.

I nod slightly, a yes as in "I give up," rather than "I am indeed afraid." Patrick removes the gun from my head. Absolutely nothing changes. I don't need to sigh with relief. I don't even move. I am once again attuned.

As Patrick lifts me up into his arms, I see great love in his eyes: love for my understanding, love for my love for him, and pain for the way he had to get it.

I think of Peter's smile, so light. Patrick heavily devours me. Our passion soon reaches the heights of human existence: the deepest pain felt not by one, but by two—and this human connection in what should be a lonely pit of darkness and suffering creates rare intimacy.

"It's because I love you that I do those things to you. Everything I do, it's only because I love you. Everything. Do you understand?"

Whispering, he adds, "Without you I don't exist."

Emotional pain of this magnitude leaves no room for kindness or generosity, which flow out of the abundance of love. The killers, the slaves, and the brokenhearted only know passion: the painful cry for love in its ruins.

Castle Van Revelingen,
Rhode-Saint-Genese, Belgium,
a Saturday morning, August 1974

Just like the first morning after we spent the night in this room, Patrick again appears with an enormous silver breakfast tray. And just like the first time, he makes a big show of pouring the hot milk and the chocolate out of two pitchers into one bowl. I dip the tip of a croissant into the warm cocoa, sweetened with four sugar cubes.

"How long has it been, anyway," Patrick mutters. "Three, no, four weeks. That's how long I didn't see you. Boy, I missed you."

I stare at him in disbelief. He looks on, uncomprehending, and continues.

"The very day after I saw you last, I left with my parents, and I just came back yesterday."

"You were gone?"

Patrick laughs ironically.

"Where were you?" I ask, incredulous.

Patrick lowers his gaze.

"Saint-Jean."

"You were in France the whole time?"

Patrick nods, frowning.

"You didn't come back to Belgium and see my mother?"

"No!" Patrick laughs.

"She's such a fucking liar."

"Hey. Watch your language."

"Well, she is."

"She's not so bad."

There is the role we are expected to play in life, prompted by a higher, unseen intelligence, and there is the role we are expected to play as lovers. When both parts are in alignment, love is possible; when they are not, love is bondage. In this moment, I feel bewildered.

"She stopped feeding me!" I yell.

"You know," Patrick ponders, "I have trouble believing that."

"You remember when you first talked to her, the morning after we first had sex in that villa not far from here, with the enormous lawn, and you went to see her while she was waiting in the car? That was after I told you she'd been taking me to this mansion where she'd left me to starve for five days, and you went to make sure she wouldn't take me there behind your back. Or am I wrong? Were you just asking for her phone number?"

Patrick shakes his head, doubling over with glee, like a kid who'd been stealing candy and finds out his mommy was in on it from the start.

"But now that I've gotten to know her better, she doesn't seem that bad. I don't know...." he says playfully.

"What, did she bake cookies for you or something?"

"Well...she has given me food."

"So, you *did* see her in the last three weeks!"

"No, no. That was when you were still in France," Patrick answers with a meek voice, a guilty look, and a pleased smile.

"If only I could cook," I sigh out loud, and bite into my croissant, trying to give Patrick a meaningful look, but I don't catch his eye, and feel stupid.

When Patrick glances at me, I turn ugly; my lips shrink, my eyes get smaller, and my skin turns sickly pale. I stuff the last piece of croissant in my mouth, but it's kind of too big.

"I want to leave," I state, detesting the sound of my voice.

"You want to go see your mother, is that it?"

"I just want to get away from you!"

"I came back from France just to see you and this is what I get!" Patrick screams.

He gets up, rushes off and turns around by the door.

"They're giving me this room for a whole week, and I'm not going to drive you back to Antwerp and then drive all the way back to France just because you're in a mood. Just sit here and stew."

Patrick leaves, slamming the door, then locking it. But after a few minutes, I hear the crick crack of the key in the door. Patrick enters and caresses my neck.

"It's not your fault, little one," he says softly.

Castle, Rhode-Saint-Genese, Belgium,
a Saturday evening, August 1974

There is an orgy tonight. All the adults are seasoned regulars, so it is not crowded, but there is a lot of noise and the atmosphere is weird and wild, as though having had to forego their Dionysian debaucheries on vacation, everyone is excited to be back. Florence is here; I avoid her. It is as though my magnetic field is so weak, my presence would not register anyway. The sickly fairy, too, absently roams the halls. Her eyes have a haunted nothingness about them, like two black holes. I search for Patrick without expecting to find him. Twice, I catch a glimpse, and he moves away. I have a vague notion that he is spending the night doing cocaine, going up to many rooms with many women, but the information never settles, and never solidifies into feeling.

It must be four in the morning when the music stops. I feel very strange and stringy, as though on cocaine with only negative side effects. An eerie silence is followed by a rumble and hushed voices. I notice some regulars filing into a library. Passing another open doorway, I am compelled to look in, and see Patrick and Florence talking. Patrick looks like he did when he picked me up in France, his face red, tense, and angry. When our eyes meet, his turn to ice.

I disappear into the library, as if the regulars will protect me from Patrick. They are huddled together, watching something. The dark-haired baron—my little friend Wouter's executioner—faces a small group. He is holding something. There is also something on the floor. Burlap. Light brown...dark brown...no, red. I don't know what he is holding. I can't see. *I don't want to.* I pass behind the group, wondering why I entered this room. After all these years, I would hope to know better. *I should leave now, before I see anything else.*

Whispers reach my ears: *"Il l'a décapité...."*

"Décapité..." What does that word mean again? Even though I know I should leave, my gaze turns in the direction everyone is looking. Through

the small herd, I see long, ash blonde hair, swaying. The baron is holding a thin braid. He is holding the sickly fairy's head by a braid, swinging it, like a pendulum, as her loose hair gently wafts through the air. Her blood is the red, the brown, drenching the burlap on the floor.

I rush out, back to the hallway, remembering that I had thought that the sickly fairy might not survive, and in my state of horror and bewilderment, I am convinced that this thought of mine is the reason for her death.

Patrick's hand brusquely grabs the back of my t-shirt. He pushes me down the hallway and outside, into his car.

Haemers residence, greater Brussels,
a Saturday night, August 1974

From a knife block set, Patrick pulls the largest one, an enormous chef's knife, and raises it at me.

"So, you've been fucking around."

I run. *Florence!* Patrick is after me in a flash. There is nowhere to go but up the royal blue carpeted stairs, with Patrick close behind.

"I thought you'd slept with my mother again!" I yell.

His limp may slow him down, but his legs are much longer than mine.

"You fucked him even before you fucked me!" Patrick screams.

"That was a rape! Florence set it up!"

Patrick grabs my right leg; I fall forward and struggle to get out of his grip.

"Oh yeah? And when you tried to see him afterwards, what was that? Was that rape?"

I squirm wildly while Patrick pulls my jeans down, and off.

"I'll make you know what it feels like!" Patrick cries.

As I squirm wildly, Patrick repeatedly cuts the back of both my knees.

I manage to pull myself free, push up, race up the landing and further up the stairs, blood flowing down my calves. Patrick catches up with me near the top landing, grabs me by the shoulders, and pushes me down. I fall; he pins me down and pulls me round on my back.

He'll stab me in the heart, I think, but I see no knife, just his eyes, and am amazed to see them beg in desperation.

"Is it because of my limp? Is that it?" Patrick cries, beside himself with grief and rage.

"What?"

"Is that why you don't love me?"

The discrepancy between his words and actions is so great that I can't hold on to both. I split, and leave reality. Breaking out in tears, I stretch my hands up as if nothing happened. Patrick releases me and looks on uncertainly. I put my arms around him.

"I love you too much."

Patrick's lips tentatively seek mine. Right there on the landing, with my feet resting on the steps and my knees bleeding, his hips rub between my thighs. Patrick also cries. Our tears merge, drift down my face and neck, as I escape to the velvet world in which I love Patrick more than I will ever love anyone else, and in which he loves me the same, where everything is soft and smooth and good, even the pain.

"It's you I love," I mumble through tears. "No one else."

"Me too."

After the make-up sex, we inspect my knees, crisscrossed with bleeding cuts and slashes, though none nearly as deep as his initial assault with the penknife. Patrick looks at my knees, then at the knife on the steps, then looks around in a daze.

"Is this where it happened to you?" I ask.

Patrick nods. I caress his face.

"It wasn't your fault."

"If you knew everything, you wouldn't say that."

"Tell me."

Patrick turns shy. With downcast eyes, he considers what to say. He slightly shakes his head.

"I can't."

"It's alright, you know."

"No, it's...I did something; I couldn't help myself. And my father...he was really hurt by that. Because he...because I...."

Patrick blushes, looks down and shakes his head.

"How could you have hurt him so much, when he was the adult?"

Patrick looks like he would like to speak, but again he shakes his head.

"You were innocent," I whisper.

Patrick smiles. Tremendous sadness fills his eyes.

"How old were you?"

"Twelve."

A very awkward moment passes between us, as our intelligence begs us to take note of the obvious, and yet neither of us allows it to land.

"Who took care of you afterwards?" I ask.

"My mother," Patrick answers with an embarrassed laugh.

I have been felled by a common head cold. Resting in Patrick's twin size bed, my head is stacked on four pillows to facilitate breathing. Patrick comes and goes. This morning he washed my knees with soap and water and prepared the bed for me, with a pillow under my knees and several towels on top to catch the last streaks of blood. He caressed me for a while and left, returning a few hours later with pastries and buttered bread with chocolate spread, placing the plate next to the bed. Then he went out to buy packs of paper tissues, dropping them off an hour later.

I have been awake, worrying about the lymph oozing from the wounds. It has dried, but now my knees are hot and bothersome. I can't stand to have anything covering them, even though I get bad chills. The cold began this morning, without warning, and immediately moved to the worst stage, exhibiting all possible symptoms at once. Even the backs of my eyeballs hurt, and terrible headaches pop up in different places. Tears keep flowing from my eyes because of the irritation.

Because of a strong but by now vague impression of something that happened earlier, I feel fat. I have been trying all day not to eat the bread on the plate next to the bed, but my memory, thoughts and feelings are all fractured, and so is my resolve. I eat the sandwich. And the croissant. The purple poster on the wall keeps reminding me of the time Patrick sang that song to me, as if I were his angel. I feel so guilty and worthless now, so dreadfully far from angelic. Patrick enters with a bowl of warm food, picking up the empty plate and replacing it with the full one. He smiles, and without saying a word, leaves.

On the fifth day, Patrick decides that I can walk well enough, and late that night drives me home. He is exactly the same he has been the whole time I was in his bed: gentlemanly, friendly, and calm. I feel that I have been an enormous burden.

Family home,
a Friday morning, August 1974

Last night, I quietly entered through the unlocked backdoor when Patrick dropped me off, and I have not seen Mama yet. She is now at breakfast in the kitchen with my little brother, and looks up with annoyed surprise. I pass through to the living room in my pajamas, walking carefully so as not to upset the itching scabs on my knees. Upon entering the living room, with its large picture windows looking out across the front lawn and the fields beyond, I suddenly see him. I can't believe my eyes. His back is turned, but it is Peter, sitting on his parked motorbike.

I sneak off to my bedroom, dress and quickly pack some clothes in my book bag. I feel the blood pulse through my head as I walk through the dark hallway, listening for Mama's sounds. She is still in the kitchen, in the back of the house. I think my brother might be playing in the backyard. I quietly grab a windbreaker and casually walk to the front door, yelling, "I'm going outside!"

Peter must hear that someone is walking down the driveway, but he keeps looking across the field, as if he were observing the landscape. When I am very near, he finally turns his head and looks extremely surprised and happy. I hurriedly want to hop on, but Peter stops me, looking me up and down, as if surprised to see me in one piece. He takes note of the wounds, and hugs me, holds me.

"Boy, I've been so worried. And look at you," Peter says, "I was right to worry. Come on, let's get out of here."

I hop on, Peter starts the bike up, and we are off. During the ride, my knees get numb. I don't care. I hold on tight to my hero.

Peter's family home,

Schoten, Belgium, a Friday, August 1974

When Peter and I arrive at his house, he helps me off the motorbike. My knees have no feeling at all and when I try to stand, I collapse. Peter carries me.

"I've been parked many hours in front of your house in the last few days. I'm so happy that you're alive, but what happened? What did they do to you?"

"Stabbed," I answer, looking lovingly into Peter's eyes as he carries me in the house and up the stairs to the bathroom.

Peter sets me down. I can stand. He hum-hums with little dry coughs as he gets to work, inspecting the bathroom cabinet for salves and bandages.

"Peter? I really need to wash up. Do you think that would be all right?"

Mild warm water runs over my head and body as I stand in the small tub, hidden by a tan, orange and yellow flowered shower curtain.

As I sit on a stool, Peter tends to my wounds like Mama never could. He looks me in the eye, with a serious look that is at once comical; and a surge of love wells up in me. Even though I can walk again, Peter insists on carrying me down the stairs. He sets me down in the yard, commenting how lucky we are that no one is around, and goes off to take care of a few things. After twenty minutes or so, he reappears with the tent and begins to set it up in the back of the yard while I sit and watch.

"I better hurry. My father's going to be home any minute."

"Great. I can't wait to meet him."

"I haven't talked to him yet. I will; I just want to do it right, to make sure he's not going to say no."

Peter throws me a sideways, troubled glance.

"But I'm going to try to keep you here as long as I can," he adds.

"Maybe your father won't want to help, no matter what."

"No, he'll want to. He's good. He's just simple, and it's complicated. I'm kind of young to have a girlfriend, but you—you're really young. And he will wonder how we met, because you're not from here. And he doesn't know anything about Danny and those guys of course. And that's without even bringing up your awful situation."

It suddenly strikes me that I had completely forgotten.

"But there's something else we could do."

"What?"

"We could run away."

Peter stops hammering the tent pole into the ground and stares at me for what seems like a very long time.

"I don't know if running away is a smart thing to do."

"On your motorcycle! We can ride all the way to the South of France. There are a lot of kids who get jobs for the summer. I'm sure we can still find something, and we can take the tent and live in it."

Peter frowns, and puts the wooden hammer aside.

"You know, kids who run away, they're found. And if we managed not to be found, it would be very hard. We wouldn't be able to go to school, and then we'd be forced to take low jobs for the rest of our lives. My dad is a worker at the sausage factory down the road. I don't want to do that when I grow up. I wouldn't want that for you. You're very pretty and sophisticated, and I want to be able to give you nice things, and if we run away, that can't happen."

"But if we don't leave I'll be killed!" I yell, angry.

Peter takes me in his arms.

"No. I will find a solution. I promise. Just let me work on it, so that I'm sure that I'm not messing up."

"But there's no time. You can't keep me in this tent and as soon as you take me home Patrick will come and get me again."

I proceed to angrily list all the things Patrick did in the past days, and conclude, "He's crazy. He says that he does these things because he loves me. He's going to kill me!"

Peter, tears in his eyes, tries to rock me, but I push him away.

"The motorbike is right there. It's not that hard," I continue, searching for the bike, nowhere to be seen.

Peter gives me another pained look. He sharply inhales as he intently focuses his gaze on me, but the force of his intent dissolves as he catches my eye, and he gently shakes his head.

"It's more complicated than that."

"But even if we have to work hard," I press on, "we'll find some way to change our situation later on. It'll be nice, because we'll be together."

Peter sort of shakes and waves his hands low down in a tense manner. He gets back to work, pulling at a loop and fastening it with a picket.

"Anneke, you just have to let me work on it. Trust me. Okay?"

Peter has made a bed just like Patrick did, with many pillows under my head and a few under my knees. He now enters the tent holding a big plate of spaghetti with tomato sauce and proudly presents it to me. I break into tears.

"Oh Peter, I can't eat that...."

Peter puts the plate aside and comes to sit by my side. I can't stop weeping. Peter lies down next to me, caresses my face, wipes my tears and gently shushes me.

"I can't even tell you," I sob. "It's too horrible."

"You can tell me."

I shake my head as the tears keep flowing.

"Why do you love me?" I wonder out loud. "I give you nothing but trouble."

"I gave you very big trouble. And you were very nice about it. Your trouble is not even your fault."

I remember Peter apologizing to me; his dark side had been recognized and accepted, and maybe that is what makes us feel loved.

"But maybe it is, Peter. Maybe it is all my fault. I'm not that good, you know."

"Oh, but you are," Peter says without skipping a beat.

"If you knew me better, you wouldn't say that."

"Try me," Peter says.

I think of Patrick, and how I just said to Peter what Patrick said to me, and how Patrick got shy and blushed.

"No, you don't understand. You see, Peter, I love the gangster. I love you too, but I don't know; I can't help loving him. I think I love him more than you. He found out about you; Florence told him. That's why he got so mad that he stabbed me."

"Right! He got so mad he stabbed you when he heard you had someone else, but he made you watch him have sex with your mother, and that was okay with him? He can do whatever he wants but if you do something he doesn't like, he's going to stab you, or who knows what else?"

Ashamed, I begin to cry, and avert my head.

"But don't you think it's horrible that I feel that way, that I told you? Don't you think I'm horrible?"

Peter douses my face with soft kisses.

"You?"

I pull Peter closer, but he refrains.

"Your knees. I don't want to do anything that might hurt you."

"Peter, I'll be alright, really."

"Okay, but you don't move. Promise."

Later that evening, Peter turns towards the cold plate of spaghetti, gives me a look, pulls the plate closer. Now I can eat.

That night, a dream takes me back to infancy, to someone who took care of me, who loved me. Mémé ran the community-funded daycare center in Brussels, near the TV studios where Mama worked as a stenographer. I am held by Mémé, cuddled, cooed to, feeling warm. Wrapped against Mémé's body from the moment Mama leaves, Mémé takes care of four or five toddlers without having to put me down. Numb and dull from Mama's abuse,

I am safe in the makeshift wrap, but, angry at Mémé over our separation, I turn my head aside, averting my gaze. It is alright to be angry now; she understands how much I've been hurt away from her. I enjoy her fussing over me, caressing my head, saying sweet things in a consoling language, soft and melodious. I can feel that Mémé loves me; I am sweet and cute. I warm up to her, trust her again, can be myself again—a baby. What joy! I feel these sweet vibrations as waves of pleasure passing through my body. Love is bringing me back to life.

Mémé hands me back to Mama, the other mother I love so much—no, more—because if I don't love Mémé, she still loves me; whereas with Mama, I love her and love her and love her to pieces—and might my undying devotion not keep her wrath at bay for a few more minutes, so that I can live a few more minutes?

There is Mama's fear of me; her gaze makes me feel evil and powerful, powerfully evil, even though I am powerless, unable to form intelligible sounds, no motor control, no control over anything. I lie alone, crying, and hear the sound change as I continue to be ignored. My cries sound ugly, as they must sound to Mama. After endless agony, long after the cries have died out, long after I have turned dull and numb, Mama brusquely grabs me. This touch, albeit rough, this attention, albeit in anger, is good. The pain in my ankles and feet is intense as Mama pulls me up to change a soiled cloth diaper. I feel incredibly filthy and bad and undeserving. Hanging upside down, Mama's furious anger is solidified into a thousand cold knives, going through me. Then the pain, the pain, the pain in the genital area—too much to bear. The extreme sexual sensations that accompany the pain—I can go there. I focus in on the arousal, until it is clear that Mama loves me; she gives me these sensations that feel good.

I wake up in Peter's tent, feeling aroused, in pain, and in fear. *The memories in the dream seemed so real.* What is this arousal that I have for Peter? Could it be a body signal I mistake for love, whereas it really serves as a catalyst for aggression? Is my sexual magnetic output programmed to draw me back to either side of the power pendulum, to enact the role of either the victim or the aggressor?

CHAPTER FOURTEEN

Castle, Belgium,
afternoon, early September, 1974

Patrick softly sways his head to a blues ballad as he cuts a line of cocaine with a razor blade on the glass-topped salon table, rolls up a twenty franc note, sniffs half the line through one nostril and the other half through the other.

Lamentations about unrequited love and loneliness and a mournful slide guitar set the mood. Patrick puts a comforting hand through my hair as he mouths along with the singer, crying that he is feeling so sad, that his love for his baby is all in vain.

Patrick shoots me a cold look, full of meaning.

We leave the salon in search of a bedroom. As we walk the halls, he opens one door after another, inspecting various rooms.

"I want to try something we've never done before," he confesses with a smile.

Standing behind me, he puts his arms around me. When Patrick decides on a room that seems in no way different from the others, he smiles excitedly and begins to kiss me on the bed.

"Do you need the coke now just to be with me?" I ask.

"Never!"

A little while later I ask, "Then why?"

Patrick laughs, exasperated at my insistence.

"Because I'd never have the guts to do what I want to do. I'd be too shy."

"What is it?"

Patrick responds with more kisses.

He is so amazingly methodical. *Why do I like that so much about him? Why can't I help liking him so much?*

He brings his hand down my back and down in my underwear, stroking my buttocks. He unbuttons my pants, pulls them off, puts me on my stomach and continues to stroke me.

"How I love your behind," he confesses.

I look back to make sure, and yes, Patrick is blushing, fiercely.

"Why?" I ask. My cheeks are burning as well.

"It's so little."

"Like yours."

Patrick laughs hard, embarrassed. He lays down on top of me, kisses me more, slightly rubbing himself against the skin of my lower back, aroused.

"Patrick, I can't. I can't do that."

"Why not?"

"I can't even tell you."

Patrick slides off a little, so he lies more next to me than on me, and strokes my head and back.

"But do. I have to know."

Patrick is so excited his breathing is shallow. The air is charged with sexual tension.

"I can't talk about that. It's too...."

I sigh. I can't.

"But I understand," Patrick says. "You're too ashamed, but it's alright. I really understand."

"No, it's...do you remember I told you about the first time I was brought to the network? About the old guy?"

"Of course."

"When I arrived, he was sort of in Nihoul's job, I think, and the couple—the cleaning lady and her husband—showed him the girls they'd brought, me included. He nodded, but he seemed put out, and then he asked if they didn't have any boys, but they didn't, not that night. So, he looked at me again. My hair was really short. My mother had it cut like that, even if I hated it. And then I felt him becoming interested."

As I am whispering, Patrick and I lie very close, unmoving, on our stomachs. As we are enveloped by the shame that overshadowed my experience, the sexual energy intensifies, and my telling of the story has become erotic foreplay.

"He used me as a boy," I whisper, and instantly Patrick is drawn onto me again, and I feel him against my lower back, and I find myself breathing, murmuring.

"That was the show you were talking about? On the stage?" Patrick asks, controlling his breathing.

"You remember that?" I exclaim in surprise.

There is no answer, and I, too, would like to stop talking and enjoy the erotic sensations in my attunement with Patrick, because, while that feels good, I am also feeling unwell, as if I'm going to be very, very sick.

"That was different. That was afterwards. With the husband of the couple that brought me there."

"What was that?"

Lying absolutely still helps with the nausea. Short of breath, in an agitated whisper, I relate the events from the past. Shame seems to enshroud us like a separate entity.

ANNEKE LUCAS   189

"They put a metal collar around my neck, with a chain attached to it. The husband of the cleaning lady walked me around the stage. I had to crawl on my hands and knees, naked."

I had thought that the sexual vibe would certainly dissipate with this, but the opposite is true: the nausea dissipates.

"Then he had to poop. He did it right there on the stage and I had to watch, and the people at the party, they were sort of watching too, and they were disgusted, making jokes and turning away, clasping their noses and stuff. He held me by the leash the whole time, grinning. When he was done, he got up and pulled me over and then pushed my face down so my nose almost touched it. He said, 'Come, doggy. Come on. Sniff it.'"

Patrick guides our focus towards the raw feeling, away from the repulsive physical facts, turning both of us into secret witnesses to the suffocating shame of this child in the story. Ashamed to behold such utter humiliation, as though it put both of us on the other side of shame in the S&M game, the excitement increases.

"So, I did. But then he pushed me even closer, and he told me to eat it. I ate it. And then he ordered me to say that I liked it, pulling the metal collar back so I choked. I said that I liked it."

After a very charged silence, Patrick, in disbelief, asks, "And after that, you stood up and shouted that they couldn't treat you this way? That you would tell on them?"

"That was later. After it was over and he had taken the leash and the collar off, he just left me there by myself. I felt like I was going to die. I had to do something, or else I surely would have died."

"But you'd already survived! You were alive!"

"I don't know."

The erotic stimulation increases. Patrick slides up and down on my back.

"I guess we never really know," he comments.

It was clear in the past that I was going to die unless I acted, did something drastic to assert my existence. Here I am with Patrick, who earlier tonight has indicated that his love for me is all in vain, but who is about to do exactly what was done to me during that night of never-ending, soul-slaying humiliations. And I have no sense that it is dead wrong, no platform to stand up for myself, no revolution to stoke.

"Don't worry; I'm not going to hurt you," Patrick says.

The shame and fear are just as great as in the past, as well as the pain. I have to give myself to Patrick; leave my body's sensations and just feel the emotions. I feel his excitement, his shame, his pleasure. *Stop thinking! Surrender.*

Uncharacteristically, Patrick moans loudly during the sex, and yells when he reaches orgasm. He instantly heads to the bathroom, which is right by the bed. The proximity between the two is the one difference between this room and the others, and with a vague presentiment of fear, I wonder if that is why he chose it.

Approaching the open bathroom door, I notice Patrick standing by the sink, his penis hanging over the porcelain rim. He cups running water into his hand and washes himself. He turns his head and gives me one of his icy stares.

"You know, you really should watch what you eat next time before you come over. This is disgusting."

Backyard, Peter's family home, Schoten, Belgium, afternoon, early September, 1974

Peter tentatively strokes my arm inside the tent.

"We can't have sex anymore," I command with a halting gesture.

"Okay," he answers, sweetly. "I wasn't trying anything."

I'm surprised at how well Peter takes my angry directive.

He should get mad at me. He shouldn't let me order him around. He should be more of a man!

"I don't know what happened, but if you could tell me...." Peter begins.

"NO!"

"I understand you, really I do," Peter says in a small voice.

I look at Peter, strongly derisive. His body seems so small and insignificant. *How could I ever have been attracted to him?* I wonder.

Peter trembles under my stare. I am disgusted at the sight of his apprehensive looks, feebly seeking my approval. I lie down on my back and block Peter out. I would like to understand my violent reactions towards him, unwelcome intruders into a brittle self-image. I like being with Peter better than with Patrick, but I like myself better when I'm with Patrick. With Patrick irrevocably in the role of the sadistic bad guy, I am the victim. That is not easy, but it is harder to be despicable, deriding Peter, whose only crime is that he does not have power in my eyes, which simply means that he does not harm me.

Is there no way to stop this dark flow, passed from one to another, down the spiral, from top to bottom, into the plumbless well, where the weakest, the lowest, the youngest, get the life beaten out of them? How can Peter regain power in my view?

"Peter," I exclaim. "We have to run away!"

I expect that my sudden shift, the hope and enthusiasm in my voice are going to immediately rub off on Peter, but his bearing remains placid.

"I told you before; it's not a good idea," he answers softly.

"It doesn't matter if it's a good idea or not. It's the only thing we can do!" I urge him on, still hopeful.

As Peter gently shakes his head, I wonder, exasperated, desperate, why Peter won't understand the greater implication of my need for him to comply. I jump up and run outside the tent.

"Don't," Peter cries weakly, "My dad's around!"

He hurries after me as I run out into the yard.

"Where's the motorcycle, Peter? Let's just go!"

Peter catches up with me and grabs my hand, gently pulling, trying to steer us back to our shelter.

"Where's the bike?"

"It's not here right now. Forget about the bike. The bike...."

Peter halts, considers something.

"We can't do this," he concludes.

"Then let's go see your father right now. Maybe he saw me already. This is our chance."

Peter's eyes glaze over and his hand, still holding mine, trembles violently. He awkwardly shakes his head.

"No. No."

The words burst out of Peter's mouth like inadvertently launched rockets, astonishing the astronaut and observer alike.

"Peter. Please."

"Let me take care of you here," Peter implores me.

He hesitantly caresses my cheek. I swat his hand away, follow him back to the tent and crawl inside. Lying on the air mattress, I soon feel Peter's hand on my thigh.

"Stop it! Stop touching me! I can't stand it right now!"

"Sweetheart," Peter entreats, "I'm just...."

"STOP. STOP. STOP!"

I hit Peter wherever I can. I turn away from him and roll up in a ball.

"I don't want you anymore," I yell.

"You mean right now?" Peter asks softly, afraid.

"No, forever," I shout. "It's over. I don't want to see you again. Just take me home."

"Anneke," Peter says softly, his hand flying to my hair. "Don't say that."

I lie motionless and submit to Peter stroking my head. His caresses decrease until his hand lies still. Then he removes it. I sit up.

"Okay. Can you take me home now?"

"I can't take you now.... You can sleep here by yourself if you want; I'll go inside, and tomorrow I can take you back, if you want."

"Okay."

When Peter turns and leaves. I suddenly experience a terrible hesitation, a loss of confidence so severe that I feel as if I am going to die. Some hours later, Peter quietly steals into the tent. I pretend to sleep as he sits still in the dark. When I hear a rustle indicating his departure, I am suddenly gripped by horrendous fear and cry out.

"Peter!"

He returns to my side without a word. I reach my arms up and we embrace. We lie together, completely still. We hold each other tight without concentrating on touch. Our sense of identity, gender, age—it is all gone; yet we are more keenly aware of who we are, connected on this subtlest, deepest level. There is some otherworldly feeling to this embrace, and something else, unsettling. I move. Peter tightens his hold. I gently push him out of my arms. He leaves the tent. A heavy pain enters my heart.

When Peter enters the tent at dawn, he looks fragile, and turns self-conscious as he smiles.

"You're sure you don't want to stay a little longer?"

I shake my head.

"We have to sneak past the side of the house, okay? Follow me."

We quietly creep through the backyard, then walk towards the woods on the dirt road. The motorbike is parked at the entrance of the little wood where we went the first time Peter had brought me here. I gather that Peter would never have parked his motorcycle this far from the house unless he wanted to hide his exit from his father.

"Are you keeping something a secret from me?" I ask with a conspiratorial smile.

"No."

We drive on the familiar narrow roads of the flat countryside dotted with church steeples, under a threateningly low sky, so gray the canals look like sewers. The heavy sky seems ready to burst any minute with fat raindrops as Peter stops the motorbike near my house. As soon as I alight, I am ready to briskly walk off.

"Anneke!"

I turn in my tracks and face him defiantly, impatiently.

"Aren't you even going to say goodbye?" Peter asks with a frail smile.

"Why should I? You don't care about me, why should I care about you?"

Peter's eyes widen in astonishment.

"Of course I care about you," he retorts. "More than anyone in the world."

"Oh yeah? Well, I don't care about you. You know that?"

"I don't believe that," Peter says with a nervous laugh.

"I don't. It's the truth. I don't love you. I never loved you. I love Patrick. You're too little for me. And you're not good-looking, like he is."

Every one of my utterances makes Peter jerk, like a swing of a sledgehammer hitting his chest. I am so indifferent, my coldness must have frozen the rain into the clouds, because it still is not coming down.

"Your nose is too narrow," I add.

"You can't just insult me like that. There's no need for that!" he yells.

I laugh at Peter. Not out loud, not very obvious, but clearly enough. Peter seems to physically whither. Then, in an amazing bout, he straightens his spine, kicks the starter and shoots back as he revs up the motor by turning the right handle, flicking his wrist up and down.

"You can't do this to me. I am going to get over this. I'm not going to let you do this to me."

Peter drives off. It still hasn't started to rain, but it should, any second now. From beneath the canopy of leaves, it almost looks like night under the dark sky. There is no hellish glow. There is no fire and no debris spouting from the depths. The devastation and destruction are not visible, but frozen into the hearts of lovers.

Uccle Fort-Jaco, Brussels,
Thursday morning, September 12, 1974

After spending the night, once again, in the upstairs corner room in the small castle in Rhode-Saint-Genese, Patrick drives me to the neighboring Brussels commune of Uccle Fort-Jaco. The Porsche screeches to a halt on the wet pavement, right in front of the bakery we have visited once before. As we get out of the car, Patrick explains, "This is one of the best bakeries in Brussels; that's why we drove here."

As we enter, Patrick orders two croissants. I remember well how self-conscious he got last time, when the baker's woman eyed him suspiciously, and I don't care to take note of how confident Patrick is this time around. I keep thinking of Peter, and that I said his nose was too narrow.

Back in 1972, during my first encounter with the network Big Shot, I had observed that he was self-conscious about his nose, and I had told him that it was good-looking. That compliment was uttered in a crucial, life-or-death moment when I was moved by sudden grace, helping me to see a little boy inside a monster, and find what I needed to say to save my life. Also, when I had first met Peter last year, he witnessed his then-friend threaten to cut my nose with a penknife. Maybe I was getting revenge on Peter for his friend's action, or for everything I have ever been forced to do.

I have been sullen and silent with Patrick, and he bestows a charming smile on the young woman behind the counter, who giggles. I sigh audibly and roll my eyes. The woman looks on in surprise, as does Patrick. I shoot him a jealous look. He laughs, which makes me so furious that I don't want to follow him out. Patrick stands in the open doorway of the bakery with an amused look on his face, as in "Are you really going to stay here?" I suddenly take note of his large bare feet, stuck in ivory and red horse-bit loafers.

Part of my training in Germany had been to spot men's weaknesses, which had become an automated sixth sense. The purpose for having my gift of perception honed with mind control tactics was to optimize my service, so as to put a soothing balm of peace on my perpetrators' deepest wounds, only to report back to my Big Shot owner for whom I was to spy. While I have employed this gift mostly to better placate my perpetrators, I have never before used it in anger.

Patrick decides we should go for a stroll, since the downpour that began after Peter left has finally let up. As we walk along the road and turn into the forest, my attention remains riveted on Patrick's shoes. *Look at him walking amidst all these fancy cars and people with those shoes as a passport into their world. As if he didn't need his gun to get their respect.*

When we enter the woods, I wish I were going for a walk with Peter instead of Patrick. We turn into a large, manicured lane lined with tall, straight trees. Well-dressed citizens cross our path, and Patrick greets them with an irritating confidence which I suspect he derives from the shoes he is wearing. Walking deliberately, without a limp, he seems to be making the extra effort to belong to the upscale crowd. When we pass a brown brick chalet, I pull Patrick by the hand towards a rugged path. He follows along, laughing patronizingly.

"I just don't want to get my shoes wet and dirty."

I stare at his feet, then at him.

"My father says the shoes make the man," Patrick says proudly.

Reminded of Patrick's tragic loyalty to his father, a dark influx of thoughts suggests that Patrick's relationship to his shoes is deeply linked to his perception of his father. As if blind faith in his father's quote hides the irreparable damage caused by that same father. *His father was probably being sarcastic*, I think.

I try to absorb the pristine beauty of the forest, but when Patrick greets a passer-by with this forced gaiety that has been grating my nerves all morning, I run off, into the woods, up a little hill. I stop and turn around, smiling insolently at Patrick. Patrick stands nailed to the ground.

"What are you waiting for?" I tease him.

Patrick indicates his shoes.

"The Guccis. Did you forget?"

"Your shoes shouldn't stop you from going somewhere," I laugh.

Patrick looks stunned and helpless.

"You can just clean them," I add flatly.

"No, no. I don't want to get dirt inside either. Come on. Come back."

"I don't want to."

I cross my arms and stand on the slope, defiantly facing Patrick.

"Get over here," Patrick says, brusquely shaking his finger down so it points to the ground where he is standing. "Get over here!" he repeats.

The memories of Patrick's derision for me melt into derision for his powerlessness with his shoes. *Look at him standing there, like an idiot, with his stupid clown shoes*, I think.

I turn and dart off, up the knoll, higher, through the wet leaves. Soon, I hear Patrick's arrhythmical tread rustling the leaves. He pounces, roughly throws me down on the soaked, muddy carpet. My wrist twists under my body weight. I turn over and shout, "You hurt my wrist!"

Patrick grabs me by the sore wrist and drags me through the bed of leaves.

"Get up and walk!" he screams.

"I can't!" I yell back.

Patrick suddenly stops, throws me down as if I were a mail package, and observes his right foot.

"There's a scratch."

He lifts his foot up to examine the shoe more closely, balancing on his other foot. He slaps the dirt off the damaged shoe to make sure.

"It's scratched," he laments. "You ruined my shoes."

"You. Hurt. My. Wrist."

"Get up." Patrick commands curtly.

He grabs me by the back of my anorak, pulls me up and pushes me out in front of him. I am smeared with mud, there are leaves in my unkempt hair, and it starts to rain. As Patrick pushes me through the woods and onto the path, a couple approaches from the opposite direction. Patrick is visibly self-conscious and meets the pair of well-bred citizens under their umbrellas with a tight-lipped smile. All the way back through the stately lane, Patrick greets passers-by with forced hellos and eager nods, met mostly with empty stares from underneath large umbrellas. When we get into the Porsche, appropriately parked right in front of the bakery, just like the morning after we first had sex, Patrick spins the car into the fastest ever U-turn and furiously races down the Avenue, back towards the castle.

Patrick throws me down on the rug in the corner room and punches me wherever he can with a closed fist. I am still defiantly staring into his insanely furious eyes.

"I don't love you!" I yell. "I love Peter. And he loves me!"

Patrick has his fist raised, aimed to strike again, but holds it up, frozen in the air.

"*Le petit Pierre?*" he asks, using the French name for Peter. "The other one?"

"That's right," I shoot back a lot less confidently, surprised by Patrick's sudden casualness.

Patrick stops beating me and straightens himself, appearing to think things over.

"He's nice to me even when I'm not nice to him. All you do is hurt me. I'm tired of being hurt. I don't care what you do anymore."

Patrick slightly shakes his head, seems not to hear me, as though my words could hinder his concentration.

"So, you love him?" he asks, deadpan, as if double-checking some neutral fact.

Now I'm scared. Patrick, still apparently lost in thought, is nodding his head.

"Okay," Patrick says, as if he is seeing reason. "Here's what I'm going to do. I'm going to kill the little bastard."

I instantly throw myself on Patrick and cling to his neck with all my might.

"NO! You don't need to kill him. I broke up with him. I'm never going to see him again!"

"I thought you just said you loved him," Patrick says calmly, trying to peel my hands apart behind his neck.

"Only because I was so mad at you, but it's true. I broke up with him because I love you. That's what I told him. You can go and ask him if you want, he'll only tell you the same thing I'm telling you."

Patrick pries my hands open and throws me off him.

"I really hate it when you lie to me," he comments as he moves to leave, towards the door.

I rush after him.

"NO! I didn't lie, I'm telling the truth. Please Patrick, believe me. Go ask him. He was really hurt. I felt bad because I was so mean to him and that's why I was in a mood; but it really is true that I broke up with him and it really is true that I broke up with him because I love you. I just felt guilty but I did tell him I never wanted to see him again and I did tell him that I love you," I repeat frantically, breathlessly, trying to grab onto Patrick, trying to stop him. I put my arms around his waist and physically glue myself onto him. He tries to kick me off, push me off. I tenaciously cling to him.

"Patrick," I cry, "I'm sorry I made you run up the hill in the woods. I'm sorry that your shoe got scratched. I know that's what you're angry about, but I'll buy a new pair for you, I promise. I can get my father to give me the money."

"Your father can't afford those shoes!" Patrick screams.

Patrick manages to pull me off him and throws me so that I fly several feet through the air and land awkwardly on my back. I roll up onto my feet and lunge at Patrick, who is opening the door. I grab his ankle, and, lying on my stomach on the floor, hold on.

"I beg you, Patrick, don't do this. I'm sorry about the shoe. I'm so sorry. I promise I'll never do anything you don't like again. I promise. Please Patrick. You have to believe me. Don't do this. Don't go."

"I can see that you really do love the little bastard, or you wouldn't care so much whether he lives or dies," Patrick says. "Now let go!"

Patrick kicks my hands hard with his free foot as he squeezes his body through the doorway. When he has finally freed himself, he shuts the door on my hands. The door closes and locks. I throw myself on the door.

"PATRICK! PATRICK! PATRICK!"

I bang my head against the door, trying to break through it. I bang my head hard. I bang my head hard. I bang my head hard. The door doesn't budge. I break into uncontrollable sobs. I scream. I sob so hard it seems that

I will suffocate. I scream and sob and violently bang my head into the door for hours. *Peter! Peter! Peter! I love you. Peter!*

After spending the day locked up in the corner room, rotating from absolute agony to deadly stupor to frantic reasoning why Patrick would not succeed in killing Peter, I hear the key in the lock and Patrick appears, looking sickly, deadly pale, a glazed, absent look in his eyes. He throws me one stern look that says it all.

"You didn't!"

"He's dead!" Patrick yells.

"But you're going to be caught. The police are going to find out it was you."

"He died of an accident!" Patrick cries out in the same angry tone.

Even though I hear Patrick's words, and even though I know they are true by looking at him, I can't believe that Peter is dead. *Peter. Peterke. I love you. Please, be alive.*

PETER BOSMANS
(5-31-1960 – 9-12-1974)

Traveling to the town of Schoten in Belgium to do research for this book in 2005, I found the house where Peter had taken me, rang the doorbell and briefly met Peter's father. On September 12, 1974, at 4:10 pm, upon returning home from work, he found Peter's lifeless body on the floor of the kitchen of their house. The stove was turned on. Gas was seeping out. The death was recorded as an accident.

In 1967, when he was seven years old, Peter was hit by a car. The accident sent him into a coma lasting two weeks. When he regained consciousness, his personality had changed: he had become aggressive. He was never tested for a neurological disorder and subsequently never diagnosed. One year after the accident, in 1968, Peter's parents divorced, after which he never saw his mother again.

Peter's father informed me that Peter never owned a motorcycle. Peter apparently had been borrowing his friend Danny's motorcycle, and had not been able to tell me.

During my brief meeting with Peter's father, who believed his son died of an accident, I could not bring myself to tell him the real cause of Peter's death. It seemed that revealing this would cause unnecessary suffering to a man who had made it clear he had never fully recovered from his loss.

CHAPTER FIFTEEN

Castle tower,

Belgium, September 1974

With enormous cushiony black leather headphones over my ears, I cut myself a line of cocaine on the salon table, as the careful drumbeat and sparse opening riffs of a current song rap their way to the comforting blast of torrential guitar music. A sharp inhale shoots the powder up my nostril, and all the good stuff fills my head. I listen intently to the words, and become entirely absorbed in them, in the music. I live in the guitar music, as if it is the only force in the universe that understands exactly how I feel, the only vibration to which I can tune in, to which I can perfectly connect. It is so perfect.

I connect even more with the guitar than the lyrics, though they are eerily appropriate, screaming for someone who has recently passed, demanding they wait on the other side of the veil. I am swept away by the music, riding the erotic guitar wave, wishing for nothing else but that music, that guitar, the vibration of that music that has become one with the vibration of my being, intimately bonded with that unending riff, totally wild, never chaotic. Only it is not enough; I want it more, I need it harder. *Play more, play harder. This is not enough!*

Patrick, sniffing, wipes his nose with the back of his hand and licks the leftover grains off. He lays me down, pulls down my jeans and penetrates.

I scoot back so my head hangs upside down off the foot end of the divan, throw my elbows back and hold the big leather muffs securely over my ears, to have sex—with the music. Just as the song comes on about the angel, which Patrick had once described as his dream for both of us, he runs his fingers over my face. I push Patrick's hand away. His eyes widen.

Hours later, or maybe the following day—I don't know—it is daytime, Patrick once again readies himself for sex. He lifts me on his hands, staggers, and leans my back against the wall, too intoxicated and exhausted to support my weight. He pushes himself inside. I feel it, but without the love, I cannot get excited, not even with all the cocaine. *This is boring.*

As soon as I have the thought, Patrick stops and looks me coldly in the eye.

"It's boring?" he double-checks.

I stare back. He nods thoughtfully. Then, keeping me on him, he lifts me up and walks over to the large, open tower window. I wonder if he is going to throw me out, and note that the prospect of being thrown to my death fails to cause panic, nor does it cause any other particular feeling, positive or negative.

After Patrick killed Peter, I knew I could never suffer more, and as soon as I realized it, a spiritual force descended on me. I became aware of a higher power, always at work within me and without me. It was as if my suffering drew me closer to this force, more real than anything, the One in a creation of eternal opposites and multiples, never one, never just life, but life and death.

Patrick sets me down on the windowsill. He pushes my upper body out the window. I drop backwards, and experience the adrenaline rush of the expectation of the fall, but instead of falling, I hang upside down from the sill, showered by a cold drizzle, with Patrick pulling at my hips to keep me up, continuing the sex.

He can barely keep my weight on his hands; there is a real chance he will let go. I see the park and the dark green landscape far below, or rather above me. I seem to be slipping. I am slipping. Patrick heavily catches my thigh and pulls me up, but his hands are wet from the rain, and he has trouble getting a hold. More of my weight is outside the tower than in. I may well fall. My fear is activated, and I notice that I am aroused.

It's true, I think. *This is not boring.*

By the same token, I note that whether it is boring or not, whether it is exciting or not, whether I am afraid or not, it's all the same to me. My indifference does not equal equanimity, but rather numbs anger and many other overwhelmingly negative emotions I could not possibly let myself feel; I am not unattached. Patrick has power over me, but neither of us are free. The powerful fear their love (weakness) as much as the powerless fear their power (badness), and fear ensnares everyone in their roles. The powerless want love, so, like children, they give it. The powerful take it, and, like adults, use it. True love is love with power, and true power is power with love.

Do with me what you will, I think. *Throw me out the window. Let go.* Patrick pulls me up in one sweeping motion. I sit on the windowsill, soaked and freezing. He gives me a look of tired defeat.

On the saggy divan near the stereo, about to put on headphones to listen to more music, I have this thought: *The worst has already happened to me; I have nothing to worry about.* Suddenly, a light, shining bright before my open eyes, bathes the room in unearthly beauty.

I'm on cocaine, I think. *Who knows what this is?*

The light persists. The room, the open window, the wooden sill, the gray sky outside, the white wall, the furniture—everything melts into the light. The beauty of these things, dissolving and reemerging in and out of the light is absolutely thrilling. The vibratory structure of the physical world, everything, me included, seems to flow out of this mellow yet bright light.

I cover my eyes with my hands, and am greeted by a great white sun surrounded by a golden ring in an indigo hemisphere. A vague dot appears in the center. Concentric circles begin to move, from the center outward, in ever-enlarging spheres. Watching the dazzling show of the rapid expansion of circles of light before my eyes, I am entirely peaceful, yet forewarned. Maybe the worst has not yet happened.

Villa near Bois de la Cambre, Brussels, Belgium, evening, October 1974

I have barely spent a day at school in the sixth grade. As soon as my bruises begin to heal, they are covered with new ones. After he beats me, Patrick wants to be tender, but I am too angry, and stay cold. This evening, we are in an upstairs bedroom, while an orgy is brewing downstairs. He observes my indifference, and angrily stops the intercourse.

"Why don't you go join the others downstairs? They're all there. All your little friends have arrived by now."

"My friends?

"Florence and the others."

"I don't have any friends."

"Is that so? Then what did you do before I started coming to the parties?"

"I tried to survive, just as always."

"After I started coming, you were also just surviving?"

I feel trapped, and look at him questioningly.

"You once mentioned that everything I do is just to survive, because I am a child and I have no choice," I answer.

Patrick laughs, loud, forced and cynical.

"Yes, I said that on the terrace in the South of France, didn't I? Where I took you because you wanted to go. So, the other kids didn't like you *before* you spent your time with me in the royal suites upstairs while they got fucked by old geezers in the dingy little maids' rooms?"

Wave after wave of self-loathing washes through me.

"ANSWER ME!" Patrick yells.

"It's true, they didn't like me," I mumble.

"It's funny that it took me such a long time to see why," Patrick mocks. "You are so arrogant. You just think you're better than everybody, don't you? In your sly little way, you find fault with everybody. You don't think you have to follow any rules. You're above it all. You never try to be nice to anybody. And then you're sad and shocked when nobody likes you."

I squint as his words enter like knives, cutting up my illusion of identity. Trembling with fear, my voice breaks.

"I thought you liked me."

It is as if the whole room suddenly melts. Patrick's feeling permeates it like a wave of astounding softness, and I collapse onto the floor, all strength and hardness seeping out of muscles and bones. Prostrated on the ground, I think, *you love me.* It may be only in feeling and not expressible in deeds; but I feel it, and feeling it gives me strength and the knowledge that I don't need to be liked, because it is much more important to be loved.

A forceful kick in my face throws me out of the crouched-down position onto my back, out of the mental process that led me to believe in a dream that has been keeping me alive for eleven years.

"I never loved you, you understand?" Patrick screams.

He delivers another blow to my face, and then another, and another, on my chest, on my arms. He gets up and kicks me in my side, kicks me hard all over my legs.

"The whole time I was seeing you, I was sleeping with other women. Women, girls, anybody; I fucked them. Florence; I fucked her many times. Your mother; I didn't just fuck her that one week; that kept on going. I wasn't in France for a whole month, I went back and forth, and I saw your mother in between, and many other women. I was lying to you the whole time. The whole time, you understand!"

Patrick pulls me up off the floor by the neckline of my shirt. I shield my face with my arms. As soon as he lets go of my shirt, I fall back down. He grabs me with both hands so I hang in the air.

"Get up! Get up and walk, already. Get up and walk out of here like a man. See if you'll be as arrogant as when you walked in here, strutting and cocky like you own the fucking place, like you can just take me for granted and treat me like shit, like I'm just going to put myself out for your sake and take care of you no matter what you do to me. Get out of here; there's a party downstairs; they're waiting for you. It's time to get back to work, little whore. That's all you are, you understand? A whore. A whore with pretensions! I can't think of anything more ridiculous and disgusting than a pretentious whore. Get out already, stupid fucking whore. Get out!"

Patrick pushes me. As soon as I am across the threshold, he shuts the door with a firm bang.

Once I hesitantly make my way down the dim stairway to the parlor floor, the first person I see is Florence. She grins, in the same way Mama did after Patrick beat me up the first time. Mama also looked relieved to see my bruises, satisfied to have physical proof that I am not loveable.

Wounded animal, I want to hide, but Florence leans against the wall along which I was trying to slither out of sight, blocking the way, arms crossed, smiling.

"I'm looking for a bathroom," I say, trying weakly to get past her.

"I'll show you."

She guides me along the wide hallway. A triangular window above the front door shows a rainy evening sky. A group of two girls and one boy, all a little bigger and older than me, cross our path, exchange looks with Florence, and join us. They are secretly having fun about something. Two younger girls walk towards us and when Florence nods, they join us as well.

Florence guides our group through a large smoky salon where the orgy, in spite of the early hour, is well underway, with busy network regulars in various states of undress, hardly taking note of the children stealing along the walls. Once our group is inside the bathroom, Florence shuts the door and switches on the glaring overhead light.

"Here you go," Florence announces, indicating the toilet.

I meekly shake my head, not understanding why the children would not just want to leave me alone. I am covered in large, dark red marks. One of the younger girls giggles. When I stare, her laugh turns hollow.

"What's the matter?" Florence smirks. "You don't like our company? You prefer to be with Patrick, maybe?"

I look blankly at Florence; mine is the only serious face in the room.

"See, we've all sort of been sharing him," Florence begins, looking at the older girls who send her significant glances. "But you didn't want to share, and it made us feel really sad, that you were so selfish."

Florence makes a sad clown face, and the children laugh.

"So, what happened?" Florence continues. "Aren't you with Patrick anymore?"

"I was just with him."

I expect I will be ridiculed, as the bruises should make it obvious what was going on, but instead Florence gets angry, and the other children turn deadly serious.

"I'm sure you're lying! You're always lying. You're such a liar you don't know a lie from the truth anymore!"

Florence gives me an incredibly dirty look, and I am thrown back into the past, seeing her glare at me in exactly the same way, by the little Mother Mary chapel, when her boyfriend Danny and I found out she had been lying to both of us about Peter, and we had exposed her.

Florence orders the boy and the biggest girl to grab me by the shoulders; they pull me back so I am awkwardly lying on the toilet, while the other girls grab my legs and hold them down. Florence pulls down my jeans and underwear, forces my legs open and examines my privates.

"Let's see," she says, "if you were really just with Patrick or not."

Her voice is controlled, but her chest rapidly lifts and lowers. She laughs a nasal sort of snicker. The other children, working hard to keep me in check, echo her laughter. My shame and humiliation over being exposed are so excruciating that I try with all my might to break loose, but the more I struggle, the more I sense Florence's excitement. Florence forces her fingers inside, masking her arousal with ever-louder snickers, enticing laughs from the other kids.

"You still don't get your period, do you?" Florence taunts. "You don't even have any hair."

Her loud cackles are rejoined by the mocking laughter of the other children. Rhythmically sliding her fingers in and out, Florence's agitation causes pearls of sweat to form on her brow and upper lip. In a casual tone she asks the other girls,

"You get your period, right?"

Each one of the bigger girls and one of the smaller ones nod affirmatively.

"I got mine when I was nine," Florence announces. "I've been pregnant already. I had to have an abortion. It was really scary and painful. I could have died. I always have to worry about that, every month, all the time."

Florence looks me in the eye, for a second revealing real pain. She stresses, "You have no idea how hard that is. You just have no idea. You have it so easy."

Florence works up a sweat, her cheeks blushing just like when she was once exposed while she was being raped. When she reaches the point at which garnering yet another conspiratorial laugh would be absolute overkill, she pulls her hand back and inspects her fingertips.

"No sperm," she concludes, shaking her head. "See? You were lying. You were not with Patrick."

"What are we going to do with her?" asks the boy.

It is the first time any of the others have opened their mouths, and I am surprised to hear a boy's voice, as if the male force were irrelevant in this settling of affairs. Patriarchy or not, The Mother has the power. Mama would have killed me early on if not for the other mother who loved me. Mama gets the men of the network to rape me. Florence once got boys to rape me; Florence's mother gets men to rape her. Florence snitches to Patrick and I am stabbed, Peter killed. Patrick is a bit-player in this drama ruled by envy: one female telling another to give up her power. I once believed that I deserved to be loved unconditionally. In the eyes of Florence and Mama, that self-esteem made me powerful in a way that girls are never supposed to be. We are to derive our power from our sexuality alone—compete for men and then manipulate them—and I have not played by the rules.

"Nihoul will tell us what to do with her," says Florence.

"Let's drag her over!" shouts one of the girls, gripping my leg in excitement.

Suddenly, my feet are forced up and swung into the air and my head falls back. I am pulled along by my hands and feet, across the room where the orgy is going on, the children laughing as they drag me. I try with all my might to lift up my head, to push my feet down and get my bearings, but this only exacerbates my fear.

The children place me down near Nihoul, who does not look too interested. As he takes a deep drag from his cigarette, he throws me a tired, sour glance, as in, "Are you never finished causing trouble?" Florence whispers something in Nihoul's ear that visibly enlivens him. My fear dissolves. My hour has come, but standing upright, self-esteem pours back into my body, molds it into a physical form of dignity, filling me with mental strength. I am ready to meet my fate.

I notice, behind the children, Patrick's figure at about a ten-foot distance. He is standing alone, casually observing the spectacle. Nihoul grabs me by the right wrist and pulls it, twists it, so my arm folds back painfully.

Nihoul points his burning cigarette at my forearm, a few inches from the elbow crease.

Patrick laughs sarcastically, making it very clear: *Don't expect any sympathy from me.* Nihoul digs the burning cigarette into the flesh of my arm. I smell the hairs and the flesh burning. My being concentrates into a single thought, which flows out of my body, straight to Patrick.

I don't need you! I will survive without you!

The burn on my arm fails to register. Patrick's wide-open eyes hold me, merge with me. Just like when I first met him, the surroundings, the room and all the people in it cease to exist. The energetic flow between our eyes reveals another universe, consisting of pure feeling, all of it passing through Patrick's crystal-clear eyes, as if the iris had receded, its hard color given way for emotional clarity.

The other children, extremely agitated, move about me and block Patrick from view. Nihoul says something I can't make out, and I am grabbed by the shoulders and forced to walk with the children and Nihoul, through the salon, out of the salon, through the hallway.

Nihoul directs some of the children to take me into a large bedroom. Passing through it, we reach a smaller, hidden room without windows, with an enormous old butcher's table, chapped and scratched and black with dried blood. I am made to lie on my back, ordered to spread arms and legs, and strapped down. The boy, the two older girls and one of the younger ones are here. Without Florence to lead them, they timidly retreat towards the door. Nihoul directs them to help tie me down.

"Come closer, come closer," Nihoul calls out abstractedly. "We all have to learn."

Barely paying attention to the children, his gaze downward, absent, this is the most relaxed I have ever seen Michel Nihoul. The various parts of the pasty, nondescript businessman have integrated into a real person, with thick, dark brown hair, alabaster skin, upper eyelids dropped and greenish eyes at rest, without his mandatory jokes and sleazy smile trying to please the big shots; without his sour reactions to Patrick's orders or my defiance. Nihoul rummages through a crate he has pulled out from underneath the butcher's block.

"Let's see what we've got here," he mumbles.

Under my gaze and over my body, he passes the children various instruments of torture. A penknife, scissors, a screwdriver, a razor blade, a fishhook.

"You see," Nihoul teaches the children, "It's very easy. All you do is something like this."

He sticks something that looks like a medical tool with a cone-shaped point into my arm, close to the messy, gaping wound of the cigarette burn. I breathe in slowly, and listen to the sound my breath makes in the back of my throat. Nihoul twists the cone into the ripped skin, digging deeper. I breathe out, making the same sound against the back of my throat, listening intently.

"See?" Nihoul says casually. "That's all it is. For now. For the beginning."

He nudges authoritatively, switches instruments, and drops the teeth of a mini-rake into the wound, creating three stripes of blood. The children gasp, and shoot into action to prick and cut my arms, legs and torso. They hardly touch the skin, and immediately pull back. As I focus on the breathing, every part of my body seems to fill with oxygen. Soon, I reach a deep state of relaxation and—to my amazement—I am pleasantly high. I expect that Nihoul is going to correct the children, and instruct them to puncture the skin.

"No, but you're barely getting in there," Nihoul comments. "You have to relax a little, and then just do it. Go in. Go on."

How funny that he said that about relaxing. That's what he is doing. That's what I am doing. That's what they should do.

The room is no longer a space with four walls and a butcher's block; everything is breathing, just like me. Everything is alive and part of life, and people are the most concentrated forms of energy: beautiful, complex life forms endowed with the keenest consciousness.

My smiling eyes find Nihoul's; he looks simply at me. For the first time since we have known each other—now that he definitely, finally has the power—we connect.

Immediately, a shift is reflected in Nihoul's eyes: they look less clear, as if a curtain of slime were pulled over them by an invisible pest that lives on his shoulder, whispering into his ear, "You're losing the relaxation contest with this little brat, you idiot. You better do something!" Nihoul smiles again, this time with his mouth only, whereas the eyes remain slimy. He grabs my cheeks and plies my face into a grimace.

"There, pretty girl. Not so pretty now, are we?"

He squeezes and pushes and twists my face, having fun with the results, laughing and showing the children. I breathe. The sound changes as Nihoul pulls on my lips and mouth. I hear the breath. I listen. And I see Nihoul.

What a little kid he is! How can such pettiness, such smallness, exist in a grown man? To think of the ridiculous importance, the weight, to think of the power given to evil! O darkness! O Lucifer! Here it is, in all its glory, making fun of my face.

Nihoul fishes for a thin bar of warped steel, like a drill bit with a square tip, which comes flying towards my eye. I squint, and feel the metal ripping skin as it hits my cheekbone.

"There, a souvenir," Nihoul jokes. "Go on," he orders the other children. "What are you waiting for, an official invitation?"

Nihoul is back to his Nihoul-role, forced by the creature on his shoulder to act funny. The room is a room again, with a bare light bulb hanging from the ceiling, and I see my bruised, bloody body being attacked by frightened children. Nihoul looks so bland, he is hard to describe, except that with weary eyes and a wrinkled white shirt with rolled-up sleeves, he looks like he has had a long day at a stuffy, smoky office.

Nihoul's hand touches the inside of my right thigh. *Surprise!* I have seen Nihoul make out with pretty teenagers, sixteen or seventeen, but never noticed him being sexual with younger children. *I never thought of this before.* It makes me appreciate him a little bit. I am thinking that maybe he has a backbone after all, if he hasn't raped little children just to belong. *But what is this hand?*

"Look at this!" Nihoul exclaims, observing the stab wounds on the inside of my knee. "Your boyfriend tried to make you like himself. How touching."

Nihoul smiles to remind me of Patrick's betrayal, reminding me that though Patrick may have threatened to kill him when he once made an innocuous joke about me, here he is now, and Patrick is not killing him, but Patrick is letting him kill me. *Ha ha.*

In the German mind control facility, I was strapped down frequently and learned to withstand anything, but there was always a specific purpose to the torture there. It was to get me into a state, to get into my subconscious mind and unlock parts of my brain so I could do something specific that would serve some purpose. But the purpose there was not to kill me.

I am close to feeling. I could easily cry. I could let myself feel the pain over Patrick's betrayal, Nihoul's cruelty. I could remind myself that I am the child. I could think about the fishhook which painfully pulls and stretches the skin from the inside, bruises before it rips; or I could think about the blood flowing from several dozen wounds, creeping all over my skin, tickling like mad, and I cannot wipe it off. I could realize that I am powerless. But if I do that, I will slide into the role-play. Then I will be powerless, and Nihoul almighty. I will be one side of the coin, and Nihoul the other; one divided into two, inseparable, bonded by the play, by the lie. I would love him, because I would give him all my power. Tonight, I have seen Nihoul looking like a human being, and I have appreciated him; I have gotten on his wavelength, and could easily begin to hope that connecting with him in a mental space where no one else would, and understanding him when no one else does, would spark some feeling in him—at least enough to keep me alive. My love for him would fire up my hope for his love, for his benevolence, and render me incapable of believing that he really means to hurt me, that he really wants to torture me to death, which in turn will make me incredulous, more stunned with every blow; in short, a wide-eyed victim.

Nihoul, for his part, would take good note of my disbelief. Right inside those wide-opened eyes of mine, he would see the lie. He would know that I know better, even if I don't. If I slip into my role, then Nihoul can play. For me, the feeler, the play would seem increasingly real. *What is wrong?* I would think. *I love him but he keeps on hurting me. It's not fair!* I would feel increasingly powerless, as my signs are unseen, my cries unheard. For Nihoul, the player, only his power would seem real. He would have the advantage of point of view, a godlike detachment from the events being played out. Heads getting rid of Tails. Whereas I would feel horribly trapped, Nihoul would experience a rare bout of freedom. When he first strapped me down, Nihoul was free from the gnawing pressure of the gnat droning orders in his ear. He is trying to free himself again, but for all his casualness, he is totally caught up in his part of the lie. But if I don't play my part, maybe I can die free.

I stare defiantly at Nihoul: *You think you have me now, don't you? You don't have me. You never will.*

My defiance is met with the familiar gaze of sour resentment. He shakes his head as if trying to shake the expression off his face. He ducks, noisily rummages in the torture tool bin, lifts out a strap with nails, and furiously digs the nails into my right arm, underneath the deltoid, systematically stabbing, hitting several points at once, creating an armband of blood.

"What are you waiting for?" he shouts to the other children. "Get down to business already, or you're next!"

They do as they are told. Nihoul, after puncturing the circumference of my right upper arm, hands the bloody nail strap to the girl across from him at my shoulder level, and she copies Nihoul's job on my left upper arm.

Nihoul picks an apple corer out of the bin. He raises his arm up high and hits my right leg, around the scarred knee area, the upper thigh. He whacks away at my shin, hits the bone. I resume breathing in. And breathing out.

The girl who is putting the nails in my left arm unties my wrist, to better reach the inside of my arm. I lift my forearm, to test if it is still working. The younger girl directs a penknife at my raised forearm. I can tell that, because of Nihoul's temper, she wants to try to stab me hard. Looking intently at her, I mentally shout, *Do it!* She lunges, and the knife hits, and sticks. When the girl sees the knife stuck by itself in my arm, she panics, and, not knowing what to do, she tries to pull it out, and in her terror, twists it.

A tremendous, deep, raw pain enters and spreads through my entire body. My nerves awaken, and it is as if I am being stung by thousands of giant bees at once. The stinging and singeing are intolerable, but the torture does not stop; Patrick is not here to save me; there is no light before my eyes, nor any comfort from beyond. I bite my lip in a last attempt to fight off identification with my body, fighting back the tears pushing through tightly shut eyelids.

My return to the play has not failed to attract Nihoul's notice, and through a blur of salty tears I see him smile, as in *I'm finally beginning to get through to you.*

He nonchalantly throws the apple corer over his shoulder.

"I have an idea!" he pronounces. "Since your boyfriend didn't even get you to limp, why don't we do him a favor and finish the job for him?"

He looks at the boy, who has been poking my right ankle with a screwdriver.

"You, go to the kitchen and bring me a cleaver. Or a saw. We're going to cut off her foot."

Turning to me, Nihoul adds, with great satisfaction, "So you can hobble along, like your boyfriend."

The boy hurries out of the room. I glance at my right foot, trying to ignore the bloody mess on my shin. I am bleeding profusely, covered with wounds of different shapes and sizes all over the front of my body. Nihoul seems to be considering the same, because he says, "There, children. Help me untie her. We're going to turn her over."

When the straps are undone, I involuntarily turn to the left, away from Nihoul. I try to lean on the butcher's block but don't have the strength to heist myself up. My left arm barely looks like an arm. I realize that, whether or not Nihoul is going to hack off my foot, I am going to die, because I will never heal from these wounds.

The older girls pull me up. As I sit, dazed, looking down at the disgusting, chapped butcher's block, which now has plenty of my blood that will mix in and blacken, a flash of all the children that were murdered here passes before my eyes, and knowing myself to be next, the horror sets in. *This is really happening to me. I am being murdered. I am being tortured to death because nobody cares whether I live or die.* I am one of the faceless, nameless ones, passing away into oblivion, because no one loved me, not even enough to keep me alive, not even enough to keep this from happening.

I see Patrick in my mind's eye, and see him how I saw him last, connecting—at least I thought—on this ethereal level, on which—at least I thought—we always connected, from the beginning. But if that last look did not even make a difference, if Patrick really does not love me, if I have just been dreaming, then I guess there is no telling if there is anything besides this world. I don't know if I will continue to exist in some form or just be wiped out. *I don't know anything anymore.* I don't feel ready to die.

"Push her down already!" Nihoul cries, extremely annoyed.

Nihoul forcefully pushes me down himself. The bruises get hit, the wounds scraped, my chin hits the wood. *But why is Nihoul so annoyed?* I wonder.

Nihoul is in a horrible mood. He furiously, quickly, ties the straps around my ankles and wrists, all four of them, much too tight. I am surprised it is all going so quickly. Nihoul had mentioned something about going slowly, because it was just the beginning. I don't know how long we have been in this room—half an hour, one hour?

"No, no!" Nihoul cries impatiently. "You have to go into the muscle. Otherwise she doesn't even feel it."

I feel a sharp stab of something going deep into my left calf muscle, throbbing with pain, which makes me move, which makes everything hurt. A few seconds later I feel the same in my right calf muscle. The children continue to poke me, but Nihoul turns away from the spectacle, brooding. I am exhausted, but curious. I would like to know why Nihoul is in such a mood.

The door opens. *That's it. The boy is back with the cleaver. Now my foot's going to come off!* I think, but I hear the voice of an adult, one of Polo's friends.

"Okay, Michel. You can let her go now. That's enough."

"You're joking."

"Nope. That's it."

Nihoul furiously unties the straps.

"You're making a big mistake," Nihoul warns the man exiting the room. "She's going to give us trouble."

MICHEL NIHOUL
(4-23-1941 – 10-23-2019)

Arrested on August 15, 1996, Michel Nihoul was one of four
defendants in the Dutroux case, dubbed the Belgian pedophile
scandal in the press. Four murdered girls and two survivors
were referred to by the New York Times as "the victims of
a deadly pornography ring." (New York Times 9/96).

In the fall of 1996, several survivors of the network approached
investigators of the Dutroux case, testifying anonymously under
the code name X. Michel Nihoul featured prominently in all the X
testimonies. The testimony of X1, Regina Louf, stood out because of
her extremely precise, detailed descriptions of network activity in the
1980's. Investigators linked Regina Louf's testimony to several unsolved
child murders involving Michel Nihoul. In October 1996, the magistrate
in charge of the Dutroux case, who eagerly promised the public to "get
to the bottom of this," was fired from the case, causing protests around
the country. (New York Times 10/19/96) Soon after, X1/Regina
Louf's investigators were put on leave, and remained so even after the
complaint triggering their dismissal was found unsubstantiated.

On January 27, 1997, it was decided to reopen the investigation into
the unsolved murder of Christine Van Hees, which regained attention
thanks to the testimony of X1/Regina Louf. On February 13, 1984,
sixteen-year old Christine Van Hees was repeatedly raped, tortured,
and finally set on fire. The original murder file already contained leads
to Michel Nihoul and Marc Dutroux. These leads were neglected,
and yet the same examining magistrate who handled the case from
1985 onward was placed in charge of the re-investigation. It should
have been known by the Belgian judiciary that this magistrate's sister
was godmother to the son of Michel Nihoul, and that he furthermore

had once acted as a lawyer for Michel Nihoul's longtime girlfriend. Moreover, this magistrate thanked his appointment to the extreme right-wing political milieu of Michel Nihoul and friends, which his investigation should have scrutinized. In 1998, the Van Hees murder file was once again closed. The other unsolved child murders brought back into focus by Regina Louf's testimony were left untouched, and by then the statute of limitations had run out on all of these cases.[1]

On October 22, 2001, a file named *"Dutroux-bis,"* was officially split off from the Dutroux case. The Dutroux-bis file contained all the X-testimonies, as well as thousands of hairs and trace evidence which did not belong to any of the victims or defendants, found in Marc Dutroux' car and dungeons.

On March 19, 2001, Newsweek Magazine published an article titled: *"Justice Delayed in Belgium."* Three years later, on March 1, 2004, eight years after the bodies of four murdered girls were found, the Dutroux case went to trial. Because of the notoriety of the case, the trial was moved to the city of Arlon, where the public and thousands of journalists who could not fit into the courtroom could follow the trial on large video screens.

In April 2004, the Belgian journalist Douglas De Coninck published a book titled: *"30 Witnesses Dead: Those Who Won't Testify at The Dutroux Trial,"* tracing, in great detail, the activities of thirty people who were either about to reveal "something big," or to deliver important testimony in the Dutroux case, but who were murdered, inexplicably committed suicide, or died in suspicious accidents.[2]

---

1. *From the book by the French Title:"Les Dossiers X: Ce que la Belgique ne devait pas savoir sur l'Affaire Dutroux," Flemish Title: "De X-dossiers: Wat België niet mocht weten over de zaak-Dutroux" (The X-Files: What Belgium was not supposed to know about the Dutroux Case) by Annemie Bulté, Douglas De Coninck and Marie-Jeanne Van Heeswyck. Publisher: Epo/Houtekiet, copyright 1999*

2. *Book by the French Title: "30 Temois morts," Flemish Title: "Dode Getuigen: dertig mensen die niet zullen spreken op het proces-Dutroux"(30 Witnesses Dead: Those Who Won't Testify at The Dutroux Trial,) by Douglas De Coninck.*

On June 17, 2004, the Dutroux trial concluded. The lawyer of one of the surviving victims stated, "Three quarters of the questions we had at the trial were answered with, 'We don't know, but we are going to investigate this in the Dutroux-bis file.'"

Michel Nihoul was found guilty of the minor charges of peddling false documents, dealing drugs and trading in stolen vehicles. (*New York Times 6/18/2004*) Even though the majority of the jury deemed Nihoul guilty of complicity in the kidnappings of the young victims, the judge ruled Nihoul not guilty of that charge. Nihoul received a five-year sentence for drug dealing and gang formation, and was granted early release less than two years later, in April 2006.

On November 26, 2004, months after the trial, the Dutroux-bis file was officially closed, without another trial, and without any new information being released to the public.

Michel Nihoul published a book titled *"Rumors, Facts"* to clear his name, and enjoyed minor celebrity status for the remainder of his life. He joked that he was a WC, an acronym for *Wallon Connu*—Known Walloon—but WC is also the acronym for Water Closet and the commonly used term for toilet.

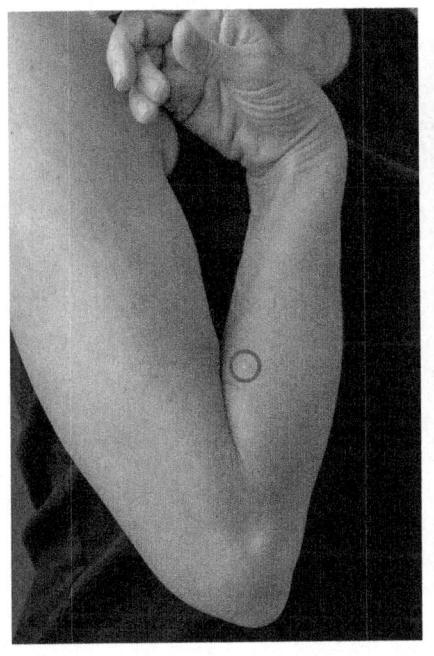 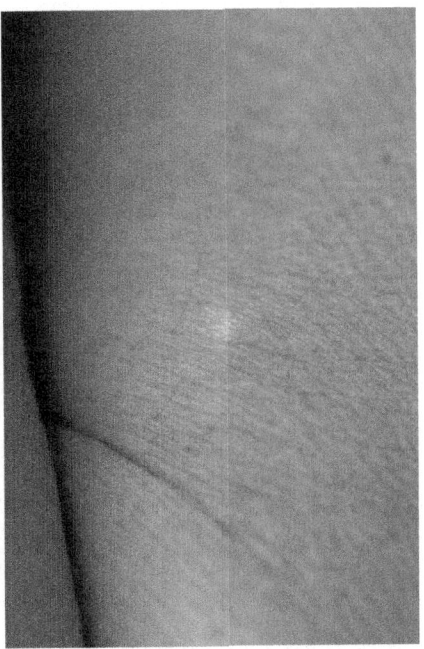

"Nihoul grabs me by the right wrist and pulls it, twists it, so my arm folds back painfully. Nihoul points his burning cigarette at my forearm, a few inches from the elbow crease. [...] Nihoul digs the burning cigarette into the flesh of my arm."

"He [...] drops the teeth of a mini-rake into the wound, creating three stripes of blood."

Photos taken in 2022, 48 years after the wounding. Notice the circular, raised burn mark (with arm similarly positioned), and, in the close-up at right, with scars from the "mini-rake" towards the bottom right.

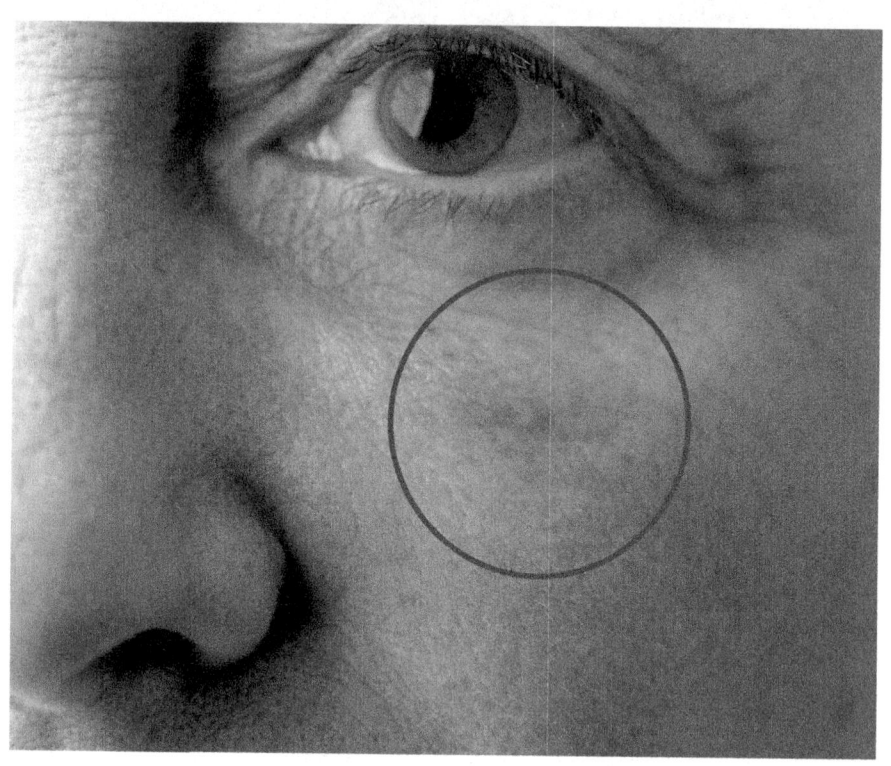

"Nihoul fishes for a thin bar of warped steel, like a drill bit with
a square tip, which comes flying towards my eye. I squint, and
feel the metal ripping skin as it hits my cheekbone."

Photo taken in 2022, 48 years after the wounding. As I grew up, and over
time, the scar moved from the cheekbone towards the middle of my face.

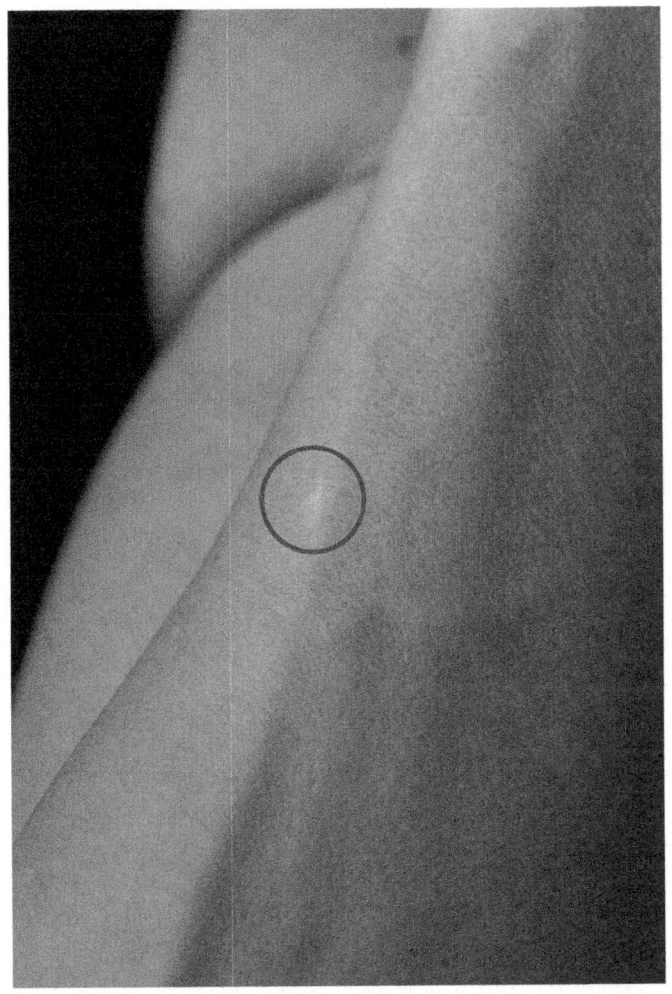

"The younger girl directs a penknife at my raised forearm. [...] She lunges, and the knife hits, and sticks. When the girl sees the knife stuck by itself in my arm, she panics, and, not knowing what to do, she tries to pull it out, and in her terror, twists it."

Photo taken in 2022, 48 years after the wounding. This scar moved about 4" as I grew, from about 2.5" above the elbow, up towards the middle of the left forearm.

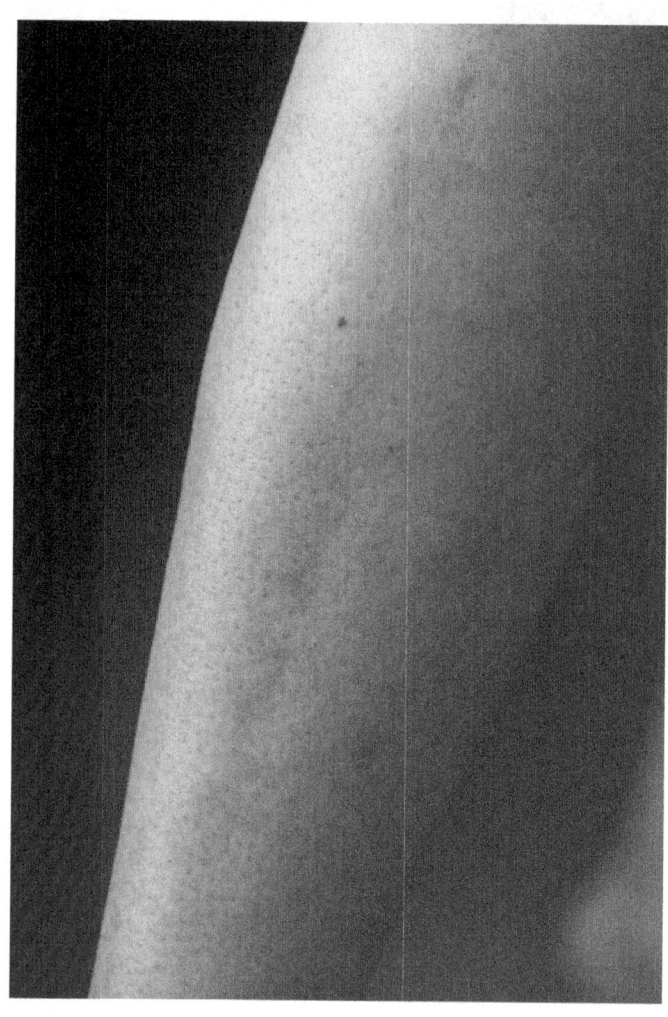

"Nihoul picks an apple corer out of the bin. He raises his arm up high and hits my right leg. [...] He whacks away at my shin, hits the bone."

Photo taken in 2022, 48 years after the wounding. Right bottom leg. Notice the scars from right below the knee down the shin, the vertical depression at the center, and the white, patterned scarring from the apple corer.

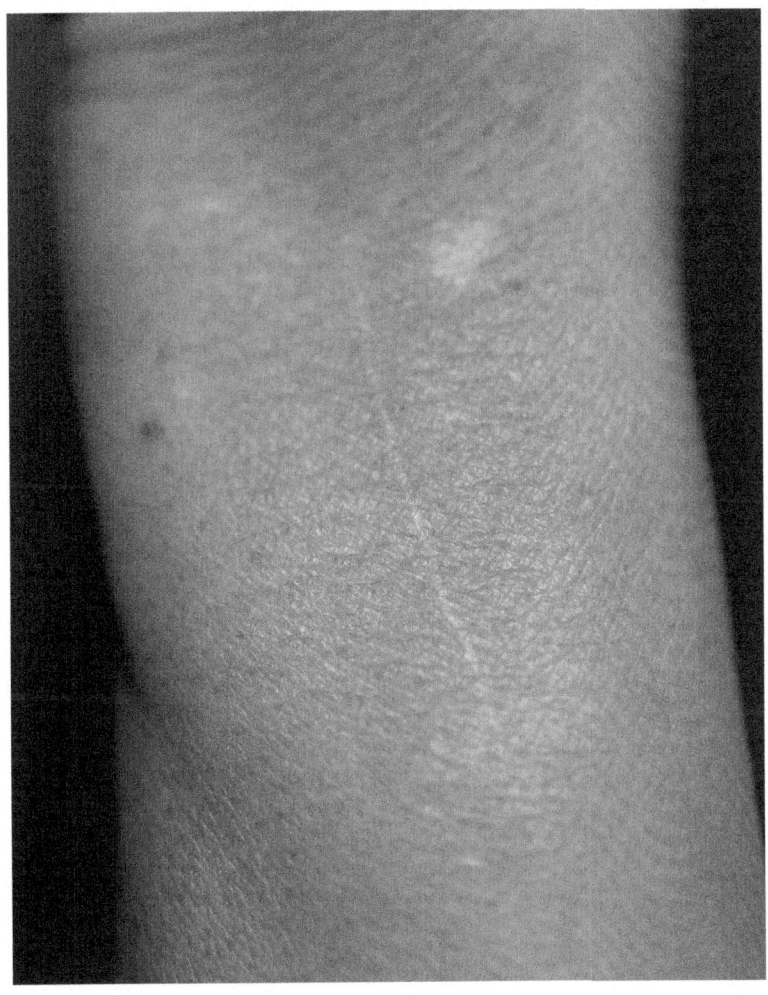

"Under my gaze and over my body, he passes the children various instruments of torture. A penknife, scissors, a screwdriver, a razor blade, a fishhook."

My right wrist and top of forearm. Photo taken in 2022, 48 years after the wounding. The two marks on the top left are from a fishhook; the white mark on the top right is from a screwdriver; the vertical line is from a razor blade, and the marks towards the bottom of the vertical cut were made with scissors during my torture in 1974 led by Michel Nihoul.

CHAPTER SIXTEEN

Night, villa, Belgium, October 1974

A strong metallic taste imbues my mouth. I am lying face down in a pool of blood, running from my wounds in narrow gullets, dripping steadily off the butcher's block.

I am horribly exhausted. *Maybe I should close my eyes, and then maybe I'll just drift off, sleep.*

And bleed to death.

I'm not ready to die.

I wriggle my toes. The right foot hurts as though it were crushed. There is pain in my ankle. The burn stings more than anything else. The pain in my right shoulder is severe. The left shoulder hurts as well. I raise myself up on my hands and knees. On my arm, a purulent, sticky brown wide-open hole looks frightening. I break into tears. I don't know how long, but I sit there on the butcher's block and cry. Blood keeps flowing. Tears keep flowing.

I shuffle to the edge, but the floor looks like it is too far down. I slide, sink down onto the floor. Crouched down, I raise my head to look for my clothes, and remember they were pulled off in the bathroom, ages ago, by the children.

I spot the familiar little pile of my clothes in the corner. At first, I can't believe what I see. When I crawl over, it is clear that everything is there, even my underwear. I break into tears again. Sobbing uncontrollably, I am overwhelmed with feelings of gratitude that one of these children, who had been pushed to bully me and then forced to participate in my torture, had the thoughtfulness to bring my clothes here. It reminds me that no matter what we need to do to survive, we child victims are always connected to each other.

Incredibly, I can get up, and though I am lightheaded, I can slowly walk. I exit the door into a bigger room. There is the beginning of a thought, but it can't form, as I have no energy for thoughts. I enter a lavatory. My hand has deep, bleeding scratches from the fishhook and I turn on the tap to let the cool water mingle with the blood.

Looking in the mirror is hard. My skin is blue-gray, the color of death. Blood runs from the wounds, but some cuts and scratches are drying. Bloody pulp emerges from my left arm and right shin. I carefully pull on my underwear, then the jeans. These are wide-legged jeans that don't irritate the wounds; I am overwhelmed with gratitude for this, and more tears flow. My navy-blue t-shirt hides the blood stains. It does have short sleeves, showing my arms. *Oh well.*

As I gently open the door into the hallway, I see Patrick, leaning against the wall, holding a girl on his hands, having sex with her.

Patrick notices me, puts the girl down, zips up, and pats her naked bottom, thus sending her away.

"Come along," he says to me. "I was waiting for you."

Walking beside Patrick in the hallway, I feel calm, and grateful that someone waited for me.

Patrick slows down to my pace. Blood is seeping through my pants.

Patrick guides me into an office with a large desk, and gives me a little pinch before removing his hand from my shoulder. *Pay attention!*

Awaiting us are the young girl with whom Patrick just had sex, Polo, and his friend who stopped the torture, who is acting as if he were here on some other business. It looks like Polo is at home here, that this is his own office.

Patrick closes the door, goes to stand behind Polo, and leans against the wall, hands behind his back.

Polo looks me up and down, one hand lightly positioned on the desk, drumming his fingers, pinky to pointing finger, a few riffs, observing my condition, calculating something.

He takes a deep drag from his pipe, blows out smoke, and speaks.

"All right. Here you are. So, your life was saved. But this is not what we do. We don't begin this type of thing and then stop and then you're free to go. There's a price to pay. Someone is going to have to die. Who that's going to be, is up to you. It's going to be you, or her."

Polo points to the little girl.

I have an intense craving for chocolate.

I don't want to know which answer I am expected to give. And if I had a choice...I really would like to have chocolate.

Patrick catches my eye and smiles encouragingly. He looks nervous. I look up at Polo, checking to see if I might ask for a last meal. Polo raises his eyes to the ceiling and rolls his head impatiently: *Decide already.*

Angry, I think, *Don't expect me to hurry up.*

I observe the girl to see if she can give me a clue. She is maybe eight or nine years old, slight build, thick wavy dark brown hair, and thick, long bangs. The frame of her hair almost swallows her tiny face, which is quirky, delicate, with brown eyes and very thin lips that tremble as she purses them shut and squints her eyes in an involuntary grimace of fear, oddly resembling a smile.

I stare into the floor, trying to sense what is expected of me. When Polo asked ten children to choose between their lives and the lives of ten rabbits, nine children immediately chose to give their lives for the rabbits, yet no children were killed that day. But all the rabbits were.

When I was trained in Germany, it was also made very clear that if I made the "wrong choice," my punishment was having to observe what the consequences of my choice would be for the intended victim. The "right choice" made me feel all the more evil, and I think that was the point.

I think I know what I am supposed to say, but I would like to not have to say it. I become aware of a hasty rhythmic patter in the room. Patrick is restlessly tapping the heel of his foot on the floor, and when I raise my gaze he gives me another cheerleader smile. *He was having sex with that girl, right in the hallway, right outside the door out of which he knew I would appear. Now I have to decide who is going to die, the girl he was just having sex with, or me.*

The patter stops. I look at Patrick again and he smiles knowingly, relaxed now, happy. I shoot him an accusatory glare, which he acknowledges with a look that is amazingly sweet and loving, the way he used to look at me, a long, long time ago. I stare at the floor and nudge towards the girl.

"Her," I say to Polo in a near-whisper.

"That's why we like you," Polo comments flatly. "You always make the right choice. But you're going to have to kill her."

Bathroom, villa, Belgium, night, October 1974

Patrick sets me down on the sink of yet another lavatory in this house. He carefully takes off my clothes, and wets a dark-colored towel. When he is about to dab it on my skin, he hesitates, just for an instant, but I see in his eyes that he is wondering if I am going to live. He decidedly brings the towel to my left arm and shakes his head: *You're in bad shape, but I can handle it.* He dots the area around the gory armband, wiping up lymph and blood to reveal blue, blue skin. The towel keeps lapping up more blood, and Patrick gets busier, swiping more towels out of a cabinet. He uses wet ones, dry ones, binding my left arm, binding my right leg. He carries me out through the hallway, the lobby, and out the front door to his parked car. He unlocks and opens the door, carefully placing me in the bucket seat.

When he is behind the wheel, his eyes cloud over, and he looks sad.

"We're going to meet them and some of the others at somebody else's house."

He puts a hand through my hair and sighs.

"You'll do fine. I'm going to be with you every step of the way."

During the ride, every one of my breaths is a belabored sigh, and my eyes move strangely about in the occipital orbits. The anticipation of taking a human life, a child's life, is more torturous than any physical torture could ever be.

I don't understand how I could possibly have ended up in this situation. For me, the price to belong to the most exclusive club in the world was to kill. I had been invited in about a year and a half ago, after I had heard all about my glamorous future and had been praised and admired for my sensual performance by a select group of powerful friends of the Big Shot. The induction ritual was to end in a killing. I knew then as I do now, that in the network there is no point in refusing to kill when you are ordered. I had discovered at the start of this part of the training in Germany, that attempting to save the victim by refusing, only ensures that the victim will suffer more. This is why, during that induction ritual, I had to through with it. But the next time I saw the Big Shot—who felt that I was the luckiest girl alive to have crossed paths with him—I defied him. I was unwilling to pay the price, unwilling to sell my soul to the devil, unwilling to kill to be part of the secret gang that forms the world's elite, who put their own slaves and puppets in roles at the top of the global power structure of privilege and entitlement.

It was clear that if I were to accept the future for which I had been so expertly trained and prepared, owned by the Big Shot networker and paid off with celebrity status and riches, organized child murders would occur again, and I wanted no part of it. However, when I broke with him, I was only rejected from the inner circle of the global network, not from the outer reaches, where the Belgians did their best to copy their role models with psychopathic traditions such as satanic ceremonies and exit rituals.

After a twenty-minute ride, Patrick parks in a private driveway and we walk, slowly, up a path towards a white villa, partially hidden by a cluster of evergreens. The autumn moonlight shows that the informal garden is sparse but well-tended. A network regular opens the door of the brightly lit lobby, cold and empty. The man stares blatantly as Patrick ushers me in. My clothes are hardly a decent cover, so stained are they with blood; the bulk of the towel around my leg is visible under the jeans; the towel around my left arm has turned a disgusting brown; my right arm is covered in ugly wounds, and my blue skin is covered with dark gray bruises. Another regular meets our host; the two of them mockingly observe me. One turns to the other.

"She's the one who's supposed to...?"

He doesn't say "do the killing" out loud. The friend snickers and gives the host a meaningful look that makes it clear that I am not meant to survive.

"Come on!" Patrick calls angrily as he pushes past the two regulars, sending them a quick, disdainful glance down his nose.

The two men's eyes follow Patrick and me as we file into a hallway. *They weren't intimidated*, I realize, stunned. *They weren't afraid of Patrick at all.*

Patrick turns his head and gives me an embarrassed, apologetic look.

We enter a large chamber on the ground floor, covered with industrial wall-to-wall carpet, impersonal billows of dusty transparent curtains and dim fluorescent lights. The girl has been tied to a flattened dentist's chair, three tan vinyl pillows mounted on an ivory metal frame atop a single round pedestal. She is naked, exposed to a small group of men of five or six regulars including Polo, but not Nihoul.

The girl and I are the only females here. The men, distinguished-looking members of a dying patriarchy, pretend to lazily lull about, as if they are casually discussing, smoking, their whiskey goblets posed on narrow metal stands in the same ivory as the dentist's chair.

As Patrick and I enter, followed by the two regulars who were at the front door, Polo throws me a tired, almost angry look.

Patrick guides me to an area off to the side that has a black leather sofa and plain chairs arranged in a semi-circle around a glass-topped salon table, much like a dentist's waiting area—which it might have been, before the wall came down. Patrick pulls a clear plastic bag out of his pocket, pours cocaine onto the glass table and begins to separate the lines.

The group encircles the girl. Tension pervades the room like the whirring blade of a circular saw, flown off its hinges and spinning in the air above everyone's head, ready to plunge down and attack the next victim. No one knows for sure that they won't be next. Fear is everywhere; and when the perpetrators strike, they beat the blade. It's the network match: strike, strike, strike, strike and don't miss, because the ball is a blade.

I take a rolled-up hundred franc note from Patrick and sniff both big white lines off the table. The cocaine eases the mental torture and freezes the pain.

Patrick kisses me, and I kiss him. I escape into feeling his love one more time. All that goes through my mind is how long it has been, how long it has been, how much I missed this, how much I missed him, how much I love him.

"Mon amour. Mon amour. Mon amour. Mon amour." I whisper.

I give myself to Patrick with utter abandon, utterly focus on him until I absorb his essence and he becomes the sole object in my existence. Everything else vanishes, and soon I am locked in the familiar cocoon of intense sensual intimacy.

I overhear a comment of someone who has drifted away from the dentist's chair.

"What an idiot. Sold his life. And for what? For that dumb little bitch. I'll never understand such folly."

"I understand it. Just look at them. Look at that," someone responds.

"What are they talking about?" I whisper to Patrick.

"Oh, nothing," Patrick responds with an embarrassed glance.

"What did he mean, 'You sold your life'?"

"It's nothing. I'm just going to go to work for Polo. That's all."

"For life? For the rest of your life?"

Patrick shrugs.

"I guess I didn't want you to die after all," he laughs sheepishly.

I now understand what Polo was calculating when he sized me up in his office after the torture.

"But if I die, then you don't have to work for him...."

"No, no, no, it wouldn't change anything. It's all set. I'm going to work for him no matter what."

"But no. If I die, then you don't owe him anything."

"All right, children," Polo's voice booms as he approaches us. "It's time you two shot into action...or at least, a different kind of action."

Everyone laughs. Even the men around the dentist's chair utter appreciative chuckles. Polo, indicating the Gillette razor blade Patrick used to split up the cocaine, thunders in an exaggerated showman's tone of dismay, "You've got stuff right here on the table. Here's another one. Get moving."

Polo throws a large fold-out barber's razor on the table and turns on his heel, heading back towards the victim. Polo is clearly ordering Patrick around, making him feel who is boss in front of everyone, letting Patrick know exactly what he has gotten himself into with his silly sentiment for me.

Some of the regulars quickly exchange mocking glances. As Patrick sets me down, the pain and frustration over the humiliations flash in his charron blue eyes. Then, he puts his attention on the two razor blades, inspects them in the relaxed manner of an expert, gives me the barber's razor and guides me to the dentist's chair. Patrick is completely at ease as he observes the girl. Polo and the other men hold their breath as they watch Patrick in tense silence.

"What you do," Patrick explains to me, "is you tune in with the girl at the very moment you cut her. The cut is going to tense her muscles, and if you're feeling it, your muscles are going to go into a spasm, and that is going to feel nice. Like this, watch."

Patrick approaches the girl with great deliberation, energetically moving towards her, pulling away in subtle physical ways, skillfully performing the dance of attraction. He is the star of the show, and the audience is enthralled.

The girl locks eyes with Patrick. Patrick smiles at her. As she smiles back, Patrick, without taking his friendly eyes off hers, slashes her thigh, as if saying, "See? I'm doing this, but don't take note; the cutting is not important; what is important is that I like you." The girl keeps her eyes glued to Patrick's, still surrendered even as her muscles bulge and her body tenses in shock.

Patrick casually turns to me.

"See? Did you feel that, too?"

I did not. Being tortured was so easy compared to this unbearable tension, this intolerable mental torture. A myriad of thoughts invade my mind; the voltage in my brain is a million times what it should be. My head must be about to explode.

"You try," Patrick says, turning to me and sticking his tongue deep in my mouth.

"OH NO!" Polo roars. "You two are not going to start again!"

Though Patrick obediently stops kissing, he laughs.

"Why don't you try?" he asks me again, still amused.

Where should I cut her? I don't want to cut her!

"Use what you feel," Patrick says, putting his hand on my behind, sliding his fingers to my genitals.

Breathing shallowly, I bring my arm forwards. The long handle of the barber's razor keeps me at a relative distance; it must be why Patrick chose it. When I was tortured, the cuts in the middle of the quadriceps, at the exact front of the leg, bothered me the least. I aim for that spot and cut, immediately entering a state of enormous confusion and dissociation. Nevertheless, I see the girl's muscular reaction and empathically feel the shock she feels, and I feel Patrick's fingers, and a shock ripples through my body.

"See?" Patrick laughs in my ear. "You're just like me."

Patrick whisks me away to the waiting area.

"Where do you think you're going?" Polo calls out.

"We need more coke," Patrick replies impassively. "You guys have fun."

I snort up the coke with the greatest, longest, deepest inhale and engage in savage sex with Patrick. His gaze fastened on mine says that he loves me more than anything or anyone on earth.

During our trips to the dentist's chair, the girl's body is covered with increasingly more neat, narrow cuts inflicted by razor blades, and round brown burn marks from cigarettes. The men don't try to catch her eye, but stare at her genitals, gathering up erotic steam and anger so as to strike and experience a thrill. She stares up, out into space. Only when Patrick gets near does she move her head to be able to look him softly in the eye, and Patrick looks straight back at her with a warm smile.

A sensation settles in me, of being in a lake of mud, struggling to move, drowning, surrounded by monsters trying to rip me apart. Though not a single ray of sunlight has seeped through the flimsy curtains, it seems like I have been in this room—in this lake of mud—for several days before the familiar voice with the extra decibel of someone used to addressing crowds announces, "Alright, children. Stop playing now. It's time for serious business."

Sitting on Patrick's hands, I turn and see Polo standing in front of the salon table surrounded by all the men. With great bravado, he pulls a dagger out of its sheath. Patrick puts me down and whispers.

"There you go, little one."

Solemnly, Polo hands me the unsheathed dagger, the blade pointing upwards.

"Watch out. It's sharp."

I stare at him as the men laugh softly. Patrick encouragingly taps my shoulder.

"You can do it, little one. I know it. You're just like me."

"Just cut her throat," Polo says, sounding bored.

I hold the dagger up as it was given to me, and examine the fat, rounded, shiny chocolate-colored wooden handle with an inlaid bronze scroll. The handle feels smooth. The back of what appears to be a 10-inch long blade looks like the bone of a feather: thicker at the bottom, the steel sprouting out of the bronze. Though the handle looks antique, the blade looks new, with crisscross marks along the cutting edge. I carefully stroke four fingers across, while my thumb runs up to the point. It is very sharp.

Polo sighs impatiently, looking as though he regrets making such a big deal of presenting me with the weapon. It was just a joke. Now let's move on with the show already.

I look him in the eyes, thinking, *It's not a joke to me.*

Polo answers my thought with the same tired, angry look he shot me when I first entered this chamber, as if I have it much too good; too much fuss is made about me, about my life. To him, I am nothing but a nuisance, not worth the trouble. I am nothing.

My thought response is: *I am human.*

Polo angrily fastens his gaze on mine, and our combined concentration creates an intense fusion. I seem to absorb Polo's entire being, as if his soul were pouring out of those doggish eyes. In a flash, I remember what

Polo told me after he once beat me black and blue, "Get out of here. You're so dead there's nothing to be done with you," and I now understand he was speaking of himself.

To him, the whole world is lifeless. He imagines himself riding a mighty dragon, sword ever at the ready, chopping down every stirring of real life to make it fit into his cardboard fairy tale. Everything is a show; and he really does have a flair for the dramatic.

In the same flash, lasting maybe a second in all, I get a sense why Polo went so far out of his way to make me scream, ordering the bugs, securing the house and Nihoul, setting up the scene in the cellar. To one who knows no love, nothing seems real except himself and his power. It's fun to ride a dragon. It's fun to play, but if Polo doesn't win, he is suddenly hanging on to the underbelly of his galloping mount. From the vantage point of the dragon's gut, everything on earth, all those creatures down there, become a bit too real, stirring his greatest fear, that he is more worthless than all the slaves and plebeians combined. If he is not on top, then his grand persona, which makes him appear more lively than everyone else, collapses together with his whole cardboard world. And all that is left is a weak little boy, so hurt he is beyond the capacity to feel pain. And because of that, all his feelings are dead.

Polo's energy retreats back into his body, and he suddenly looks sad— like a dog that knows it can never be human—and tired, from steering and maneuvering, forever trying to stay on top of that mighty beast.

Patrick's hand is on my shoulder, gently goading me on, like a mother would her child. In a world mothered by insecure men, women are the children fighting for the parents' attention, killing each other if they must. Mama wants to kill me, so I will be out of her way and the men can pay attention to her alone. Out of my unrequited mother love has sprung my love for Patrick, which got me here. I will do what pleases him, which is what pleases Polo, a dead soul leading a deadly, deadening show.

There is no way out. I know I can't refuse or this poor child's end will be made even worse. I do have a plan, but first I have to go through with this. I do not want to do this; and I know that I cannot do it and also live with myself afterwards. So I will die. That is my plan.

I begin to march like a soldier. Without thinking, I put myself in motion to rouse dormant energies. Pace firm, I circle the victim tied to the dentist's chair. Images roll before my mind's eye to stir up anger this girl could never inspire, images that feed those dark energies that are usually only stirred in defense of one's life, when fear of death creates a hormonal storm of aggression to kill the enemy. I march like a soldier to bring myself into the state necessary to carry out my plan. As I march, I can't even feel weakness or pain from my wounds anymore. Situations from the past in which I wished I could have defended myself float through my mind. All the men of the network pass the revue. I see them looking at me the way they looked at her tonight, like a collection of legs, thighs and genitals. I remember countless faces, countless scornful gazes. I see the icy stare of the sterile Gaspard, the clumsy first-timers acting like I am so adept and they are so adolescent, the charmers needing eye contact, confusing me with their coy looks, connecting as if they saw me, the way Patrick looked at this girl tonight.

I recall the hundreds of men who came into that little room with the dirty mattress in the mansion. And not one of them said, "No. This is a child. I cannot do this. I came to this event but now I'm alone in a room with a child and I will not stoop to this." *Not one of them ever stopped himself!*

My pace picks up as I become more agitated, furious at all the men who did not stop themselves from committing a crime against me. I am furious. Everything and everyone in my life has pushed me to this moment, to this act. I am completely enraged, even if all my anger is finding expression through a coerced, externalized channel, in the same way every networker is drawn over that boundary from which there is no return.

I am furious at Mama! She never once relented the slightest whenever she saw a chance to inflict subtle mental or life-threatening physical pain.

I remember when she pulled me by the hair to drag me to the network; when she stuffed me full of Valium. I see scenes roll by from when I was little up to just a few months ago, in which Mama blamed me, yelled at me or threatened me, while my offenses were either non-existent or completely incommensurate with her reactions or punishments. I see Mama in hundreds of situations. And never did she show any tenderness, never did she give me any love. I see Mama calling out, "You thought you could have them all!" as she was lying under Patrick.

Mama never stopped herself!

This girl is not Mama!

Shallow, panicky breaths overtake me; a vague, choppy scenario plays before my mind's eye. In these rapid images, I announce that I am not going to go through with this. Polo is livid and wants me to suffer maximally. I am strapped onto the chair and my torture begins again. The scenario continues: the girl is killed before my eyes, and Polo makes sure that I witness that it is a painful and agonizing death, to show me just how wrong my choice was. Would I be sure that I did the right thing then? She is not going to live, and I am the better executioner, because I will be quick, because I never wanted her to suffer.

I am now in a big funnel, together with all the villainous, creepy, murderous thoughts flowing through the earth's ether; I am swirling with all the dark entities feeding off these thoughts, taking over the bodies and minds of tragic humans diving into this dark, downward-spiraling stream. I have dived into the lies that have been attached to me in my eleven years on this planet by deadened adults; adults who had the same lies attached to them by deadened adults; lies straight out of the dark ages, all cascading down, descending into these rapids, into this fall....

I wish it was Mama strapped to the dentist's chair! It would then be easier to go forward with this darkest of dark actions. *Mama had sex with Patrick!* Another flash of Mama's exultation: "You thought you could have them all!" I remember the expression on the girl's face sitting on Patrick's hands. *That is how he holds <u>me</u>! That's our special way of making love!*

Now she is lost to me; that look in her eyes is my mother as she gazes lovingly into Patrick's eyes, thrilled to finally have this *thing*, whatever she believes I have and she doesn't. The same insanity that besets my mother and parents and lovers and killers has overtaken me; the innocent girl before me is not the innocent girl before me. *Mama, what did you do to me? Mama, what did you do to me? Mama, what did you do to me? Mama, why did you have me! I hate my life! I hate having to be here! I hate myself! I want to kill myself! Mama!*

I raise the dagger high up in the air, holding it in both hands, stretching my arms up high. My anger and its accompanying dark stream of thoughts now have me fully identifying as the victim, no longer bogged down by responsibility or accountability and nothing left to stop me. My mouth opens and I hear a strange sound, the unrecognizable sound of my own voice. A scream, so loud it fills the whole room. It is solidified in the air; it freezes everything and everyone here. It is a thing apart from me, emerging from me. My eyes roll up and back in their orbits as my gaze disappears inside my head. All is darkness.

Time slows to a near standstill, each nanosecond dense, charged with the fullness of a new experience: paradoxically, the more the knife lowers, the more of my burden is lifted. All my pain, physical and mental, all the suffering I have had to endure, all the pain of my mother's betrayal, all the pain of Patrick's betrayal, the unbearable weight that Mama made me carry, the unbearable weight that Patrick made me carry—in my pure victim state—now rolls off me.

My role as the grown-up in a world of infantile adults is finally, for once, completely turned inside out. I feel it now, what it is like to be innocent, to be an infant. I feel what I should have felt when I was first born. I am in the very first stage of life, the stage I could never experience, the stage I could never leave behind, the stage I sought in Patrick's arms, in Peter's arms; the stage of life that I need, that everyone needs, to feel alive. I feel light and free and limitlessly powerful, floating in a sea of bliss, not quite of this world, not quite of any other, now happily drifting, like a baby, without the responsibility to make Mama happy, without having to love Mama, without having to please her, without having to survive. This state of pure power is far more intoxicating than any high I have ever experienced, including the insane, drug-induced states designed to shape me into a crazy sex thing, including the hallucinatory sex with Patrick. This state pervades my entire body with such incredible power that all trillions of cells are equally infused, equally magnetized, equally vibrant. This power is so pure and rich that only those who have been made aware of their powerlessness as repeatedly and unrelentingly as myself could fully appreciate it. I have never experienced such freedom.

The very core of the addiction of all my perpetrators, the essence of the delusive nature of this realm, all that is false, all that which leads erring humans astray, everything power is about, the idea of freedom sought through all the traps set out in the world to pull humans down into the domain of Satan, away from God and truth and love—this dark chasm is opened wide before me, engulfing me. I experience the most extreme high, the most powerful substitute for true love, in this dense, dense moment in which everything that makes me human is lost to the beast. The beast has been set loose. The beast has free reign. The beast reigns.

The blade plunges heavily into the girl's body, slicing through her lower belly. I hear the dull thud of the point hitting bone. The knife stands vertically, the blade incised below the navel, across the pelvis. I now have killed myself before birth. I now have killed my mother. I now have killed this little girl. I am now ready to die. With my last strength, I pull the enormous dagger out of her flesh. I fall, and all goes black.

CHAPTER SEVENTEEN

Villa, Belgium, October 1974

O h, how soothing, the stillness. My energy slowly, gradually, retreats
from the senses. I don't know if my eyes are open or closed; my sight
is gone. I don't know if my mouth is open or closed. I don't feel my tongue
touching the roof of my mouth. My mouth has no taste. A very faint string
of breaths still keeps me attached to life. I hear a rumble of male voices;
Polo's voice is louder than the other men's, shouting orders to Patrick. The
voices fade out, and I wonder if my sense of hearing is gone. I assume that
my breath is soon going to stop, and the thought brings a little bit of fear.

A familiar light appears. Beautiful, inviting, it expands into a large
sun that rests peacefully before my eyes. I am not afraid anymore. This light
is my home. This light has always been my home, more so than life on that
other plane, boxed into time and space...a little box...I am ready to leave
that little box, to go back into the light.

I hear Patrick's voice clearly, right beside me.

"Annie...Annie...Little one. Come back. Come on. Come back."

Oh Patrick, my love, I think. *If I came back, you would have to go to work
for Polo.*

"*Allez, ma petite*...Don't go. I don't want you to go. Please."

I cannot feel Patrick touching me, but I have the sense that he is doing something with my body. The light is still before my eyes, but I seem to be floating, or tumbling, in the air.

"Okay, that's enough now," Patrick says decidedly. "Come back now. It's been enough. *Ma petite Annie*...Come on. *Allez*...Come back. Do it for me."

As I hear Patrick's soft sobs, I wish I could comfort him, tell him I am so fine. I wish I could let him know that I am closer to him than ever before, and that even when I leave, I will never truly leave him.

As I unhurriedly wait to pass through the light, Patrick's sobs are abruptly interrupted. He gasps.

What is that? Why did he gasp?

The energy in the room is entirely changed. Patrick is intensely focused on something. My mind drifts into attunement with his, and I realize that the girl, whom he believed dead, has stirred. Patrick is too scared to move. Patrick, I sense, decides to wait it out. He figures that she will die. But the girl stirred. The girl is not dead. I am not dead either, but I don't stir; I don't need help. The girl is holding on to life because she cannot die; she needs help. The sun is still shining before my eyes, warm as ever, inviting as ever, and it seems that I know what is happening in this room because the light is telling me everything. The light, increasingly personal and familiar, is telling me everything for a reason. The girl needs help, and Patrick is not going to help her.

I don't want to help her! I want to help Patrick!

Patrick is not going to help the girl. I can't lie here with the same peaceful feeling, with the same happiness and readiness to depart, knowing that this girl needs help and no one is helping her. If no one else will do it, I will.

All right! I think, angry, addressing the light, which I feel is prodding me to do this thing I don't want. As soon as I accept the task, I become aware of my lips lightly touching one another. The electricity has been switched on again, and the energy is flowing outward, through the senses, back into the physical world. Pins and needles make me aware of my fingers and toes. I take a breath, aware of my chest rising. I take a deeper breath. And yet another. I lift my fingers lightly. I can move. I open my eyes. Darkness, apart from the internal sun, shining clear as ever. A blur appears. A black grid. White fluorescent light behind it, truly lit by the gold of the vibrating sun.

I turn my head. I hear Patrick gasp again. I see the body of the girl. A still outline in a halo of gold. Everything appears as formless—I can't make out shapes—but I know it's her. We are both lying on the floor. She is maybe six feet from me. An endless distance. I turn over onto my stomach. *The effort*. I do not want to do this. I liked my plan to die, which would have also helped Patrick. It was a beautiful, romantic plan. It might have worked. And here I am, in spite of myself, getting up again, to help the girl.

I place my right hand flat on the floor. I place my left hand flat on the floor. I push up both arms at once. I sit on all fours. I move one hand over to position myself facing the outline on the floor, and nearly fall. I have no pain, but every tiny move requires superhuman effort. I move my hand one inch. I move my other hand one inch. I feel like giving up and collapsing. I move one knee one inch. I move the other knee one inch.

No pain. *How strange, that I feel no pain.* I try to move forward again, but fall. *The effort*. I see the outline of the girl, unmoving before me, bathed in the light of my internal sun. I place my right hand flat on the floor. I place my left hand flat on the floor. I drag myself forward on my elbows. I fall down. *The effort!* I inch forward like a snake, scooting a knee forward, flopping my hands in front of me, pulling myself forward, dragging the lead weight, the incredible load of my body, over to the formless pale shape lying on the floor. When I notice the big bob of dark hair on one end of the shape, I drag myself towards it. I reach her side, exhausted.

I look into her face. Her eyes are open. She is dying; she is nearly dead, yet she is pleading. All feeling that had been shut out comes flooding over me. I want to cry, but a strange, sweet force is holding back my tears, balancing my energy, helping me concentrate on the task at hand, guiding me. I am not tired anymore, but alert. It is as if the great, gentle force of love imbued every particle of the atmosphere within and around us, and that this love, eternal and omnipresent yet deeply personal, is guiding me. I attune myself to the force, coming from the light.

"You're going to go, you know," I say simply, supported by this energy of incredible, unconditional love that is shining through my heart, and the divine compassion that is effortlessly flowing through my gaze.

Her eyes widen slightly, in fear.

"You don't have to be afraid," I say. "It's better, to go. You're the lucky one. I'm going to have to stay here."

I motion to the room, our world.

"You'll see a light. Do you see it already?"

Ever so slightly, the girl nods, as if she does not want to acknowledge that she is seeing the light, as if she is afraid of the light, as if the light were death.

"Well that's good," I say with an encouraging smile.

The girl's little mouth smiles weakly.

"You're going to go through the light," I specify. "You'll still be you."

This, it seems, is what the girl needed to hear. That she would still be. That she would not cease to exist at the moment of death. With the light right here before my eyes, simultaneously shining through me and guiding my every move, my every word, it seems only the most natural thing; of course, we exist eternally, without beginning and without end.

The girl's eyes let go of mine. Her gaze turns upward, becomes absent, as she prepares to die. I sit with the girl, gently caressing the spot between her eyebrows with my thumb. I don't know why, and I don't know how long. A fraction of a thought wants me to feel deep grief, but the light stays my feelings, as if urging me to remain in this state of calmness and deep peace, so that I can be a better instrument of service in this moment. The internal sun remains shining before my eyes, vibrant, more real than ever, closer than ever. When the sun lets me know that I can stop rubbing the girl's forehead, I remove my hand.

The light expands. *Oh.* It suddenly dawns on me: it was so hard to crawl over here because I was still selfishly attached to my little plan, dying for Patrick. I was battling the ego, which always wants to get its way, which always tries to keep us tied to the lower realms.

Suddenly, I am showered with shafts of glittering golden rays emerging from the internal sun, which envelops me like a celestial dome. Bathed in the greatest, sweetest love, I experience a long-forgotten joy, incredibly uplifting, without excitement, because this joy is the expansion of peace. I am aware that I am physically lying on the floor in the room even as I am lifted amidst the dazzling abodes into the sphere of light.

As my consciousness passes through the ether, a figure begins to materialize inside the source of the light. Though instantly familiar, I cannot tell whether it is a man or a woman, but I do know that this is the manifestation of the consciousness that has been lovingly guiding me, present since before the beginning and throughout life. Long black hair flowing over ochre robes. The most beautifully sculpted face I have ever seen, with bronze skin gleaming more radiantly than the most precious metal. Knowledge of worlds upon worlds emanates from wide-set, bottomless black eyes, each twinkle suggesting volumes of profundities. In this gaze, I see the most extraordinary pride, which is the willpower, the inexorable determination of one who never gave up in his search for truth. Woman or man, this is the primordial source of beauty, truth and love: The Teacher.

I prostrate myself at the Teacher's feet and bow, ineffably happy, feeling completely understood and loved. My state of bliss is that pure happiness sought through various states of intoxication in life. Intuitively, I absorb the knowledge that this unconditional love is more subtle, and it takes much personal effort to reach, but it offers the freedom sought after in the other ecstatic states—the bliss consciousness which we are, behind the veil of the world, behind our psychology, behind our circumstances, behind our human bodies.

About ten extremely beautiful beings, their features refined by self-control, right actions and noble thoughts, their faces glowing with serenity and intelligence, appear around the Teacher. The girl is also here. She is being commended on having passed a very difficult test, but it is made clear to me that this is not my business; I am just to know—for my own benefit—that she is here, and that she is well.

The Teacher's gaze bores through me, eyes dancing with indescribable mirth.

"Now do you understand?"

Instantly, I am taken back to a past well before this life, in which I had been unable to find any love or understanding for those who hurt or kill children. Now that I have just experienced the essence of that energy, it is clear that it can serve as a catalyst to find that understanding, and expand my love to include all.

The Teacher divines my burning wish, *Can I stay?* The answer is immediate; I will have to return. I receive images that clarify why. Visions of future events roll before my eyes; multi-layered purposes are revealed, about my life, about this experience. I receive everything instantaneously, outside of time; and each piece of information is consistent with a particular present or future need.

I wonder about Patrick. If I have to return, will I be with him, in the near or distant future?

"After tonight, you will not see him again," says the Teacher.

"Who will love me?"

"You have divine love; you want human love as well?"

Through the irony, through glorious beauty, through straightforward truths, the Teacher is speaking directly to my nature, expressing the aspects to which I am most drawn. Thus, I understand that I am loved no matter what I have done, and this knowledge I will have to find once again as I return to the world and live my life, even as I bear the guilt over the murder; guilt so enormous it will be a mental disease. I will need to learn to love and understand myself in order to learn to love and understand others.

My audience is drawing to a close, and longingly, I take in the beloved Teacher one last time. I bow before his feet and before the exalted beings. I stay prostrate. I stay prostrate for a very long time. I don't know how long.

PARAMAHANSA YOGANANDA

(1893-1952)

Swami Yogananda brought the teachings of yoga, and particularly the sacred technique of Kriya Yoga, to the West. He is the founder of Self Realization Fellowship (SRF) / Yogoda Satsanga Society (YSS) of India, the organization disseminating these teachings. He published the book *"Autobiography of a Yogi"* in 1946 and spent the latter years of his life writing commentaries on the Christian Gospels (*"The Second Coming of Christ"*) and the Hindu Bhagavad Gita, (*"God Talks with Arjuna"*), offering intuitively perceived, spiritual interpretations to these scriptures.

CHAPTER EIGHTEEN

Villa, Belgium, October 1974

Lying on my stomach, I lift myself up to lean on my hands, and I hear quickly receding footsteps behind me. I open my eyes to see the white flesh of the bloody remains of the girl, and swivel round to avoid the sight.

Patrick, cowering in the corner of the den, stares wide-eyed at me. I bound up and run over to the narrow space between the wall and the sofa where he is taking refuge. He sticks his hand out to stop me from getting nearer. I realize that I jumped up and ran over fast, and when I glance down at my body, I notice that all the wounds have stopped bleeding. Not only that; they are much smaller, and clean and dry as if I have been healing for at least two weeks in optimal conditions. The bruises are all gone. My skin is clean and glowing luminously. I have gained a few pounds.

Patrick stares at me as though I were an apparition, which I guess I am.

"It's just me," I try.

I advance towards Patrick, who adds another hand to his barrier and gasps, "No!"

"Did you see the light?" I ask.

"No, nothing. Don't tell me about it."

There is something very different about me indeed, not only my physical appearance. I am treading lightly. The awareness of the body of the girl, and my failure to die after having killed her, is creating a split. While I have just had an experience of Truth, I am now back in the relative, dualistic realm, my consciousness tied solely to this world—a world in which I just killed a girl, and where I will have to live knowing that. I want to flee from that knowledge, and this flight makes me light as a feather.

"You know, it was wonderful. There were beings there, and I was told...."

"I SAID DON'T TELL ME ABOUT IT."

"Could you just listen for a second...."

"SHUT UP! I don't want to hear any of that nonsense."

"No, but you're into science, right? Why wouldn't you want to listen when you've got scientific proof right here?"

I anxiously indicate my body.

"Just leave me alone," Patrick says in a threatening tone.

I move my hand to Patrick's face; he violently swats it away.

"Patrick...."

"GET AWAY FROM ME. LEAVE ME ALONE."

"But Patrick, I love you."

"LEAVE ME ALONE. ARE YOU DEAF?"

"I'm just trying to tell you what happened. I'm not doing anything to hurt you."

I reach out and touch Patrick's cheek. Patrick flies up and hits me in the face before he runs off and yells, "You made me do that!"

"What are you doing?" I sob. "Are you going to just leave me here?"

"You give me no choice."

I run after Patrick, crying, holding my hand over a freshly bruised cheekbone. Patrick stands glued by the door, hand on the handle.

"Patrick, please. You can't do that," I say in tears, vaguely indicating the dead body.

"Why not? You killed her."

I turn away and break down in heaving sobs.

"But I didn't want to do that! I had no choice, and if you wouldn't have...influenced me."

"Oh, you're going to blame me for that now?"

"I'm not blaming you for anything; I'm just...I'm just...."

"You're just what?"

"I can't think of it right now."

"Okay, go and wait for me outside the front door. I'll take you home."

Patrick opens the door with a stentorian glare. Overcome with sadness, I leave my guilt-induced state of denial, breeding ground for hypocrisy, arguments and violence.

I sit down on a round, smooth rock under big fir trees, feeling the sweet air and balmy breeze on my skin, smelling the trees, especially fragrant after the rain, and feel deep gratitude for life.

I hear Patrick rummage by the car and try not to think about what he might be doing. After what seems like a half hour or so, Patrick calls me and I timidly approach. He leans over the roof of the Porsche, his face ashen, visible even in the brittle first light of a cloudy dawn. He gives me a heavy, stern look in which I recognize tremendous pain and guilt.

As we drive off, Patrick stares stoically at the road. Once we get onto the brightly lit expressway, it starts to rain again. I listen to the sounds of the rain, the moving window wipers, the car motor. About fifteen minutes pass. Then Patrick speaks in a detached, authoritative voice.

"Okay, here's what you have to do. You're going to live with your mother, in that family, but you have to get out of that house as soon as you can. When you're fifteen, sixteen years old, you should move out. Then eventually, you have to get out of the country. In the eighties, you won't want to be here, you'll just have to trust me on that. Move to London, Paris...New York. You should study English and move to New York and live there.

"You should never become a prostitute. Never take any money for sex, never let a lover give you any money, never have sex to get anything from anybody. Never do it. Wear decent clothes. It can be sexy, but keep it simple. Don't wear the frilly, lacy stuff that whores wear. As for drugs, you can take anything as long as it's given to you, but never buy any drugs yourself, and never do anything for anyone to get drugs. That includes, of course, sex. You understand? And don't become an alcoholic, either. You can have a drink, or two, or three, but make it wine, and don't drink hard liquor often. Twice a month will do for liquors and cocktails.

"You should marry. Make sure it's not an older man who made his own money. Marry a man your own age, from a wealthy family."

With an amused smile, he adds, "Preferably a family of New York bankers."

I begin to whimper.

"Now you need to stop crying and listen, because this is important. You understand?"

I cry harder.

"STOP CRYING ALREADY AND LET ME SAY SOMETHING! YOU HAVE TO STOP CRYING NOW."

I stop crying.

"Alright, you have to forget everything. Forget Polo, forget everyone you've come across at the parties, forget the parties and the places where you were taken, forget where I took you, forget me. Never say anything to anyone about this experience, you understand that? Never."

I nod, and tears flow again. I'm still crying when we reach the driveway of my family's home, and when Patrick stops the car, without turning off the motor, I cry more.

"Now you have to stop crying and go inside."

I shake my head, covering my face with my hands, and mumble, "I need you to hold me one last time."

I lean in and rest my head on Patrick's arm, certain that I am entirely unlovable and he will physically remove me from the car, but he puts his arm over my shoulder and sighs. I reach my arms around his neck, scoot onto his lap and embrace him. Patrick switches off the ignition. I am not consciously aware of a deeper motive, but it seems vital to feel all the closeness I have experienced with Patrick once again. With the awareness that this really is the last time, I absorb his familiar odor, like a mammal recognizing its own. With unrivaled presence of mind, we reconnect through sex. His lips quiver against my cheek. We remain glued together, unmoving, enjoying bliss—not the pure bliss I experienced not long ago, but an emotional union that would engrave Patrick's directions deeply into my consciousness, so that in the future I would follow them, no matter what.

When I open my eyes, daylight filters clearly enough through a heavy mantle of clouds, momentarily holding the rain. As I move to open the door, Patrick stays my hand.

"I'll come and look for you, in New York, ten years from now."

I look down, avoiding Patrick's eyes.

"So we can be together as a couple," he adds with a soft chuckle.

In his survival instructions guided from beyond, that had him speak like an oracle, Patrick carved no space out for himself in my life. I am never going to see Patrick again. I look at him. His eyes glaze over. He laughs self-deprecatingly as tears roll down his face. He puts his hand over his eyes and, between sobs, utters, "Forgive me."

He quiets down and we become still.

"I love you," I answer.

The misty daylight persistently creeps through the gray clouds, and I notice, over Patrick's shoulder, a man passing on the dirt road at the bottom of the driveway, walking a dog.

"Don't move," I whisper.

Once the man has passed and a few more seconds have elapsed, Patrick says, "Did they see us?"

"I don't know. He looked at the car. I guess I should go now, before someone else passes, or my mother comes out the door."

"I couldn't care less about your mother," Patrick says, looking at me intently, sadly. "Wait...."

He opens the glove compartment and removes a little plastic bag. He inspects its contents and then hands it to me. There are pills inside.

"If it gets tough, in the coming days, maybe weeks, take one. It's like heroin, so never take more than one at a time. No, maybe just take a half; that will be plenty for you. And certainly not more than one half a day. And try not to take it every day, or not at all. But if it gets too difficult, it will help."

I silently communicate my gratitude. As he absorbs it, his features become imbued with profound wisdom, while his eyes look physically larger, cleared up. We sit for a long time in peaceful silence, savoring the intimacy, until I move to get out of the car.

"There's something I meant to tell you, but I never did," Patrick says. "But I always wanted to say it to you. I don't want to hide anything from you."

I remove my hand from the door handle.

"It's very hard to talk about, though," Patrick says with an insecure laugh.

He glances uncertainly.

"I told you what my father did...."

The ensuing pause seems too long, so I say, "He stabbed you."

Patrick chuckles.

"But I couldn't tell you why...."

Silence.

"It was because he found me. In bed. With his wife. With my mother."

I picture the twelve-year old boy Patrick in the impossible situation he just described, with an incestuous mother, violently punished by his father, saddled with all responsibility, with all the blame, all the time, with every step he takes entrenching the lie that it was all his fault. I am overcome with sadness and love for this young boy, confused by the physical pleasure, made to feel he had seduced his mother.

I am flooded with memories of things Patrick has said about women, remembering his anger when he would call them whores. On the other hand, he became like a little boy after the first time we'd had sex, apprehensive and insecure. No wonder his views on women are so polarized: his is the quintessential story to activate a mother-whore complex, when trauma splits the sexual predator mom off from the idealized mother figure on the surface.

Being made into a sexual partner by his mother must have pushed him to act more macho—a child trying to prove he is a man. I see that my mother must have been a stand-in for his own, and that he took on the role of his own father by sleeping with her; the role of the scary male adult. I'm sure Patrick never healed from that trauma, and in his urge to be relieved from that extremely twisted burden, passed it on.

"First he was going to kill me," Patrick says. "He held a gun to my head, but then he changed his mind...."

I think of Patrick holding the gun to my head. I think of Patrick telling me about holding the gun to the heads of the men that he kills. I think of Peter, and understand that Patrick killed the young rival he himself once was, and that he killed a part of himself with Peter.

I ask, "But why was your father so mad at you, and not at your mother?"

Turning beet red, Patrick averts his face.

"I guess he felt that I betrayed him."

After a few dense seconds, the puzzle pieces fall into place, and Patrick's impossible cycle comes into view, in which he has to betray to shield his parents from their betrayal of him. Indoctrinated with notions of a ridiculous secret bond of loyalty between so-called male friends, he runs from the emasculation brought about by his father straight into the creepy arms of his mother where he has to be a man, never a child. His innocence and self-esteem compulsively, secretly and violently robbed by both parents, Patrick robs—that is to say he makes his living compulsively, secretly, and violently. Pushed into crime and pedophilia by his own father, Patrick loyally plays his assigned role of the bad guy while his parents get to look decent.

For the whole time Patrick has been speaking, I have just listened, but now my hand floats to his head and I stroke his hot blushing cheek, his beautiful face, so ashamed.

I freeze. A cluster of people is treading down the path, nearing the driveway. They are dressed in outdoorsy rain gear; all have backpacks, and a few carry walking sticks. I bury my face in Patrick's neck and cover it further with my hand, peeking through my fingers, because three or four people are staring blatantly in our direction.

"There's a lot of them," I whisper.

Several more people pass the unguarded lawn, bordered by a thinning row of young birch trees on both sides and open to plain view in the front. It seems all the trekkers, without exception, are interested in the car, or what is going on inside.

"How many?" Patrick whispers back.

"About twenty...at least."

After the second or so it takes for Patrick to fully appreciate our situation, he lets out a muffled snort. I am also finding it hard to contain my mirth.

"They've stopped," I report. "About five of them are staring."

They stand at a distance, enjoying the sight, not of pastoral plains or deciduous forest, but of a small Porsche with two people inside, sitting very close together, one sitting on the other's lap, or at least one would surmise.... "What might they be doing?" "Do you think...really?" I seem to follow their bits of conversation by watching their body language, and sure enough, there come the roguish grins. I press my body more deeply against Patrick's, bury my face entirely in the curb of his neck, and kiss it. Patrick keeps absolutely still as my hand strokes the entire front of his body. *Could I?* Yes. As I rhythmically move on Patrick's lap, he keeps still, apart from his hands, which lift me up and down. I peek over his shoulder at our audience. One man, wearing a floppy little rain hat, has dropped his jaw and gapes, mouth open wide. The other men seem no less shocked. They are glued to their spots. A lady approaches the stationary group of men. She places her hands on her hips and frowns, wearing a condemnatory expression as she addresses the men. Still in a daze, they unglue themselves and robotically follow her. Slowly, very slowly, they continue on with their promenade, looking back for as long as they possibly can, staring, staring, staring. Finally, the whole busload is out of sight. Patrick stops making the effort not to move. Several more unsuspecting walkers, taking advantage of the rain reprieve on this Sunday morning, pass the driveway before we are done.

We sit in stillness for a long time. I lightly kiss Patrick's lips and get out of the car. Before I close the door, Patrick silently says goodbye, gravely serious, sending a look full of longing and greatly tender.

I walk towards the house, repressing the urge to keep looking back, unnecessarily dragging out the pain of separation. But once I have turned the corner onto the little dirt path towards the unlocked back door where the parked car would disappear from view altogether, I turn, catch his eye and savor, for the last time, the deep and effortless intimacy I have known with Patrick Haemers.

PATRICK HAEMERS

(11-2-1952 – 5-14-1993)

PAUL (POLO) VANDEN BOEYNANTS

(5-22-1919 – 1-9-2001)

Paul Vanden Boeynants, popularly called VDB in Belgium, started out as a butcher. He quickly built a meat-processing empire. In 1948, he joined the Conservative Party and in 1949 was elected into Belgian Parliament. He was council member for the city of Brussels from 1952 until 1995. From 1966 until 1968, he was Prime Minister of Belgium. From 1972 until 1979, he was Minister of National Defense. During his tenure, he supplied entire army units with new weaponry via large international contracts. He tried to reform the army and militarize the state, but large public protests put a stop to his plans. From 1977 until 1979, he led the extreme right wing CéPIC organization, which was disbanded after conflicting interests were discovered with the fascist militant group *Front de la Jeunesse* (Youth's Front). In 1978 Vanden Boeynants once again became Prime Minister for one year, while simultaneously maintaining his post as Minister of National Defense.

In 1978, Patrick Haemers was sentenced to 3 years of prison for the rape of a prostitute. He served 14 months of his term. In October 1981, he attacked a bank in Deerlijk, Belgium. (This is generally believed to be Patrick Haemers' first robbery, rather than that this was the first time he was caught.) His father, Achille Haemers, was spotted in the environs of the branch during the hold-up. The booty (350,000 BF) was retrieved from Achille Haemers' car. The father admitted he was near the bank, "to prevent his son from making a mistake." In June 1982, Patrick was sentenced to two years of prison for the hold-up. His father was acquitted.

In March 1985 Patrick married Denise Tyack.

On November 4, 1985, Patrick Haemers and his gang robbed a postal money transport in Verviers, killing two postal employees: a 30-year-old mother of two, and a 31-year-old man about to become father.

From 1982 until 1985, Belgium was terrorized by a gang (French: *Tueurs de Brabant*; Flemish: *Bende van Nijvel*) that killed a total of 28 and wounded over 40. In the fall of 1985, the gang focused on a popular chain of large supermarkets, killing anyone in sight, including children. On November 9, 1985, only five days after the deadly robbery in Verviers, at a supermarket in Alost, nine-year old David Van de Steen saw one of the killers' mask fall off, before being shot in the hip and leg. David lost his entire family to the shootings and became crippled for life. Upon seeing a photo of Patrick Haemers later on, he instantly recognized him as the man who shot him. Strangely, even though David Van de Steen has never doubted himself, the judiciary and the press have never believed him. Many questions surrounding the terror attacks and the subsequent police investigations remain unanswered to this day.

Also in 1985, Paul Vanden Boeynants was convicted of fiscal fraud concerning 137 cases of tax evasion and forgery. He was ordered by the court to pay a fine of a half million Belgian Francs (about 12,400 Euros) and was given a prison sentence of three years, suspended by the court in view of his "services to the state." The conviction had embittered Vanden Boeynants. He was quoted as saying, "I was treated like dirt. [...] I will never, ever forget this."

In 1986, Patrick Haemers was once again arrested and imprisoned, a suspect in nine armed robberies.

On August 13, 1987, a small group of armed men, with the help
of Patrick's wife, successfully staged Patrick Haemers' escape from
prison during a transfer from court. The two guards in the transport
vehicle were shot in the legs and remained disabled for life.

In 1988, while the appeal process of Paul Vanden Boeynants' conviction
for fiscal fraud and forgery was ongoing, the minister of Interior Affairs
refused to confirm Vanden Boeynants' appointment as mayor of Brussels,
which he had reported to a colleague to be his "lifelong dream."

On January 14, 1989, Paul Vanden Boeynants was kidnapped.
One month later, after a ransom of 63 million francs (about
1.5 million Euros) was paid, he was released. Not long after, he gave
a widely attended press release, wearing sunglasses, claiming the
light bothered him because he had been chained to a wall in a dark
basement. Referring to himself mostly in the 3rd person as "VDB,"
he said he'd given himself courage with the mantra, "VDB, tu ne
vas pas crever!" (VDB, you're not gonna croak!). The press and the
entire country were enthralled; Vanden Boeynants was more popular
than ever, and was treated as a hero. A song was released titled "Qui
(M'a Enlevé?") (Who Kidnapped Me?) using soundbites of Vanden
Boeynants' super-dramatic voice at the legendary press conference.

Two investigators for the Paul Vanden Boeynants kidnapping got on the
trail of Patrick Haemers. Their numerous, convivial conversations with
Patrick's father, Achille Haemers, eventually led them to the fugitive's
hiding place. They described the series of events that led to the capture
as miraculously slipping through the system, as though they were not
meant to succeed. On May 17, 1989, Belgian public enemy number one
Patrick Haemers, his wife Denise Tyack, and a friend were apprehended
in Rio de Janeiro. In the following days, the Belgian press descended
in droves on the office of the Federal Police Commissioner in Brazil
where Patrick Haemers gave interviews. He admitted to his role in
Paul Vanden Boeynants' kidnapping and also in a series of hold-ups,

including several with fatalities. He remained in custody in Brazil for almost one year and was extradited to Belgium on April 1, 1990.

Early 1993, Paul Vanden Boeynants' record was officially cleared. His good name was entirely restituted, and any charges and further investigations into fraud, forgery, drug trafficking and suspected corruption in army equipment purchases were dropped. He immediately ran for Mayor of Brussels, but did not win the election.

Patrick Haemers remained in a Brussels prison for three years in solitary confinement. His trial for the kidnapping was scheduled for April 19, 1993, but he arrived in court only to be told that his trial was delayed. On May 14, 1993, shortly before his trial, Patrick Haemers allegedly committed suicide in his prison cell by hanging himself from a 4'3" high radiator. He was forty years old. No autopsy was performed, nor was anyone allowed to view the body.

On October 25, 1993, at what was termed the "Trial of the Century" by the Belgian press, six months after Patrick Haemers' death, with other members of the Haemers gang as defendants, Paul Vanden Boeynants magnanimously "forgave" his kidnappers.

Paul Vanden Boeynants retired from politics in 1995 and spent his last years as editor-in-chief for a satirical magazine. He died in 2001 of pneumonia caught after cardiovascular surgery at the age of 81.

Note: The above information was compiled by the author over a number of years from books and various Flemish, Dutch and French-Belgian mainstream articles and interviews. Certain elements were never addressed in these materials, such as Vanden Boeynans' desire to become mayor of Brussels as a potential motive for staging his own kidnapping. I included only what I was able to verify using more than one source, or quotes made by the subjects in filmed interviews.

EPILOGUE

The weeks following my rescue from the network were difficult. My mother, whose name was Sabine Michielsen, (1939-2019), was unhappy to have lost her income, as well as her main method to keep me under her control. With visible reminders of network abuse in the shape of large scabs all over my body, my mother kept me out of school, yet continued to aggressively ignore the obvious. Just as during our previous drives to network gatherings when I had received a powerful script that *what was happening was not actually happening*, so too, my wounds did not exist as far as my mother was concerned. To get a sense of such a mindset, and how it is possible to be deluded by it, perhaps it could be compared to being pick-pocketed, or swindled. Thieves often create a similar illusion, catching you inside a thought trap where all is well, as if they are just a passer-by or a friendly citizen, confusing you even as they steal from you. Or in another example, I remember a yoga guru who molested his victims in plain sight, in front of an audience, and no one batted an eye, as if *what was happening was not actually happening*. Everyone was as hypnotized, under the spell of this guru considered too elevated do be doing anything wrong. This profound level of gaslighting is not that uncommon.

When in those weeks after my rescue I verbally confronted my mother about how I had obtained my wounds, it only roused her impulse to silence me at any cost. After one strangulation attempt, and one final trip to the network behind the back of the leadership, my mother regained her control over me by sexually assaulting me. My shame over this assault was so great that I split, and gave up. Without any room for truth, without any mirror or context, the prohibited reality gradually escaped from my conscious mind, and I slipped back into placating behavior, accepting my mother's fantasy in which she was the perfect mother. Everything that did not fit that narrative simply never existed. After the scabs fell off, physical scars remained, but I was so dissociated I barely noticed them, let alone wondered how I had gotten them. Everything connected to the network, the early incidents that had been revived when Patrick had asked me about them, as well as the trauma Patrick himself had inflicted—and which I had shared with Peter—everything was gradually pushed down into my subconscious mind. Ultimately, Patrick himself had insisted that I forget everything, including him. While I knew him, I would have never believed it possible, but I did forget him, or it would be more accurate to say that the memory of him was repressed, even though my sense of self, my beliefs, thoughts, and actions were influenced by him.

My mother was never diagnosed as mentally ill. It was in fact barely recognized that something about her was off. At most, people might have judged her for her compulsive flirtations and overtly sexual behavior, likely symptoms of sexual trauma. However, by today's standards, in the way that massive brainwashing has pushed the entire Western world into unbridled sexual focus and addiction, such behavior would still not be generally recognized as an unconscious symbolic repetition of some aspect of a previous sexual trauma. In my mother's case, I believe that a young, girlish part inside her was constantly trying to feel loved by being sexual with all men, cardboard stand-ins for the Father, placing her in direct competition with all females, cardboard stand-ins for the Mother. As far as I can tell, my mother's emotional life, which motivated her every word and action, was stuck inside an impossible incest triangle.

According to my mother, her parents had been perfect. Nevertheless, when in my early years in therapy I would try to confront her with anything she might have done that was not perfect, she would scream that I had no idea how bad she'd had it. When I would query her about what, then, had happened to her, she would become vague and fall silent. I do know that she was born in in 1939 in Belgium near the Dutch border, and that the town where she grew up suffered famine during the Second World War. Her father was held as a prisoner of war in a German concentration camp and returned home in 1944. In 1945, weeks before her sixth birthday, her mother died in childbirth. If she was a victim of incest, I can imagine that after her mother's death, any negative feelings towards her mother (for not protecting her from abuse?) would have been locked away behind many thick layers of shame. My mother's intonations were often those of a five-year old girl, and while she only ever uttered praise about her mother, all other women received only criticism from her, at least behind their backs. With me, her own daughter, her black and white thinking went between seeing me as evil and all-powerful (the "bad" authority) and a bland receptacle for her abuse (the little girl part in her who carried the blame for her own experience of abuse). It seems clear to me now that once upon a time, my mother must have made the firm decision to never again feel shame. This resolution, while it surely protected her from all the uncomfortable, confusing and painful feelings hiding behind shame, made her shameless.

My mother's prevailing need to believe that she was good, and her drive to prove it, caused her to project a powerful spell onto her environment in which no proof to the contrary could exist. In this way, my mother was a lot like the powerful psychopathic leaders who use their nearly limitless, stolen resources to create the illusion that they are benign and benevolent. Casting a blinding spell, they manipulate politics and the media to hypnotize us into believing that their abuses do not exist, even as the signs and results of these abuses are everywhere.

Fighting off their deep-seated fear that they are worthless, the psychopathic elite use modern-day Eugenics to justify their profound disdain and lack of respect for the rest of humanity (a reflection of their own self-hatred). Normalizing pedophilia is part of a greater plan to centralize power and control people, devised and pushed by emotionally infantile psychopaths who would rather brainwash the entire population into emulating them than to face their own childhood trauma. Instead of confronting their childish idealization of their own abusers, they embrace the lies, bolstered by pride of family and blood lineage. Without access to their innocence and goodness, they believe goodness to be either false or stupid. In their eyes, innocence does not exist, not even in babies and children. Embracing evil, they signal to each other with secret hand gestures, code words, symbols and colors, announcing they have sold their soul and are—or want to be—part of that club where the highest ranking are the most depraved. Unconsciously trying to exorcise their childhood trauma, they endlessly inflict various psychological and physical aspects of their previous abuse onto new victims in the role of abuser, intensified and multiplied by their entitlement and privilege. Through organized abuse, our false leaders can experience the raw and intoxicating release from the burden of their own abuse, while basking in the religious glow of being part of something greater than themselves. Satanists, hidden in the top tiers of many secret and religious societies, partake in practices and rituals that support and encourage freedom through depravity (the abused child part getting revenge on powerless victims instead of their abuser) even as they are entrapped and enslaved in a cult which turns everything on its head. Bad is good. Darkness is light. The worse one is, the better.

If we see the insanity of what is happening in the world, we have a duty to also see the insanity of those who are behind it. We are not only witnessing the devastating results of greed, which, as far as emotional maturity goes, puts its host at the level of a toddler. We are talking about people who are emotional newborns, who without their power and status which makes them look the opposite of what they are, would be as helpless and rudderless as their infant victims. Our leadership is attempting to create a world in the image of the utter chaos and devastation in their own hearts, which they, in their role of the powerful perpetrators, plan to inflict on everyone while they themselves plan to escape: Heads getting rid of Tails. We regard these people as either better than us or as powerfully evil, but both those viewpoints give them power, and hide their utter insanity.

The hierarchic societal structure supports the stubborn superstition that we need authority figures to rule over us and that we should blindly trust government and its servants to decide what is best for us. Without those at the top needing to be there, and without us handing over our power to those who automatically abuse it, all injustices on earth would be instantly eradicated. The power imbalances embedded into the hierarchy hide the simple truth that we are one species, inherently equal.

After my escape from the network, I managed to get through elementary school without obvious trouble, but in middle school I repeated the eighth grade twice, switching schools each time. By age fifteen, I quit school and started drifting, often staying with people whom I had met in bars and cafes, preparing to leave home as per Patrick Haemers' repressed but active instructions. At age sixteen, bar hopping with some café acquaintances, I ended up in the red-light district of Antwerp. The owner immediately wished to recruit me, and I accepted my companions' dare to have drinks with customers. The atmosphere was entirely familiar and the owner protected me from pushy customers, so I could still honor the first of my life's rules as directed by Patrick, which was to never become a prostitute. Around that time, I moved in with a man twice my age, whom I had met at a bar. He had offered me his couch, but three weeks later, in a drunken rage, he bullied me into a sexual relationship. After he helped me find a steady job, I left him and moved into my own apartment.

In February of 1982, I met my biological father, who also coerced me into sex. Three months later, I left Belgium, first escaping to the South of France, where I got a job selling ice cream for the summer. That fall, I moved to London, the following year to Paris, and in 1985 to New York, getting by doing low-level office jobs, waitressing, or as an au pair. Patrick Haemers' directions operated as unconscious internal guiding principles: I never bought drugs, never had sex with anyone to obtain anything, I did not drink too much alcohol, and avoided wearing "the frilly, lacy stuff." Also, since I had been trained to move among the elite, my trauma did not show—at least not at first glance. My frequent moves may have covered certain giveaways, such as my inability to maintain stable relationships or to hold onto a job. And the world culture itself, shaped by my powerful perpetrators, hid what I would now deem obvious symptoms of extensive sexual trauma.

In 1987, I traveled to Los Angeles and sometime afterwards started therapy. I told my first therapist of my sexual relationship with my father, from the perspective he had pushed on me, which was that we were equals. After all, I had been eighteen when we met, officially old enough to give consent. Sex had only been possible because he had not raised me. In response to my justifications, the therapist stated, "Your father abused you!" I broke into tears, and at long last got in touch with all the grief and disappointment that my real father, when I had finally met him, could only muster interest in me if I had sex with him. In the weeks following that therapy session, as I grieved, I first noticed the magical effect of neural integration, observing my transformation as I saw the world through new eyes and found the world responding to me in a new way. I was emotionally maturing and gaining in wisdom, and it was clear that the insights I received would be worth any pain.

Sometime in the late 1980's, walking in downtown Los Angeles near Skid Row, a faint whiff of human feces sent me into a powerful flashback of the S&M show to which I had been subjected during my first time in the network. In my panic, only one thought was clear: *If this is true, I'm going to kill myself!* The memory disappeared as quickly as it had surfaced. However, from that time onward, I was often plagued with dark flashbacks of horrors from the network, accompanied by confusion, disbelief and suicidality. In the ensuing years, I would see various therapists who helped me with memories of incest and sexual assault, but not Satanic Ritual Abuse (SRA). I never came across any therapist who suggested memories to me, or who put ideas into my head. On the contrary, if there was an issue with therapists, it was that they were not open to all of my experience, and put up walls once I started to venture in the direction of my mother's dark side, or extreme abuse.

In 1988, a film director for whom I was working in Los Angeles gifted me a session with a psychic who told me, towards the end of the hour, that we had a visitor who had been picking up on our conversation through the ether. I was nailed to my seat as the inner parts that held the experiences with Patrick Haemers filled me with a heavy sense of deep truth. The psychic said, "He was a young man, and you were a child. He wants you to know that he *did* betray you. He can see that now. But, you know, the flesh is weak." She smiled at me in the way that he might have. However, I was not ready, and left this message untouched, recorded on an audio cassette with the rest of the session, which turned out to be an accurate prophecy of my future.

Without a Bachelor's degree, I was accepted into a Master of Fine Arts program for screenwriting in 1991 based on writing samples, and received a certificate of completion from the American Film Institute, where I met my future husband. I did not consciously remember the instructions I had received during my rescue back in 1974, but my husband did match the profile Patrick Haemers had outlined. The only way in which the guidelines manifested is that there was a strong internal "yes" present for me in this relationship, which was simply not there with others. In 1994, at the Bodhi Tree Bookstore in West Hollywood, I saw a large poster of a face that looked strongly familiar. At first, I could not tell if it was a man or a woman, and then saw that it was the cover for *"Autobiography of a Yogi,"* by Paramahansa Yogananda. My future husband and I started to meditate after reading the book. The spiritual path would become most important for my recovery, opening up a viable perspective for the dark experiences of my past.

In May 1993, I had a dream about the North Sea in Belgium. The atmosphere and colors were those of the time I had walked on the beach with Patrick Haemers in 1974, when he had appeared joyful and free, and I'd had the powerful sense that I was looking at his actualized Self. The silvery water in the dream inundated everything in a gigantic flood, and I woke up with the intuitive certainty that the most important person in my life had died, even though I did not know who this person was, or what this meant. I told my therapist about the dream; she was dismissive, and I decided then and there that I needed to look for someone new. Even as memories from the network started to crystallize, I could not find a therapist with whom

I felt safe to share these invasive and what then felt as extremely shameful events from my past. In 1996, the Dutroux Case offered yet another glimpse into the possibility of my memories being real, but they had nowhere to land until I moved back to New York City in 1997, and after an arduous search, finally found a therapist who was able to hold space for me. This doctor was new to SRA, but not blind to the potential for human darkness. Supported in my marriage, I was able to focus completely on healing from childhood trauma, meditating, writing, and going to yoga classes and therapy several times a week. During this period, the overwhelming truth brutally imposed itself. With each new memory, I prayed it would be my last, convinced each time that there could not possibly be more, so enormous and devastating was the truth. I never accepted the new information out of hand. However, usually, it soon became clear that *if* this were true, it would answer many questions. Behaviors, words or actions of mine or others, or circumstantial occurrences I had always remembered and might not previously have understood, would make sense *if* this memory were real. Sometimes I experienced days of heightened lucidity, when these puzzle pieces of my life were falling into place, followed by grief so intense that it took all my physical strength to bear. However, even in the most painful periods of such a healing cycle, I would notice the benefit. I wasn't looking for or finding benefit, but rather, the process of awakening brought all feelings to life, not just the repressed negative ones, and I might feel joyfulness or gratitude more keenly than ever before as well.

My life did not always outwardly seem to improve: after my divorce, carving a path towards financial independence while confronted with a massive guilt complex which had left me feeling undeserving, was not easy. But, as my circumstances shifted to reflect my growing self-esteem, the hardship was easier to bear, because I also felt divine purpose and connection. More painful memories were buried more deeply and emerged in later years. These tended to relate to the mind control training and my experiences at the seat of the dark circle of power. Because I had the previous decades of healing and exponential growth, it was, relatively speaking, easier and more fluid to go through this journey of continued integration and growth.

Committing to truth and personal evolution may in some ways seem reckless, as deep trauma work may temporarily incapacitate a person to the point of getting fired or needing to take time off from work. To anyone who has never experienced real personal growth, such a path must seem crazy, and my story and healing must seem baffling or unbelievable. The tide of the world takes us outside of ourselves, asking us to do, to perform, and to climb. Healing has us going against that outward tide, asking us to stop, to reverse the flow and to go inward.

On my lengthy inward expedition, I have come to understand much about my mother and the class to which she catered in her desire to belong. The psychopaths who attempt to rule the world have no access to their inner selves, and are trying to know themselves only through outward means, through status and control, needing to feel superior in order to feel worthy. The outer world is set up for all of us to follow their direction and get swept up in their lies and terror campaigns without inner recourse to deeper truth. Their brainwashing leaves us emotionally numb, without empathy, mocking and deriding each other so we can feel superior, just like them. And if we should dare to turn the tide, if we dare to express our own free will when it does not coincide with their plans—such as me telling my story—we can expect to experience gaslighting on a scale that could only be matched with the enormity of their fortunes.

Meditation practice and the cultivation of a personal relationship with true authority figures such as Jesus Christ or Yogananda have properly challenged my notions of power. Starting out, parts of me were convinced that they, too, must be power-hungry hypocrites. Their consciousness being all-pervading, and meditation and prayer being the channels to commune directly with the enlightened ones, allowed me to open myself up increasingly to receive divine love. These great teachers continue to show me, in the sweetest, most personal way, that love is the only reality. To counter the dark forces and the occult practices of my childhood perpetrators—especially those at the seat of world power who were surrendered to dark entities—I needed to turn to the greatest beings of light. The power of love they embody—and help us to recover within us—is necessary to overcome the darkness threatening to overtake the globe. Even as we steadily move into a more enlightened era, the slaves to power, bound to earth and its riches, are fighting tooth and nail to protect their lies and way of life, which is creating the turbulence we are experiencing today. Our task is to retrieve our innate power through personal connection with earth and the divine, and to break out of the massive indoctrination that has taught us to passively rely on temporal authorities.

My path has changed me—and as a result, my outer circumstances—more than I could have ever imagined. Healing breaks our heart so that love can enter. Healing from trauma is to feel suppressed feelings so that we can expand and feel everything. It means to go inward, to connect with our own truth and so connect with greater truth, so that we can know what we know with certainty, because we can feel it, because we are in touch with our true selves. Commitment to truth and personal evolution takes us within, which is how we can bring the light in, and "dispel the accumulated darkness of ages."

Made in the USA
Middletown, DE
04 February 2023

23783528R00169